# Humane Development

# Humane
# Development

Participation
and Change among
the Sadāma
of Ethiopia

John H. Hamer

The University of Alabama Press

**Library of Congress Cataloging-in-Publication Data**

Hamer, John H., 1926–
  Humane development.

  Bibliography: p.
  Includes index.
    1. Sidamo (African people) 2. Acculturation—
Ethiopia—Case studies. 3. Rural development—
Ethiopia—Case studies. I. Title.
DT380.4.S5H35 1987    306'.089935    85-28975
ISBN 0-8173-0302-2

To
Irene and Betana

# Contents

# Illustrations

## Tables

## Figures

## Maps

# Photographs

I shall follow the simplest possible format. This will involve contrasting short and long vowels by use of the macron for the latter. The short consonant will be contrasted with the long or geminated consonant by using a double letter for the geminated form. The alveopalatals č and š are marked by the inverted circumflex, thus č as in 'chin' and š as in 'she.' In addition, sh in proper names is pronounced š. The English equivalents of the important vowels in Sadāminya are as follows:

a as in 'father'
e as in 'say'
i as in 'see'
o as in 'go'
u as in 'fool'

Humane Development

"Now that money has made people equal, they no longer wish to honor and love one another." The speaker, Borassa, a Sadǎnčo from southern Ethiopia, is referring to a situation common to many Third World people.[1] It is one in which the cash economy brought about by international capitalism and its consequences—the nation state, religious and ideological proselytization, and increasing emphasis on participation in the marketplace—has seemingly brought about equality. By equality, Borassa means that money has provided men, if not women, the opportunity to pursue many individualistic alternatives in business, farming, religious ideas, and formal education for their children. When, however, he says that people no longer love one another, he is suggesting that they do not honor their obligations as they once did to their kinsmen and other members of the community. Borassa is raising by implication the major questions to be discussed in this book. Has an individualism replaced the idyllic condition of cooperation that he so wistfully recalls? Did such a condition ever exist? Furthermore, have the Sadāma willingly participated in these significant changes that have occurred within the lifetime of the old man?

The Sadāma have always experienced conflict between self-interest and community obligation, but their system of consensual authority has provided a means for maintaining a balance between the two. Moreover, the continuity of this process of reconciliation has ensured the redistribution of wealth that has provided for equality of participation in the community. So even as the Sadāma have become articulated with the state and have experienced the impact of a cash economy, they have been able to modify their institutions to enable them to decide and act upon their destiny. Rather than leading to the demise of their culture, the introduction of a cash economy and state controls has provided new options for individuals.

Indeed there is little evidence for communalism in African societies. Kinship ties enable a man to hold rights in the use of property, the title to which is conceived of as belonging to the ancestral heroes. In reality, however, the individual householder works his own land, sometimes in conjunction with neighbors and friends in the completion of large tasks but often by himself with assistance from members of his household. It is now widely accepted in African studies that cooperation in one aspect of social life does not mean that it will exist in others.[2] Nor do people necessarily like to cooperate in groups, as is evidenced by their willingness to abandon cooperation when there is no longer individual advantage or when community pressures and sanctions have been removed.

Unfortunately, African leaders have assumed the existence of a traditional communal way of life.[3] Consequently, they have believed that superimposition of collective farms and cooperatives would lead to increased agricultural productivity and rural development. Now, after two decades of independence, it is recognized that such beliefs were inappropriate, that Western concepts of production and marketing cooperatives will not mesh with African kinship systems and beliefs about cooperation.[4]

Rather, indigenous African economies have been based upon small-scale production, with redistribution among kinsmen of any surplus produced. Redistribution of surplus rewarded achievement by enhancing social esteem, rather than by providing a base for increasing productivity. Then, in many areas, colonialism undermined this system of equalitarian community participation by the introduction of wage labor and individual land titles. In turn the old division of labor was modified with men engaging in cash cropping and wage labor, while women were left with the responsibility for subsistence gardening activities.

Given these circumstances, the few African cooperatives that developed before and after World War II were not essentially community-oriented organizations. They were successful only insofar as they could be used to oppose colonialism and foreign economic interests. Participation was based upon perceived personal gain rather than upon providing communal benefits. Moreover, the very structure of these cooperatives, based on impersonal efficiency, was antithetical to traditional kin-directed values. In some areas there were the further complications of the clash between developing class interests and kinship ties.

At independence many African governments sought to encourage rural development by establishing cooperative programs. In many instances, after sizable inputs of government resources, there was no significant increase in productivity. In Zambia, for example, the massive government superimposition of rural cooperatives on a presumed communal base was recognized as a failure by 1970.[5] And it is now conceded that the ujamaa scheme in Tanzania has not been viable.[6] Under these circumstances it is not surprising that there is much disillusionment about development programs in Africa.[7] The new states have simply not been able to provide the infrastructural supports, cash incentives for increasing productivity, or reliable expertise for instructing farmers in new techniques.

Nevertheless, there have been significant changes in the life-style of rural Africans in recent decades. The Sadāma mirror these changes. Most notable has been the transformation to peasantry status from a social system of autonomous clans, linked by periodic markets and trading relations with neighboring societies. Until the end of the nineteenth century the Sadāma were essentially self-contained, relying primarily upon their own language and customs, which made them distinct from their neighbors. In terms of producing and distributing the essentials of food, clothing, shelter, tools, and weapons, they were largely independent of others. When, however, the Sadāma were incorporated into the Ethiopian Empire in the late nineteenth century, they became part of a more inclusive whole.

In the process they took on the attributes of peasants by becoming subordinate to an elite ruling class.[8] Further constraints were provided by a literacy system necessary to gain access to state-controlled agencies. Moreover, the people were subjected to universalistic religions and a state ideology. Since 1945, however, the Sadāma have begun to acquire the characteristics of farmers by becoming "agricultural entrepreneurs"[9] engaged in cash cropping, which has linked them to the international market system. And their children have begun to acquire the rudiments of literacy through formal education. The people have responded by creating their own associations to cope with change. The impact that these historical developments have made upon their culture forms the subject matter of this book.

The Sadāma differ, however, from peasants in other Third World areas in that there is no landless understratum that wealthy individuals who hold higher status can exploit or coerce. There have always been differences in wealth, with individual Sadāma being esteemed for their success in acquiring more land and cattle, exhibiting greater than average oratorical ability, or demonstrating unusual courage in warfare. Such individuals have been honored but have also acquired more obligations than most people in terms of expectations about redistribution of their largess through hospitality. Consequently, few Sadāma in the past have acquired noticeably more material possessions than others. Such inequalities as have existed have been based essentially on age and sex, as well as on differentiation of cultivators' clans from small artisan clans. And this structure continues to be predominant in the countryside.

With the exception of a few landowners in the southern part of Sidāmoland, the state-imposed authorities and northern merchants confine their interests and activities to the few administrative towns. It is important to point out that the Sadāma have not experienced the impact of European thought and material interests that were a part of colonialism. The Italian occupation lasted only five years, as compared with the generations of European colonialism experienced by Africans in other parts of the continent. Also, the youth have been free of the pressures and inducements to participate in migratory labor. Hence there has been no depletion of the abler part of the labor force in the countryside, nor has there been the cultural discontinuity between generations resulting from prolonged separation.

## Participation in Development

Therefore, despite the late-nineteenth-century conquest by the Amhara, the Sadāma have maintained control of their land resources, practicing subsistence food production and only recently engaging in cash cropping. They have continued by maintaining community controls to ensure the redistribution of wealth and by adapting to changes imposed by the state and world capitalism. In this book I examine how the Sadāma have reinterpreted traditional consensual decision making to fit new organizations for coping with cash cropping and changing living standards. Through these organizations the people have been able to participate in community planning, the acquisition of public facilities, marketing innovations, and other improvements. The problem of balancing self-interest with community responsibility is a recurring theme throughout their history, as will be demonstrated in the following chapters. It continues to be so in the contemporary societies, as will be shown in the process of planning new roads, in settling disputes over boundaries, and in other matters that require a delicate balance between motivating individual participation and preventing self-aggrandizement, threatening the rights and well-being of others. This has provided the essence of the grass roots participation mentioned in the title.

The idea of local-level participation has not been popular among Third World development theorists. Those who consider development to be predicated strictly upon investment, economic planning, and political action at the national level consider such grass roots participation as irrelevant.[10] The stress in African development has been on stabilization of the state through avoidance of decision-making activities at the regional, ethnic, or local levels that could constitute a threat to national unity. On the other hand, it is argued that reluctance to accept participation as fundamental to the change process shows impatience and disillusion with the human condition.[11] Indeed, Africans have preferred "local democracy" and "mass participation" as a means of resisting external domination and imposition of government decision making from the top down.[12]

Important socioeconomic changes inevitably lead to numerous conflicting purposes within communities. This has led some social scientists to be skeptical about the benefits of industrial nations intervening in the Third World. They argue that individual initiative in acceptance of external innovations entails risks and increases dissension within communities.[13] These persons assume that only by adhering to a survival standard of living can peasants or farmers avoid actions that would jeopardize this minimum security. Other analysts, however, question the reality of a value system entailing altruistic sacrifices of self-interest in favor of such a minimum standard of community welfare.[14] The latter scholars argue that the individual cannot know when a contribution does indeed support something as abstract as community welfare unless there is some tangible change for the better in his or her position. Furthermore, people like the Sadāma, who control their own land and are not dominated by other socioeconomic classes, are economically more secure than many Latin American and Asian peoples. They need not reject external innovations as long as through their self-help societies they are able to cope with self-aggrandizement, planning, and cooperation in the change process. Indeed, the final chapters of the book will be devoted to an examination of theoretical positions regarding external intervention, as it affects development at the grass roots level.

## Fieldwork and Methods

It is important for the reader to have some understanding of how this study was made. For approximately thirteen months during 1964 and 1965 my family and I lived on the edge of the towns of Yirgā Alēm (see map 1) in the heart of Sidāmoland. Our original goals were to study child-rearing practices as well as to develop an ethnography, since minimal systematic information had previously been collected about the people and their culture. It was only toward the end of our fieldwork that we began to appreciate the many ramifications of a developing cash economy and the gradual incorporation of the Sadāma into the world marketing system for coffee. At that point, we began to focus attention more on what the people were doing in adjusting to this situation. We were fortunate to be present shortly after the initial formation of small societies for picking coffee and at the beginning of discussions on how to gain more influence in the marketing process so as to improve the general standard of living. The tangible expression of such improvement was more schools, increases in the number of health clinics, establishment of water systems, feeder roads to ease the burden of travel, improved access to manufactured consumer goods, and better housing. Then for a period of six months in 1973, just prior to the Ethiopian Revolution, we returned to see how, or whether, the societies had become more formally organized in the previous eight years and the extent to which the dreams and plans of the 1960s had become the realities of the 1970s.

Our approach to fieldwork involved concentration on four small communities of approximately four hundred people in the Āletā area (see map 1). This is the home of twelve clans known collectively as the Āletā, whose ancestors left the main body of the Sadāma, north of the Gidabo River, 150 years ago. We were introduced into these communities by my assistant, who had close paternal cousins in one of them. These hamlets differed from those in more remote parts of Sidāmoland in being near the single all-weather road as well as being located in the heart of the coffee-growing region. Thus, coffee may have provided the people with better than average cash incomes but not necessarily wealth, since their areas are more conducive to cattle herding and cultivation of the food staple ensete, a large, bananalike plant. There was only one household head in these communities who was considered wealthy by local standards. So the area of research concentration was probably as typical as any in the region.

# Map 1
*Clan Divisions*

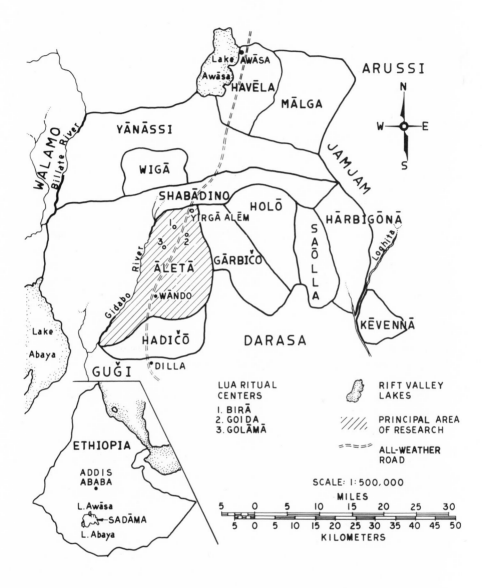

WALAMO

Billate River

Lake Awāsa

Awāsa

AWĀSA

HAVĒLA

MĀLGA

ARUSSI

N
W — E
S

YĀNĀSSI

WIGĀ

SHABĀDINO

YIRGĀ ALĒM

HOLŌ

JAMJAM

HĀRBIGŌNĀ

Loghita

Gidabo River

1
3  2

ĀLETĀ

GĀRBIČO

SAŌLLA

WĀNDO

Lake Abaya

HADIČO

DARASA

KĒVENNĀ

GUǦI

DILLA

ETHIOPIA

ADDIS ABABA

L. Awāsa

SADĀMA

L. Abaya

LUA RITUAL CENTERS
1. BIRĀ
2. GOIDA
3. GOLĀMĀ

RIFT VALLEY LAKES

PRINCIPAL AREA OF RESEARCH

ALL-WEATHER ROAD

SCALE: 1:500,000

MILES

5    0    5    10    15    20    25    30

5  0  5  10  15  20  25  30  35  40  45  50
KILOMETERS

7

Much of my time in the first three months was spent in collecting genealogies, learning gardening procedures, attending elders' councils, and simply observing everyday happenings. As our assistant was well known and liked by most of the householders, we were soon accepted and able to participate in community life. Perhaps we were a welcome change from many of the descendants of northern Ethiopians, who disparaged the culture and avoided the people socially. By contrast, our eagerness to learn about the culture and our struggles with the language soon brought many willing teachers. It was from this group that we were able to select our initial informants. When people became more aware of our interests in their history, we were gradually led through the network of informants' kin and friends to learned old men in more remote areas of the countryside. Thus within seven months we had established rapport with a few distinguished notables in most clan areas in all parts of Sidāmoland. This enabled us to collect and cross-check historical material, as well as information on kinship, ritual, politics, and the economy. Later these contacts were to prove invaluable in our efforts to gain new informants in the self-help movement and to participate in executive committee meetings in widely scattered areas.

In all of the interviewing and participant observation, reciprocity was the key to maintaining relations with informants and friends. We were fortunate to have a Land Rover, which made it possible during the dry season to travel as far as donkey trails would take us, before resorting to leg power. This vehicle was an important factor in reciprocity. We were able to assist farmers in hauling coffee to market, in participating in rituals involving distant relatives, and at least once a week in taking the sick from our research communities to the outpatient clinic in Yirgā Alēm. In this connection our residence on the outskirts of the town was most useful. It enabled us to offer our hospitality to the many Sadāma who gave so freely of their own in the countryside. Consequently, on those days when we were not in the field there was always a group of guests at mealtimes, often staying overnight. These sessions provided us with answers to pressing questions as well as clues for further investigation.

Though I was able after several months to understand much of what was being said in interviews and group conversations, I never did become fluent in Sadāminya, the local language. As a consequence, we relied heavily on our assistant, who was fluent in English. By the time we returned in 1973 he had acquired a degree in economics from an American university and had been appointed to an Ethiopian high school teaching position. He had also entered into politics, having shortly before our arrival contested and lost the 1973 elections for the Ethiopian parliament. This experience further enhanced his knowledge of local politics and widened his network of acquaintances. All of this background increased his ability to work with us in understanding the problems and directions of the self-help movement in the mid-1970s.

The sequence of chapters begins with a discussion of the people, their location, and the characteristics of their physical environment. Then, by examining mythology and descent group pedigrees, it is possible to outline the origins and broad historical outlines of the Sadāma in chapter 3. The social structure of the people as it relates to their use of the factors and relations of production is the subject of chapter 4. Chapter 5 deals with the important matter of marriage as it pertains to linkages between descent groups and the division of labor and helps to complete the discussion of how kinship affects the mode of production and distribution. The first five chapters thus provide the background for understanding the fundamental beliefs and rituals that underpin the juridical-political system. Chapter 6 treats these topics and, with chapter 7, considers how authority works in linking household and communities for cooperation in production.

Chapters 8 and 9 are concerned with the impact of international capitalism and how the Sadāma have responded by developing their own self-help societies. It will then be possible in chapter 10 to consider these changes from a broad theoretical perspective. The concluding chapter contains a brief summation and speculation about the future of the Sadāma.

# 2

# The People
# and Their Environment

As a beginning, it is necessary briefly to identify the people called the Sadāma, who they are, where they are located, and how they relate to their environment. They are singularly fortunate in inhabiting an optimum area for grazing cattle and for producing an unusual, but very durable, food staple—*Ensete ventricosum*. This plant is well adapted to the climatic conditions along the escarpment of this particular sector of the Rift Valley. As will be explained, ensete is easily stored and more resistant than maize and other cereal grains to drought conditions. After categorizing the people, my purpose in this chapter is to examine the topography, soil, climatic conditions, communications, mode of cultivating ensete, and distribution of the population.

## The People

The term designating the people discussed in this work has been used in many different forms and in reference to so many groups as to be confusing. Murdock, for example, uses the term *Sidāmo* to include virtually all the ethnic groups of south central Ethiopia.[1] Then, rather surprisingly, he mentions a Sidāmo tribe as part of what he refers to as the Konso cluster to the east of his original reference group.[2] These usages are much too broad for identifying the people I call the Sadāma. Of somewhat narrower focus is the term *Sidāma*, used to refer to the Gudela, Kambata, Tambaro, Alaba, and Walamo in the sixteenth century, peoples dwelling in the general vicinity of Lakes Abaya and Awāsa.[3]

Furthermore, there is reference in the sixteenth century to a Sidāmo people who were part of the kingdom of Bali, living in its southwestern extreme near Lake Abaya (see map 2).[4] It is said that at that

**Map 2**

*Peoples of Southwest Ethiopia and Historic Migrations of the Sadāma*

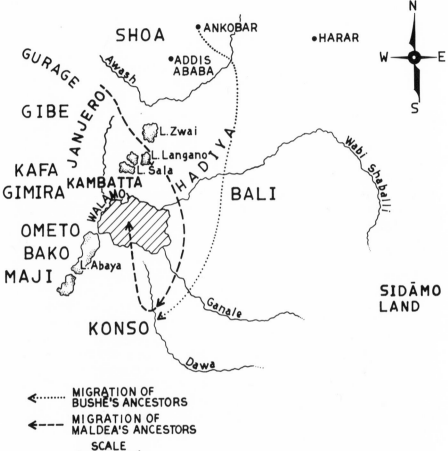

MIGRATION OF
BUSHE'S ANCESTORS

MIGRATION OF
MALDEA'S ANCESTORS

SCALE

0    50    100
km

11

time Sidāmoland formed a link between the coast and the interior of south central Ethiopia. Indeed, the Sidāmo are supposed to have prevented the Oromo invasions of the sixteenth century from penetrating to the west of Lake Abaya. In fact, to this day the term *Sidāmo* is used by the Oromo to mean "enemy."[5]

It is this more specific categorization of the people to the east of Lakes Abaya and Awāsa that I refer to as the Sadāma. This is what the people call themselves. And in keeping with the historic formulations about the area as a buffer against the Oromo incursion, I will use *Sidāmoland* as the term for their territory.

## Environmental Setting

Sidāmoland resembles a trapezoid in shape, extending 95 kilometers north to south and 120 kilometers east to west. In traveling the 270 kilometers south from Addis Ababa to the northern boundary of Sidāmoland at Lake Awāsa (see map 1), one encounters dramatic changes in terrain. Initially there is the gradual descent from the high elevation of Addis Ababa (eight thousand feet) to the floor of the Rift Valley. The change is from intensely cultivated fields of teff and wheat and the bracing air of the highlands to low-lying, humid, grazing lands interspersed with acacia trees.[6] This landscape is broken by the major lakes Zwai, Langano, and Šala. After leaving the low-lying lake area, one begins a gradual ascent to higher elevations. Even at the height of the dry season in February, when the ground is a dull mustard color and dust is everywhere, the traveler is impressed by the greenery of the multitudes of ensete plants that cluster around each homestead. This eye-catching verdure continues for another 95 kilometers as one continues to Dilla on the southern boundary of Sidāmoland (see map 1).

The Sadāma consider their boundaries as demarcated by a series of waterways, including Lake Awāsa in the north, Lake Abaya in the south, the upper branches of the Loghita River on the east, and the Billate River on the west (see map 1). As to cultural boundaries, in the north are the Arussi people; the Walamo are situated on the western boundary, and the Gugi and Darasa are on the south; the Jamjam (Northern Gugi) are on the east.

On the basis of differences in elevation there are three distinct ecological zones of habitation. The lowlands, which range up to approximately five thousand feet, consist primarily of savanna, where there is a minimal cultivation of maize and millet as well as the predominant activity of herding livestock. From five thousand to between seven thousand and eight thousand feet the vegetation is lush, and this is where the basic subsistence crops of *Ensete ventricosum* and *Zea maize* abound. Beyond eight thousand feet the rainfall is more frequent and there is widespread cultivation of barley, teff, and wheat. At this highest of elevations there is better than adequate pasture because some rain falls throughout the year. Possibly because of lack of the durable ensete, as well as appropriateness of the area as grazing land, the population is less dense than in the middle elevation zone.

The lowland areas surrounding the upper end of Lake Abaya and extending in a northeastward direction toward the western edge of Lake Awāsa (see map 1) are inhabited throughout the year by persons engaged solely in herding stock. When the grass withers in the dry season, the option of those in the middle ensete zone of sending their cattle to the highlands helps maintain kinship ties between the two areas. Likewise, individuals often utilize the lower elevations in the heavy rains, when pastures in the middle ensete zone and highlands become so soggy that animals can graze only with discomfort. Also, in the midlands, people plan on a cow calving every two years, while in the lowlands it is estimated that the same animal will calve every one and a half years. Consequently, if a man can spare any cattle from his regular farming activities he will seek to increase his herd by sending a few to the lowlands to be kept by relatives or friends. The owner always retains reproductive rights over these animals, but the herder obtains the by-products that will be useful for subsistence or trade.

Climate can be characterized as moderate, with alternating dry (November–March) and rainy (April–October) cycles. Rain at the middle and high altitudes is sufficient to provide a productive plant life, while at the same time the elevation is sufficient to protect people from the more pernicious effects of malaria. In the past, fauna such as lions, elephants, and buffalo were quite plentiful, but because of the great increase in human population density and the intensive hunting after the 1890s, this is no longer true.

## Communications

An all-weather gravel road runs north to south, passing through or near the major towns of Awāsa, Yirgā Alēm, Wāndo, and Dilla (see map 1). Extending from this major artery are numerous feeder roads that connect with marketplaces in the countryside. These market-places in turn are connected with a network of footpaths linking the rural hamlets. Waterways such as the Gidabo River and the many smaller streams are spanned by stone bridges built during the Italian occupation. These feeder roads and pathways are negotiable only on foot at the height of the rainy season, a time when the steep mountain trails are simply impassable.

The difficulties of travel lend to the remoteness of many hamlets for two or three months of the year. The major towns, though, are linked by the government bus line and a few privately owned micro-buses. Bicycles, because of the rough roads, are seldom seen in the countryside. Hence for the most part people travel on foot or by mule.

There are telecommunication centers in the major towns. But the unreliable phone service is used primarily by government officials and coffee merchants, seldom by ordinary townspeople or peasants.

## Cultivation and Food Preparation

Ensete ventricosum is a giant form of banana tree that produces a nonedible fruit. The food it provides comes from the trunk and root system and supplies the Sadāma with their basic, relatively drought-resistant food staple. The impressive height and luxuriant foliage of the plant (wese in Sadāminya) varies with soil conditions and time of planting. Thus gardens with seedlings planted six months previously may have plants ranging in height from two to five feet. In some instances plants in the ground for a little more than two years are eighteen feet tall, and the ado variety reaches a height of over twenty feet in five years. In general, the ensete grown in the middle elevations at around six thousand feet is considered by the botanist Smeds to be of the highest quality.[7] Some informants can enumerate twenty-five to thirty varieties of ensete, which are planted according to preference for size (as a mark of prestige), or for rapid maturity. Ensete, regardless of variety, is never grown from seed but is propagated from roots of small two-year-old plants. The cycle begins in the highlands, where there is continuous moisture, rather than in the middle elevations, where the dry season is considered by the Sadāma as detrimental to the growth of young seedlings. The small plants are buried upside down, with roots protruding, in well-prepared soil. Within a few months many small shoots sprout from the roots, which in turn are cut off and planted. The variety *ado* is considered the best for the propagation process. The small seedlings, known as *funta*, are then purchased by farmers from the middle elevations in time for the spring planting season. In the past, butter, iron money, and other items of barter were involved in the exchange, but today such transactions are strictly monetary.

During January and February, farmers prepare the land with their hoes and digging sticks, rarely using plows because of the small size of household plots. The procedure involves turning under the old brush and grass to serve as fertilizer. Two broad soil types are recognized by color: the red, which is said to need much animal manure to produce ensete, and the brown, which requires less and is considered ideal. With careful management, a small, one- or two-acre plot will provide subsistence for a husband, wife, and their children. It is essential, however, to protect the soil either by fallowing annually when the garden is large or, as is generally the case for small plots, by ensuring continual replenishment of soil nutrients with ample supplies of animal manure.

Planting of ensete should occur in March, April, or May. April is considered by many as the ideal month: dry weather conditions often exist in March, which could cause young seedlings to wither, and May could be a problem month if the early rains are too heavy, for then the seedlings could be washed out of the ground. In the planting process seven or eight men and boys will dig shallow holes with their digging sticks and drop in the seedlings, the young men following up with the laborious bending involved in scooping the soil over the roots and around the lower stems of the plants. Often maize seeds are intermixed with the ensete plants so that the more rapid growth of the former will shade the latter.[8] The maize will be harvested in late July, having protected the ensete seedlings from sun and severe rainstorms during the early stages of maturation. Meanwhile, the slowly developing ensete plants are soon overshadowed by other plants and at the end of the first year are transplanted to newly prepared plots of seedlings.

Many edible plants other than ensete are cultivated, which perhaps may be best surveyed by describing the layout of a typical garden. The variety of plant life in the relatively small space of an acre or two is immediately impressive. Assuming it is December in the midlands, as one's gaze shifts from the magnificent foliage of the ensete it is attracted by the reddening berries of the few dozen coffee bushes. Then as one surveys the less-striking features of the garden, a variety of vegetables and spices come into view. There are tubers such as sweet potatoes and *boehe* (a potatolike plant) growing along the boundary of the garden where it has direct access to the sun. *Kolčāma* is another tuber, resembling in appearance the taro plant found in Oceania. Also in every garden is a patch of *šana*, a spinachlike green that is often mixed and served with ensete. Varieties of beans are grown in at least one corner. Less frequently (though more so in the highlands), in the larger gardens of more than one or two acres cereal grains such as barley and teff will be found. Formerly, informants say, nearly everyone grew millet, but it has been largely replaced by maize because of the problem of keeping birds from eating millet. Finally, there is always a small part of the garden devoted to spices for use in preserving butter and mixing with ensete. A few gardens may contain banana plants or orange and lemon trees, though most Sadāma do not as yet include these items as part of their diet. Another crop grown by a minority of farmers is sugar cane. Cane is grown in the river valleys and is found in great frequency as one approaches the gardens and pastures of the lowlands, where it constitutes a cash crop.

From the time ensete seedlings are in the ground until the plants reach maturity, the main garden work consists of weeding. In the opinion of informants it takes a minimum of four years before ensete is ready for harvesting. Harvesting can occur any time between the ending of the rains in November through early January. It must always, however, begin on a day associated with good fortune in the lunar calendar. Mature plants are first cut down by the men, and then the women remove long strips from the soft inner core of the stem, which is then left to rot. The women build small shelters of ensete leaves into which they retire to shred the long strips. Once the sections of stem have been shredded, they are mixed with pieces of the root and the mixture is ready for storage. Alternatively, roots from small plants may be boiled and eaten in much the same manner as a boiled potato.

It is difficult to obtain exact quantitative data regarding the rate of

A Wife Preparing the Root of the Ensete Plant after Harvest

consumption of the average household. In a study of the Gurage, a people further to the north who also are ensete cultivators, it is estimated that it takes an average of ten plants a year to feed an adult.[9] This is similar to an estimate obtained from a Sadāma informant of eight plants annually per adult. The key to understanding how much is to be harvested has to do with the size of the pit in which the mixture of ensete and root is stored for several months. A woman instructs her husband to dig a pit according to the dimensions she has learned by experience in harvesting with her mother. Such pits are often dug six feet deep, six by four feet on the sides, so as to contain the remains of forty large plants that were twenty to twenty-five feet in height. Often a smaller pit will be dug to hold the highly valued but less-plentiful white variety of ensete called udi. Furthermore, farmers who derive cash income from selling ensete will dig several pits. Then the mixture is covered with large leaves from the plant and left to ferment for a period ranging from several months to as much as a year. Both prestige and food quality are involved in the process, since it is believed that the taste of the food and the position of the household head are enhanced by the duration of the storage period. There is an implication of wealth in the case of a man with so much ensete in storage that he can wait for a year before using the returns of the previous harvest.

To serve ensete as food a woman first removes it from the pit, wraps the mash in a handful of the stringlike fibers from the stem of the plant, and squeezes out the liquid content. She then kneads and sifts it into a fine flour. Transformation from raw material to food is now complete, and the finished product is referred to as wāsa. It may be served as raw, sour-tasting flour mixed with vegetables, made into small pancakes, or occasionally baked into bread.

Besides ensete, animal domesticates provide the other important resource for sustaining the people. A few goats and an occasional sheep are kept by many households, but the most important domesticates are cattle. A striking feature of hamlets above the five-thousand-foot level is the way in which households and gardens cluster around the periphery of extensive grazing plateaus. Informants invariably indicated that a large herd of cattle, as well as a sizable garden, is the measure of a man of wealth. These same individuals made much of the fact that Sadāma are not fond of meat, limiting their consumption to ritual occasions and to the dry season when milk yields are low. Indeed one can observe a much-restrained etiquette surrounding meat consumption on ceremonial occasions, such that when the sacrificial animal has been divided, individuals eat only a token amount, wrapping the rest in ensete leaves to take home to their families.

This culturally defined constraint on meat consumption is not without certain utilitarian dietary and production aspects, for it is the by-products of cattle, the milk and butter, that constitute the essential protein supplements for the highly carbohydrate diet of ensete. Furthermore, from a sample of twenty-six household heads it was found that there was a mean average of 8.5 animals per household. These animals provide not only necessary food but manure for the ensete, which rapidly exhausts the soil unless periodically fertilized with animal dung.[10] Thus every morning sees women members of the household carrying dung from the cattle kraal to the ensete garden. So, under the circumstances, to slaughter any of the limited number of animals possessed by the average household head would undermine the whole system of food production. And when the men of a village do slaughter a cow for food in the dry season, it is always an animal obtained by purchase or by bartering with Arussi traders in the marketplace. Consequently, the more animals a man possesses the more certain the milk and butter supply for his wives, children, and guests, as well as the greater the productivity of their gardens.

## Population and Settlement Distribution

According to the first official population census of Ethiopia, taken in the spring of 1984, there are 1,445,830 Sadāma.[11] This is considerably higher than a previous 1969 sample survey estimate of 600,000 persons.[12] As the 1984 figures are based only on a preliminary report, there are as yet no data on population density. Nevertheless, it is possible to comment on population density based on a survey of two hamlets in the field research area. There were twenty-five homesteads in one and twenty in the other, with an average of 4.43 persons per household. This provides a figure of approximately 90 to 110 residents in each community. Such figures are in keeping with a geographer's earlier estimate of 240 persons per square mile.[13] At the same time, the average number of persons per household is half of the 7.8 average found among Gurage ensete cultivators.[14]

In terms of spatial distribution there are two principal patrilineal clan groupings, including those who claim descent from Bushē and another who hold Maldea to have been their apical ancestor. On map 1 the Mālga, Yānāssi, Wigā, Shabādino, Hadičō, Gārbičo, and Holō clans are all reputedly descendants of Bushē. All the others, with the exception of certain anomalous patrilineages, are descendants of Maldea. The Āletā clan cluster Saōlla, Hārbigōnā, and Kēvennā are, essentially for recent historical reasons, located in the southeast, while the Havēla remain in the extreme north.

Throughout Sidāmoland, the people live in small hamlets called *kāča*. With the exception of settlements in the lowlands, these consist of collections of huts scattered across the hills and interconnected by a number of narrow, winding footpaths. Such communities are usually named for natural phenomena (as, for example, Danicāmi, after the large number of elephants present when the area was first settled) or they have a name of unknown origin, perhaps from a forgotten person. Hamlets cluster around plateaus that—along with forest land—are treated as common property for purposes of grazing and gathering firewood.

At a more inclusive level is the neighborhood, or *olau,* which consists of a number of hamlets varying in size from a hundred to as many as a thousand households. Since neighborhoods are hamlet groupings for the performance of rituals and reciprocal labor exchange, they must of necessity be ones in which people are personally acquainted. Therefore the ideal size is considered to be between fifty and one hundred households. Larger neighborhoods are often divided into subneighborhoods called *činānča.*

These habitation arrangements are convenient for preserving the symbiotic relations between people, animals, and plants, for the ensete gardens cluster around the households where the animals are penned at night. The women thus have no great distance to travel in hauling manure from the cattle pens to the garden area. Furthermore, the cattle often have only to be moved from the house through the gate of the compound to reach the pasture. And while hamlets are scattered, they are never so far apart as to exclude the possibility for labor exchange or the assembly of the neighborhood to perform rituals. There is also usually a small marketing place within an hour's walk from any hamlet or a major market center that can be reached by foot in, at most, two or three hours. So the only overnight journeys are annual trips to the highlands for ensete seedlings or for removal of cattle to the highlands or lowlands during the extremes of the dry and rainy seasons. This proximity of resources is especially important in light of the difficulties of travel at the height of the rainy season.

Despite—or perhaps because of—limited means of modern communications, the distribution of the people, the durability of their staple food ensete, and the healthful conditions of the high elevation combine to provide a rich and unique culture. I have stressed here the relationships between these ecological factors and residence patterns in order to highlight their role in the historical origins of the people and their subsistence economy, the subjects of the following two chapters.

3

# Origins and History

As is true wherever peoples have no written histories, it is necessary to resort to the oral traditions and genealogies of the Sadāma in order to reconstruct the broad outlines of their origins and early existence.[1] These oral histories are about the struggles between two different kinship groups of the same cultural tradition, in which one seeks, without success, to dominate the other. In the process of resolving this conflict and in subsequent historical events, we see something of the adaptability of the Sadāma, their development of an alternatively respectful and circumventing approach to authority, and the great significance of control of land for the lives of the people.

Mythology and one of the genealogies provided by an informant indicate a northern origin for the Sadāma. One old elder suggested a linkage with the Amhara of Ankobar (see map 2) for the ancestors of Bushē, one of the two founding heroes. Bushē's ancestors, according to this legend, left Ankobar in search of better garden and grazing land and settled in an area somewhere between Harar and Lake Zwai until driven out by Ahmad Gran in the sixteenth century.[2] They then traveled south to the Dawa River. Unfortunately, there is no real genealogical support for such a claim. It is interesting, however, that the old man who could trace his ancestry beyond Maldea, the other founder hero, claimed northern links with the Gurage to the west of Lake Zwai and the Tigre in far northeastern Ethiopia.[3] But the only connection with the Amhara that most informants who were descended from Bushē would concede was that both were created out of earth. Though disagreeing on northern origins, both groups recognized the existence of pressure to move from north to south and agreed that Bushē and Maldea came together somewhere along the Dawa River.[4] The source of the impetus to move south was presumably the Islamic invasion of Ahmad Gran. It is believed that Gran conquered several neighboring peoples before moving north to be defeated by the Amhara in northern Ethiopia.

Though it was agreed that Bushē and Maldea met physically at the Dawa River (see map 2), there was little consensus as to a genealogical connection between the two. A small minority of informants considered them to be brothers, and the fact that they both have a father with the name of Silēmma lends some credence to this hypothesis. Most, however, were adamant in denying a blood relationship.

There are also varying accounts as to how and when Bushē and Maldea happened to settle within the present territorial limits of Sidāmoland. The timing of the move may be estimated from the genealogical charts as beginning approximately eighteen generations ago, early in the sixteenth century. The accounts suggest that Maldea and Bushē left the Dawa River together and arrived at approximately the same time in the land between Lakes Awāsa and Abaya. On the other hand, several of the accounts indicate that Bushē and his father followed their cattle in search of better grazing land, until the cows discovered land with which they were especially content. This land was so fertile that they decided to farm, though they had apparently not practiced agriculture during their stay along the Dawa River. In another version, Bushē and Gugi (the son of the brother of Bushē's

Cattle Grazing in the Dry Season

father) were keeping cattle together at the Dawa River.[5] Both agreed that Bushē should go north to farm while Gugi remained behind to care for the cattle. Later, when Bushē became successful in farming, he sent a request to Gugi for his cattle, which Gugi refused. From that time the descendants of Gugi and Bushē became enemies. This version tallies well with genealogy. Indeed, it provides a historical basis for the alliance of the Gugi with Maldea's descendants that resulted in the establishment of the Āletā cluster of clans.

None of the accounts directly associates Maldea and his descendants with food production, though one says that Maldea had a knowledge of gardening but on the trip north lagged behind Bushē herding his cattle. Surprisingly, for a people whose lives are so taken up with the production and consumption of ensete, there is little mention made of this plant in the mythology.

According to some accounts, it is possible that ensete and even language were provided by a people no longer in existence known as the Hoaffa. The language itself, Sadāminya, is a part of the Highland East Cushitic groups.[6] Nevertheless, it remains questionable as to whether the Sadāma would have acquired their language from the Hoaffa, for they already had genealogical ties with the Boranna through Bushē and linkages with the Oromo-speaking Gugi, both speakers of Eastern Cushitic languages.[7]

Sidāmoland, according to mythology, was originally inhabited by the Hoaffa, whose origins are uncertain.[8] These people were ruled by a tyrant named Galelciord. The narrative history indicates that he and the Hoaffa forced Bushē's and Maldea's descendants back toward the Dawa River. Nevertheless they returned, perhaps in greater numbers, and eventually an uneasy truce seems to have been established. The relationship was unsatisfactory, as indicated in the account by the demands for tribute and various forms of degradation imposed by the Hoaffa. Examples of the latter included requests to produce a rope of sand, to make a heavy mixing board out of a bush, or to transport fresh cow's milk by hand over a great distance before it could cool. The descendants of Bushē and Maldea always responded with great cleverness to these stratagems and managed to outwit the Hoaffa.

The relationship ultimately became untenable. But it is uncertain as to whether the final break came because of increasing numbers of descendants of Maldea and Bushē, the tyranny of the Hoaffa, or a combination of the two. In any event, through use of stealth, the

Sadāma managed to trick the Hoaffa into a test of arms, in which the Hoaffa were defeated.

These events, based on genealogical estimates of from 300 to 375 years ago, may have occurred between 1590 and 1665. If the estimated date of departure from the Dawa River is approximately correct, the descendants of Bushē and Maldea would have been in an uneasy state of contact for a century or more before overwhelming their adversaries.

Shortly after this defeat the conflict began between the Maldeans and the Bushēans. The root cause of dissension between the two groups may have been the increasing control of the most valuable land by the Bushēans. According to legend, Masaiča, a son of Maldea and founder of the Hoyē clan (see figure 1), along with another son Nēwa, were south of the Gidabo River as long ago as three hundred years. Indeed, with the exception of the Havēla, all of the present-day descendants of Maldea are south of the Gidabo River. Taken together with the previous indication that Maldea remained south of Bushē keeping cattle, and was at best only incidentally involved in the defeat of the Hoaffa, the material is suggestive of relatively amicable relations between the two groups prior to claims by Bushē's descendants of control over land north of the river. Furthermore, there is indication that shortly after the annihilation of the Hoaffa, Maldeans south of the Gidabo began to experience pressure on their southern and eastern flanks from Gugi and Jamjam, who were moving north. As a consequence, there seem to have been periodic advances and withdrawals across the river by the Sadāma for the next 150 years, until the early part of the nineteenth century.[9] This may have forced the Maldeans to seek protection from their relatives to the north, ultimately placing themselves in a subservient position.

The basis for superiority of one group over the other lies both in control of land and the concept of *anga*. This term may be translated literally as "hand," but the idiomatic meaning is to avoid the hand of the impure. Elders receive anga when they are promoted to elderhood, after which they may slaughter cattle and in turn eat meat slaughtered only by other elders possessing the trait. They should also abstain from eating a number of impure foods and avoid artisan clan members at mealtimes and on sacrificial occasions. Thus possession of anga connotes the authority of elderhood and a sense of superiority over those who lack it.

As it happens, only three of the eleven clans claiming descent from

Maldea possess anga. It is notable that two of the three with the trait, unlike the others, have always been in control of their own land. In this connection, Bushēans claim that most Maldeans have lost their anga for two reasons. One explanation is that their continual movement back and forth across the Gidabo and sporadic fighting with the Gugi and Jamjam interfered with gardening and herding. This led the Maldeans to eat all sorts of wild animals in violation of anga taboos. Furthermore, as is shown by the dotted lines in figure 1, several of the clans claiming Maldea as an apical ancestor lack descent purity.

The matter of land control (that is, the sanctuary that Bushēans claim to have provided the Maldeans) and the lack of anga have given rise to claims of superiority of the former over the latter. Though the Maldeans tend to admit this reasoning, they deny that it is important, maintaining that anga is useless and simply an excuse for a condescending attitude on the part of Bushēans. At any rate, as the legend in the following section indicates, it was of major ideological importance in the conflict that led to the establishment of Āletā.

## The Founding of Āletā

In order to understand the present location and relationships between the Āletā clans vis-à-vis the rest of the Sadāma, it is necessary to review the history of this development. Indeed, it is the conflict between Bushē's and Maldea's descendants over anga and land control that provides the basis for this narrative.

The descendants of Masaiča and Dāma (see figure 1) had been living south of the Gidabo River and fighting the Gugi for many years. But periodically they were forced to return across the river to seek sanctuary with Bushē's relatives. There came a time, however, when the Gugi tired of these periodic infringements of what they considered to be their land, and threatened to invade north of the river. So to forestall an invasion, the elders agreed to give annual tribute to the Gugi in the form of a large number of heifers. Since, however, the Bushēans held greater authority and were probably more numerous, they sought to require the refugees from the south to provide the tribute. This led to great resentment among the Maldeans, ultimately leading to a break with the Bushēans.

At this point, according to the legendary account, two Maldean brothers lacking anga violated the slaughtering taboo and were cursed

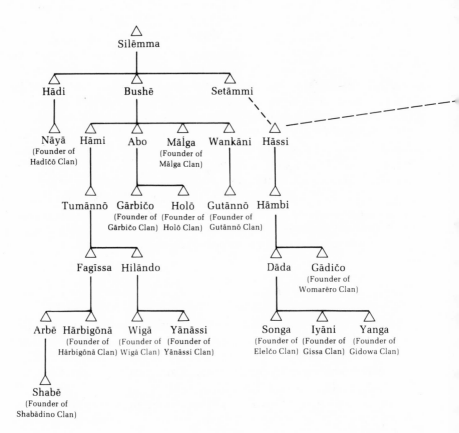

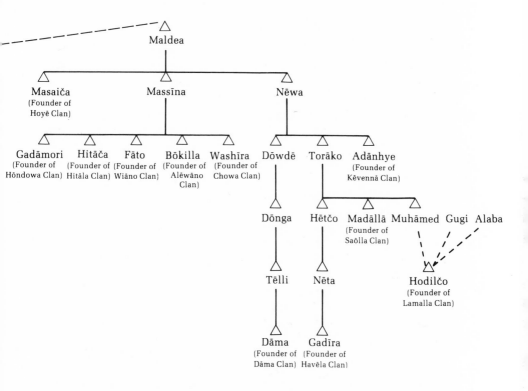

**Figure 1.** Genealogical Relations of Sadāma Clans
*Note:* Dotted lines refer in the case of Hāssi to disputed genealogical
links to Maldea or Bushē. For Hodilčo the dotted lines show a recognized connection between the Gugi and Alaba peoples as well as linkage between one of the Lamalla subclans and Maldea. *Source:* Author.

by Bushēans. Further quarrels and taboo violations followed until one of the brothers was killed. To end the growing rift, the remaining brother, Locke, contrived a plan to gain the blessing of the elders for a reoccupation of the land south of the Gidabo River.

Ordinarily the elders would have been reluctant to give such a blessing, since it would result in a loss of labor and creation of a potential threat to their own hegemony. But Locke and his mother prepared a very potent mead. And when the elders had drunk themselves into a state of intoxication, they were cajoled into giving their blessing.[10] So Locke, his relatives, and friends tricked the elders and returned south of the Gidabo.

Despite the de facto occupation, the elders soon began to realize the folly of their blessing and devised a plan to retake the land by force. Whereupon Locke, having learned of the stratagem, sent for help from his paternal uncle. The uncle lived with the Gugi and was able to persuade his friends to bring their cavalry to support Locke and his allies. The two groups set a clever trap, routed the enemy, and drove them back across the Gidabo.

Among the victorious allies were Maldeans from five different descent groups.[11] These were the people who, after the battle, initially established residences in the triangular area formed by the three major ritual centers of Birā, Goida, and Golāmā (see map 1). And because of Locke's service as leader, it was agreed that his relatives and their descendants would be entitled to half of all the land acquired south of the Gidabo, with the other groups dividing the remainder in equal shares.

According to legend it was also at this time that the people became known as the Āletā. The term came about as the result of a woman's having borne a son to one man from each group. Since women are not permitted, as a sign of respect, to mention the name of their husband's group, she would have had difficulty in referring by name to any of the peoples south of the Gidabo. So when she mentioned her problem to the elders they suggested that all the people be called the Āletā, a term she was free to use. And since that time all of the descent groups south of the Gidabo, bordered on the east by the Gārbičo and on their southern extremes by the Hadičō, have been collectively known as the Āletā.[12]

Since the initial establishment of residence, the people of Āletā have expanded to the west, east, and south as can be seen from the crosshatch area in map 1. This is partially a result of population expansion and the practices of the generational class system. Thus every seven years a new class of initiates has sought to outdo previous classes by raiding cattle from the enemy. For the seminomadic, cattle-keeping Gugi and Jamjam, this harassment, along with the expanding population of the food-producing Sadāma, has been sufficient to force them to abandon the area.[13]

## Discussion

These legendary tales passed on from one generation to another, as well as the evidence of kinship connections, enable us to gain some understanding of where the Sadāma originated and of how they came to occupy Sidāmoland. In these narratives we learn of the struggles and conflicts between the descendants of Maldea and Bushē in which the latter sought to dominate the former by claiming symbolic and ritual genealogical purity, by providing sanctuary from the Oromo-speaking Gugi, and ultimately by using force. But in time the descendants of Maldea managed to escape their subordinate status through a temporary alliance with the Gugi. This alliance enabled them to gain control of exceedingly fertile land, which is presently the optimum area for producing ensete and coffee.

There are three themes in this historical material that are relevant for understanding the economy, authority, and community participation of the people: one concerns the adaptability to change, another the respect for and circumvention of authority, and a third the conflict over land. Illustrative of the first is the story of Bushē's search for ideal soil and grazing conditions. The possible change of language, switching from grain to ensete production, and the ability to align themselves with people from other ethnic groups are also examples of adaptability to change. At the same time there is evidence for both the importance of authority in the concern of Locke and his associates for approval by the elders before crossing the Gidabo River and the importance of deferring to age and seniority as reflected in the customs connected with anga. Nevertheless, there is also indication of a willingness to manipulate authority for purposes of self-interest, as in the intoxication plot of Locke and his mother to persuade the Bushēan elders to give them the land south of the Gidabo. And finally, throughout the narratives there is quarreling over territorial access, ranging from the displacement of the original inhabitants to the dispute between Bushē's and Maldea's descendants over the control of Āletā to the expansion of the Āletāns at the expense of Gugi during the last century.

4 Kinship, Hierarchy,
and Resource
Distribution

> But Money is to the West what
> kinship is to the rest.
> —Marshall Sahlins,
> *Culture and Practical Reason*

Kinship rather than money, even today, is the key to understanding social relations and is the sine qua non of much of the subsistence production of the Sadāma. It is important to appreciate how genealogical ties provide the basis for allocation and control of land, the principal means of production. Therefore the main focus of this chapter is on kinship structure as the form for distributing and protecting resources, as well as for allocating the labor to make them productive. Secondly, I will explore the degree to which hierarchical relationships exist and affect the relations of production by examining the structure of descent and community, access to property, relations within and between generations, and social inequality.

## Clan, Lineage, and Community

Identity and rights to property are based on descent through a line of males. In keeping with the classical literature on kinship structure, I consider these lines of descent as clans (*gurrī*) and lineages (*boselo*). A lineage is usually considered as a group of unilineal kin in which members can demonstrate genealogical links with other members from a recognized common ancestor.[1] The clan, on the other hand, is a more inclusive unilineal group, in which exact genealogical articulations cannot be traced, though the members believe that a connection exists with a founding ancestor.

With the exception of the Āletā, the people are organized into a number of these virtually autonomous patrilineal clans. Āletā comprises twelve such patrilineal groups, of which seven claim descent from Maldea, four are of uncertain origin, and one has its inception

31

in the Gugi (see figure 1). The Shabādino, Yānāssi, Wigā, Mālga, Holō, Gārbičo, and Hārbigōnā all claim descent from Bushē. They refer to themselves as the Yamarīčo, which in translation means those with purity of descent. Interspersed among them are the Havēla, Saōlla and Kēvennā, which, as noted earlier, also claim descent from Maldea.

All men of these clans, which range in depth from nine to nineteen generations, claim descent from one or the other of the two founders, Maldea and Bushē, but very few can claim to trace or reach a consensus concerning the genealogical steps connecting their generation with the founders. As informants explained, few men can actually trace their ancestry to clan founders and the collateral relatives stemming from these through more than five or six generations.

Though clans are divided into lineages, the lineages are not further subdivided into major, minor, and minimal segments in any terminological sense recognized by the Sadāma. The only term indicating segmentation into less-inclusive segments than the gurrī is that of boselo. As informants explained, the basis for the segmentation of a clan into lineages is an increase in population of a particular line(s) and/or movement of one group some distance from other agnates in search of better grazing land and more fertile garden space.

It is clear that relationships within the lineage are conceived as much closer than those among clansmen. Indeed, the term hecob-minne ("house of my father") is sometimes used interchangeably with boselo, which translates as "near the fire." Clans contain varying numbers of these lineages ranging in depth from five to nine generations. And when the lineage depth is shallow, it is possible for the members actually to trace their descent from an apical ancestor and list most of their collateral relatives.

For example, Hitāča, the reputed founder of Hitāla clan, is said to have had two sons, each of whom in turn had five sons, the apical ancestors of the ten lineages associated with the clan. Bushito lineage is illustrative of one of these shallow depth units. It involves a core of male agnatic kin in the two hamlets of intensive fieldwork. Residing in these two communities are thirty-three of the forty living men and boys of this lineage who, through their ties with Bushi in the sixth ascending generation, are believed ultimately to connect with Hitāča, the putative founding ancestor of the clan. Beyond this point, however, only some of the elders will venture to claim a connection to the revered clan founder Hitāča. And this is without consensus as to the order of ascent.

By contrast, there are nine patrilineages in Shabādino clan that, being older and in control of contiguous stretches of land, are of greater genealogical depth than those of the Hitāla. Several of these lineages are at least nine generations in depth, with the alleged founder too remote for any but a handful of old men willing to attempt to trace a connection.[2] Indeed, the Yamarīčo lineages have such lengthy histories and large numbers that they would probably have become clans among the Āletā. The reason this has not happened is likely due to their close and stable spatial contiguity, quite unlike the scattered Āletā descent groups.

Patrilineages have politico-ritual functions, with the elders often being important in settling disputes and making policy concerning closely related kinsmen. And in crisis situations such as drought or widespread dissension among relatives, the elders will call all of them together to sacrifice an animal in honor of the apical lineage ancestor.

These descent groups are corporate in that they control property and are represented by assemblies of elders, the elders gathering periodically to perform ritual sacrifice.[3] Members can be called upon by the elders to defend clan territory and are answerable to them for their behavior. Conversely, should a man be involved in a dispute with members of another clan, he can expect assistance from men of his own group. By contrast, women and children have limited jural status, with their husbands or fathers being responsible for their conduct. Authority for upholding jural status rests with the clan assembly of elders, who, in addition to constituting the highest council of appeal from less-inclusive levels of organization, also perform ritual sacrifice in honor of the founding clan ancestor.

Generally, clans are exogamous. But there are some, like the Holō and Gārbičo, whose descendants claim a connection with a mythical hero founder and who thus do not marry one another. Usually, however, people without such clan connections are not restricted from marriage. There are historical accounts of formerly unrelated descent groups in which the people of one seek to gain an advantage in terms of protection or access to better land by joining the other. To signify the merger, the elders formally announce that they will be as one by becoming endogamous.

Continuity of descent and land occupation, as well as observance of certain ritual taboos, is important in determining clan prestige. For example, the previously discussed concept of anga (referring to avoidance of impure foods and stigmatized people, such as artisans) gives the Yamarǐčo clans a sense of superiority over the Āletā clans that do not possess anga. Furthermore, after the Āletā clans defeated the Yamarǐčo clans and drove out the Gugi, they became dispersed in a checkerboard pattern. By contrast, the Yamarǐčo clans occupy continuous land segments.

The residents of Āletā neighborhoods are often of mixed clan origins, partly as a result of dispersion and partly due to migration of nonrelatives and relatives by marriage, often from Yamarǐčo clans, in search of better pasture and gardening land. Therefore, a given hamlet will be associated in clan affiliation with the original inhabitants, but a high percentage or even a majority of household heads may be of varying clan origins. In the three hamlets of intensive fieldwork, for instance, 64, 60, and 27 percent of household heads had the clan affiliation of the founders. Though these persons of different clan origins are technically strangers, they are treated, except for purposes of marriage and certain rituals, as having jural identity similar to those who are clan members. Moreover, it is not unusual for a man to have land in two or more communities, having first received an inheritance from his father and later from a father-in-law, a mother's brother, or from the elders in widely separated areas. In the present situation this latter alternative is seldom possible, because of increasing population and the intensity of production resulting from cash cropping. In the past, however, when land was more plentiful, a stranger to the community had only to beg the elders for access, and he would be accommodated.

Despite the reality of clan heterogeneity in much of Āletā, the fiction is publicly maintained that all adult males belong to the clan with which the community is identified. Privately the people know and admit the different clan origins of various household heads, since this knowledge is crucial for maintaining the clan exogamy rule. Nevertheless, anyone violating the taboo by publicly discussing the different origins of others will be severely sanctioned by the elders. In the old days a violator would be fined seven heifers, four to the man whose origins had been mentioned and three to the elders who discussed the case. Today, however, sanction takes the form of a monetary fine. This helps to maintain harmony and enlist the support of outsiders in cooperative labor and defense of the land. In the present, actual fighting over land between clans seldom occurs, but rights to access must often be defended in government courts, which requires financial contributions from all household heads. Therefore, all household heads who are "strangers" continue to participate in all activities except clan rituals.

The formation of clans claiming descent from Bushē and collectively known as the Yamarĭčo involves several narratives of fraternal conflict. Thus the cleavage that led ultimately to the establishment of the Holō and Gārbičo clans southeast of the Gidabo River occurred when a younger refused to cleanse an elder brother who violated an anga taboo. The elder brother had unwittingly eaten meat slaughtered by a descendant of Maldea. The incident created so much conflict that the elder brother left, swearing eternal enmity between the kinsmen and their descendants.

In another instance, a quarrel between two brothers over a father's blessing led to the formation of the Shabādino and Hārbigōnā clans. The elder brother had been disobedient to his father and the father had decided to bless the younger by giving him greater power and authority than his eldest son. But the latter tricked his father into giving him the blessing. Later the father also blessed the younger son with wealth and an abundance of descendants. The two brothers then went separate ways and the son of one became the founder of the Shabādino, whose descendants occupy the continuous expanse of territory extending from the Loghita River to the Billate River (see map 1).

Finally, the founding of the Wigā and Yānāssi clans was based on the mythical quarrel of two brothers over a goat-milking contest. One claimed that his half-brother was illegitimate and the offended brother sought to gain revenge by placing thorns in the nipples of his brother's goat. As a consequence he lost the contest. The resulting animosity led to the separation of the two half-brothers, with their descendants ultimately becoming two different clans.

In general the oral histories show a connection between land acquisition and an emphasis on independent resource control. At the individual level there is evidence of conflict within and between generations. This is at variance with the prescribed norms of amity, reciprocity, and seniority between brothers and their fathers, which are supposed to take precedence over self-interest. It is this form of conflict that has led to the dispersion and acquisition of what constitutes contemporary clan territories.

The most important organizational level for providing large-scale labor and the carrying out of much ritual activity is a residential unit. This is the neighborhood, or olau. It usually involves the members of two or more lineages and, in Āletā, not infrequently involves members with different clan affiliations. A neighborhood consists of contiguous hamlets and, as noted in the previous chapter, should not number less than one hundred families (three or four hamlets). Because of labor and ritual functions, neighborhoods are kept at this optimum operational size. Since the neighborhood provides men for large-scale work projects such as house building, clearing trails, and cleaning water holes, a larger group of workers would be too unwieldy to manage. The ideal size is considered to be between fifty and one hundred household heads for these tasks. Their wives cooperate in preparing the food for the work parties and for the guests at the large ritual feasts. For any work project there is always a leader who serves as foreman, known as a *morīča*. His job, with the aid of the elders, is to direct the actual work activities and to fine those men who neglect or fail to appear for work. Such a leader is selected by the elders on the basis of his respect for them, impartiality, self-control, and the esteem in which he is held by others. His sanctioning authority, however, is always under the scrutiny of the elders, who watch for any sign that he may be unnecessarily intimidating workers.

The social groups that compose the neighborhoods are the hamlets, or *kāča*. Like neighborhoods, these are residential units of households, with the land considered as being a part of the clan territory of the original settler. Thus a hamlet—and this is especially true in Āletā—is likely to have household heads who constitute a small majority or even a minority of men affiliated with the clan ancestor. The rest of the household heads will be resident strangers who are treated, except for marriage and certain rituals, as if they are members of the founder's clan.

The household (*minne-māna*) typically consists of the male head, his wife, children, and cattle. The house itself consists of a circular base of wooden posts to which is attached a framework of interlaced poles covered with straw thatch.[4] Its interior is divided in half with a small fence, the people living on one side and the cattle on the other. Though the average number of persons is 4.43 per household, there are of course variations in household composition, with the occasional presence of an enfeebled grandfather, a grandmother, a father's sister, or a brother temporarily without a spouse. Sometimes a widow will be found living alone, with her house and garden tended by a son. And sometimes an older household head will have a similarly constructed dwelling in which he sleeps and receives guests.

Households in the Highlands

A Household Compound in the Middle Zone of Elevation

37

The household is the most basic unit of production. Women are responsible for the harvesting of ensete, all food preparation, and the cleanliness of the living and cattle areas. Care of the cattle area is especially important, for it involves removing dung from the cattle pen, where the animals are always housed at night, and distributing it around the ensete plants in the garden. As already indicated, this is critical for plant growth. Men, on the other hand, are responsible for preparing the land, planting, weeding, and caring for the cattle. In all these tasks husbands and wives are assisted by their children, who watch the cattle and goats during the day to see that they do not stray from the pasture into household gardens. Then as the children mature, their work lives diverge, with boys helping their fathers in gardening and girls taking on the heavier burdens originally allocated to their mothers, such as fetching firewood and water at a distance from the family compound.

If the household head needs more assistance than can be provided by household labor, as he often does in the heavy work of clearing and planting a garden, he will call upon two or three neighbors who may be friends, brothers, or paternal cousins. In turn he will be

Relatives and Friends Preparing a Garden

obligated when asked to come to their aid. Women also exchange labor during the harvest season. Thus these hamlet-centered work groups, involving three or four adults exchanging their labor, are small enough to minimize the time interval for each participant in accomplishing such tasks as planting and harvesting.

To summarize, the Sadāma receive their jural identity and initial access to land through their clan affiliation. These large descent groups are subdivided into lineages of close face-to-face relations, in which the elders may perform rituals and decide important matters affecting closely related agnatic kin. The actual labor for making the land productive, however, is provided in large- and small-scale residential groups at the neighborhood, hamlet, and household levels. Hereditary rights in land and animals will be discussed in the next section.

## Property Distribution

To understand the distribution of property it is necessary to consider its nature and limits, inheritance rights, and recent complications. The most important forms of property are those that are basic to production and the acquisition of prestige. For the Sadāma, these forms are land, cattle, and—at the present—cash.

According to mythology, when the land was first settled, a certain portion of every neighborhood was set aside for the public to graze their animals, along with a woodlot for firewood and high grass areas for providing thatch. All of the remainder was to be available to individual households for gardening and grazing animals. The only recognized title in land was held by the clan historically associated with a given parcel, with all household heads having rights of use that could be transmitted from one generation to another. Tangible signs of allocation and use were, in the early days, numerous small trenches serving as boundaries. But as population increased, land became too valuable to be wasted in boundary ditches, and the limits of household property came to be demarcated by rows of cacti and/ or red flowering plants, called *reji*. In the highlands of the bamboo forest regions, neatly placed bamboo fences serve to divide household property limits.

Since clan exogamy is practiced, women are not eligible to inherit land or cattle. In the past and continuing into the present, land ideally has been divided at marriage by a father giving equal shares to all but the eldest son. By virtue of their birth order seniority, eldest sons always receive slightly more land than their siblings, the amount being left to the discretion of the father. Nevertheless, it is usually the youngest son, because he is expected to care for his parents in their old age, who receives the household and remaining garden at their death. This land, in addition to the parcel received at marriage, usually provides the youngest son with the largest share of a father's land. If a father should die before his sons are ready for marriage, then his older brother will hold the land in trust until his nephews are ready to establish households of their own. The allocation process involves the father in measuring out garden plots with long strips of dried ensete, with a small area for cattle grazing left to be shared in common by his sons.

In polygynous marriages each wife receives a garden area in addition to a domicile for herself and her children, with the first wife usually receiving more land than succeeding co-wives. Furthermore, when a father divides the land among sons of his co-wives, the eldest son is given half the land of his mother's household, with the remainder divided equally among his younger male siblings. In the event that a junior wife lacks sons, her land will go to the eldest son of the senior wife. Then, depending on the degree of amity between co-wives, the eldest son may permit his mother's co-wife to reside on the land until her death, or he may request that she return to her own relatives.[5]

Unless a father has more than the average number of cattle (the average for the research communities was 8.5), he will not give animals with land when his sons marry. The decision to give or not to give animals and the number to give are entirely at his discretion. If he possesses relatively few animals when he dies, the youngest son usually receives them with the remainder of the land. Alternatively, the father may give cattle or money as a token of affection to a favorite son, the criterion being which son serves him the best. This form of reciprocal altruism, however, often favors the youngest son because of his ascribed role of caring for the parents in their old age.

These traditional procedures for property distribution continue, in the main, to be practiced today. Nevertheless, there have been important changes resulting from historical events beginning in the latter part of the nineteenth century. Until that time Ethiopia had remained a loose congeries of virtually independent kingdoms and tribal groups owing only nominal allegiance to an emperor. Then under the three emperors Tewodros II, Yohannes IV, and Menelik II, centralization and unification of these groups began, resulting in the formation of the Ethiopian Empire.[6] Though the empire was finally consolidated under Menelik II shortly after the beginning of the twentieth century, the situation remained precarious largely because of Italian colonization of Eritrea and Somalia. Indeed, the Italian interest in building an empire in East Africa ultimately culminated in the Italo-Ethiopian War of 1935–36. This resulted in a brief interlude of Italian occupation, ended by joint reconquest by British and Ethiopian forces in 1941.

At the time of Emperor Menelik's conquest in 1894–95, soldiers of the conquering army who remained in the south were assigned from 50 to 150 men to work their land, cut their wood, and on occasion make their wives available for preparing food. This was the *gabbar* system and was rationalized as being a means for supporting the military role of the household heads, which necessitated their being absent from their land and families for prolonged periods.[7] Sadāma were permitted one day a week to attend to their own land. As a consequence of these severe conditions, the fathers and uncles of many of my informants escaped by fleeing to the heavily forested terrain in the mountains until the Italo-Ethiopian War in 1935–36. After World War II gabbar was abolished, but many descendants of Menelik's soldiers retained large land allotments, especially in Hadičō clan territory to the south (see map 1). These allotments, known as *maderia*, were given in lieu of salary for their military service, and Sadāma remaining on such land were forced to pay a rent of one-third or more of their harvest. This system was finally abolished after the 1974 Revolution.

Land not allocated to Menelik's soldiers was placed under the jurisdiction of a *balabat*, one of the lowest-ranking government officials.[8] Among the Sadāma, balabats were chosen from ritual clan leaders known as *mote*, who were widely respected for their mediatory and ceremonial functions, but who had not traditionally been associated with the control of land. Consequently, a mote who continued to respect and protect the usufruct rights of clan members, by acting as a cultural broker with the conquerors, retained this respect. Those, however, who sought to use the balabat title to usurp land rights of others for their own gain or to win favor with the conquerors aroused the enmity of the people.

During the time gabbar was enforced, land was surveyed and divided into *gaša*. This procedure began around 1912 and slowly expanded to cover the forested and mountainous regions during the 1920s and early 1930s.[9] On each gaša, four men were made responsible for paying the land tax imposed to support the developing Ethiopian state bureaucracy. Later with increasing population and the advent of cash cropping in coffee following World War II, land shortages became a problem. As a consequence it was not uncommon for tax receipt holders to attempt to ignore traditional land use practices and to claim title to the land for themselves. As will be shown later, these practices led to considerable conflict and land dispute litigation, both in the Ethiopian courts and in the traditional dispute settlement system.

A further major impact upon traditional land distribution occurred when the Sadāma realized that they possessed an alternative form of inheritance rights enforceable through the Ethiopian courts. This alternative, followed by the Amhara (the dominant ethnic group among the conquerors), prescribed that land be divided equally among all male and female children.[10] This new set of rules provided an alternative to be pursued, according to self-interest. For example, a brother might find it in his interest to have land divided on the basis of equal shares rather than permitting his eldest and youngest siblings to acquire larger shares under traditional inheritance rules. In one recorded situation of a childless co-wife, the eldest son of the first wife wished to take advantage of his rights to all the co-wife's land, but his brothers threatened to take him to court if he did not follow the equal shares option. Another example involved the case of the descendants of two antagonistic co-wives, one of whom lacked sons. The eldest son of the first wife sought to claim the land, but the daughter of the second wife went to court to take advantage of the equal shares option. Nevertheless, social pressure applied by the elders to enforce conformity to traditional inheritance rights and continuing resentment of the conquest and imposition of what have invariably been described as the laws of "Amhara foreigners" tend to ensure that most Sadāma adhere to the traditional system. But a minority have taken advantage of the alternative land distribution process, which has led to widespread divisiveness and conflict among the people.

A combination of changing attitudes toward land distribution, the advent of a cash economy, and land scarcity have also affected the role of the stranger in acquiring land. Before World War II, a stranger requesting land would assume a fictive kinship role in respect to a land giver; if he were young he would serve the giver like a son, and if middle aged he would assume the status of a brother. Today, however, people have become reluctant to allow strangers the use of vacant land. When a stranger does receive land he must pay cash to the donor, usually on an annual basis at the time of tax collection.

In general, traditional land-use rights without alienation remain predominant in the property control and transfer process, with seniority, duty to the aged, and parental preference tending to favor the eldest and youngest sons as heirs. This system of land transfer supports the importance of seniority in the male line and gives security to the elderly by providing incentive for the youngest son to assume responsibility. Favoritism, often for the youngest son, further ensures that aged parents will receive care. Polygynous marriages provide even more support for the principle of seniority, with the eldest and youngest sons of the senior wife clearly having an advantage over junior wives without sons. But incorporation into the Ethiopian Empire has resulted in the new concept of equal land shares for all heirs, regardless of gender. This concept, by providing new alternatives for the pursuit of self-interest, contradicts seniority and the old age security aspects of traditional inheritance rules. In addition, population increase, cash cropping, and division into gaša for taxation purposes have led to alienation through title claim and, in some instances, the buying and selling of land. Finally, the traditional process of incorporating strangers into a community on a fictive kinship basis has been curtailed by demands for land rent payments.

## Mutuality and Seniority between and within Generations

Kinship for the Sadāma, however, is more than identification with clans and lineages for purposes of protection and gaining access to property; it is also the sharing of labor in the production process. To understand the significance of labor exchange, it is necessary to analyze paternal/maternal roles vis-à-vis children, relations with the grandparental generation, and relations between siblings and cousins.

Given the patrilineal orientation of the people, it is not surprising to find that the key dyadic relationship is between father (ānna) and son *(bēto)*. The two most important terms in describing the content of their activities with one another are *wājete* ("respect") and *gašōte* ("domination"). In this regard there was a consensus among informants that friendship and love are always secondary to respect in this relationship. Consequently, the father is necessarily an authority figure to the son, constituting a model of the elder-youth role of the generational class system, which predominates throughout Sidāmoland. This bond continues even after death, when the father may appear in a son's dream and demand to be served by him. At this request the son will prepare a ritual feeding, usually honey or a bull, or will risk personal disaster.

The father begins training a son for the productive work of an adult around the age of six, teaching him to herd the household cattle and later showing him how to prepare and care for a garden. Both of these activities are demanding and often frustrating, as indicated in the following reminiscence taken from my field notes of the early experience of a young man in his late twenties.

> When I began to keep cows, my father told me where I must keep them so that they might not eat other people's corn or enter into any gardens

Father and Sons Engaged in Planting Ensete and Maize

in the neighborhood. I should see that they were not eaten by any wild animals. Unfortunately, once a hyena came and ate a donkey. Sometimes leopards would come and pick out goats, sheep, or even calves. Sometimes the cattle would get into other people's gardens. Then when I came home in the evening my father would call me a "lazy boy," become angry, and sometimes beat me with a stick. Not only this, but the sun was hot, and sometimes the rain was very heavy. This way I thought that there was no harder life than keeping cattle. But it was not all bad, because I could play games with other children in the pasture, which made me happy.

As I got older I left the cattle, and my father began to teach me how to garden. I had thought that gardening would be more pleasant than looking after cattle, that it would be easy. This is because no one controls you, since it is all your own job. Second, you can pick all kinds of food and eat as much as you want. I did not then know that there are many enemies such as monkeys. I had to wake up before sunrise and watch the garden all day into the evening. Soon I began to feel there was no harder life than watching corn day and night. The monkeys came by day and wild pigs came at night. I hated this life.

Later, when a boy is fifteen or sixteen, he is considered ready to assist in house building and other work group activities. This opportunity to participate in the men's work group activities is highly desirable and greatly looked forward to by most youngsters.

The values instilled by a father in training a son are just as important for his future productivity as learning the techniques. When a son begins to take an active part in herding and gardening, greater emphasis is placed on acceptance of the idealized character attributes of obedience and respect for elders, hard work and honesty. In addition, a son will learn to admire the prestige of wealth. Proverbs are widely used to extol the virtues of work and to avoid the stigma of laziness. Three frequently quoted proverbs are as follows:

| Tōče wāro cagāgo | People who dislike work |
| Ita-vāro fa-gōgo | Enjoy only eating |
| | |
| Tōke wen-īnčo | The digging tool works |
| Ka-rēnā lo-pāuse | Only if the workers are present |
| Mō-ku tīlte tū-mi | But the spoon is always ready for the porridge bowl |
| | |
| Cāma-lāiza sū-me ditōrto | Lazy lip doesn't get dirty (a talkative person does little work) |

Youngsters are rewarded for achievement and initiative, such as taking cattle to inconvenient but unusually favorable grazing spots or showing extra diligence in performing weeding chores. At the same time, they are encouraged to revere the terms *jīrsi* and *drūma*, both signifying wealth. *Butēma* ("poverty") is associated with misfortune and low social status.

Boys are taught that the means to wealth is through planning, persistence, and the use of knowledge. Sons observe their fathers and other men in the community as they plan a balance between subsistence and cash crops so as to maximize profits from the sale of coffee without exhausting their food supply. Successful entrepreneurs are pointed out as men who, through buying coffee futures, acquire more money in the long run than those who use their cash for short-term gains such as food or clothing luxuries. Also, stories are told of how poor men become wealthy despite all kinds of obstacles, through persistence at trading and farming. The seeming paradox in inculcating obedience and responsibility to elders, while at the same time encouraging self-interest in seeking after wealth, is ideally balanced against the rule that wealth should be redistributed.

Nevertheless, should all such efforts to develop conformity to the social norms fail, there are also punitive sanctions. But fathers usually try to warn and cajole recalcitrant sons into conformity before resorting to physical punishment. A certain amount of obstreperousness and disobedience is expected from young boys, but not from youths in their late teens. And when warnings and physical punishment fail to direct them into acceptable deportment, fathers with the support of other elders will impose a form of ostracism known as *sīra*. Should this drastic step be taken, all members of the community will refuse to share food, work, or even conversation with the wayward young. Such an extreme sanction, never imposed on women or children, is seldom used by a father, since it can lead to loss of service and labor by the son.

A case in point, from my field notes, is of a son who became a Christian despite his father's objections. The subsequent estrangement of the two, combined with great distance between households, led to less frequent visits. In time the father became incensed and together with the elders of his hamlet formally ostracized his son. When, however, the son showed some remorse by visiting and bringing presents to the old man, the father quickly called together the elders to revoke the sanction. He badly needed a new house, which could not be built without his son's direction and money to feed the builders from the neighborhood.

A consideration of the position of the father's brother *(wasīlla)* shows that, as in many patrilineal systems, he may become a father surrogate for his brother's son. As previously noted, in the event of his brother's death the father's brother may hold the land in trust until the brother's sons are ready for marriage, and he also may provide them with assistance in obtaining bridewealth. This is the ideal role, but if a deceased brother's son acquires land as a stranger or if his father's landholdings are widely scattered, a lack of physical proximity may limit the potential for interaction. Nevertheless, a man should always provide assistance whenever requested by his father's brother and should keep up the relationship by periodic visits.

Those relationships between fathers and sons are the key to understanding authority, resource allocation, and redistribution in Sidāmoland. In explaining the significance of this articulation between elders and youth, Marxist anthropologists point out that land is an "instrument of labor" and that workers of one generation are indebted to the previous generation for seeds and food.[11] This contribution creates a continuous cycle of production from one generation to the next. The oldest group ultimately owes its subsistence to no living members of the community, but only to the dead elders. All other living members are indebted to the living elders. Thus this senior segment "owes nothing to any living individual," but controls the means of physiological reproduction through control of the food supply and reproduction of labor through control of access to women and of the rules of marriage. In effect this redistribution of resources to the youth by the elders is not a reciprocal return for work performed by the youth. It is basically an indication of the authority of the elders that creates a lasting indebtedness by the youth, placing them in a subordinate position.[12]

This depiction of subordination of one generation to another, in which the senior generation is lacking in indebtedness to the junior, does not adequately describe the structure of these relations among the Sadāma. The model for articulating relations between generations is not one of simple indebtedness of junior to senior, but a circular interdependency as shown in figure 2. Elders have wealth in the form of land and cattle. They also have authority, which is vested in their rights to make policy, settle disputes, and impose sanctions. The possession of these attributes gives them the means for obligating

**Figure 2.** Intergenerational Relations.
*Source:* Author

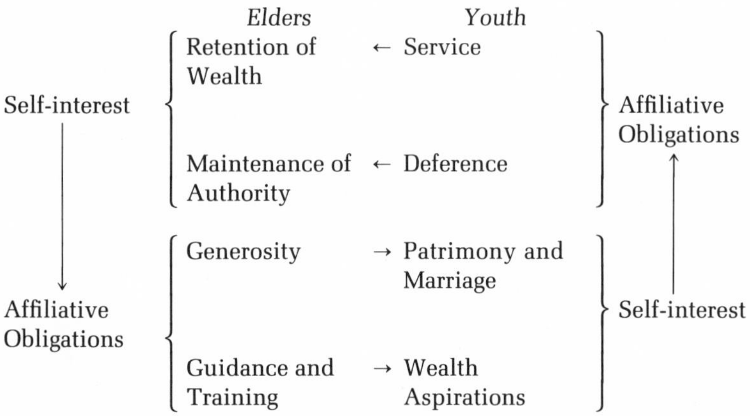

others. But they in turn must give up most (ultimately, all) of their wealth to their sons in the form of bridewealth, land, cattle. To show reluctance in parting with wealth when a son is of age and expresses readiness to marry is to invite community stigmatization as a miser or sorcerer and ultimately sanction by other elders. Moreover, an elder must use this authority responsibly for encouraging and training the youth in appropriate techniques and values of production. This obligation is taxing of an elder's time, energy, and patience. So in redistributing his wealth and expertise he is expressing his indebtedness to youth for the labor they provide in herding, gardening, and community tasks, as well as for the honor and respect they show to the elders.

In effect, the arrows in figure 2 show that the self-interest of an elder in maintaining his material well-being and his hegemony is balanced by his obligations to redistribute his resources and to educate the youth in the appropriate life-style. This provides for the self-interest of the youth in obtaining necessary resources to acquire wealth and reproduce the system. In turn, the youth must reciprocate through their respect and service to the elders.

Unlike the authoritarian father, the mother (*am-īte*) has a role, in keeping with the ideal women's attributes of humility and friendship, that is essentially nurturant in regard to children. But in addition to looking after their creature comforts, she is also expected to support the father in their discipline. Like her husband she tends to favor boys because of the security sons provide in old age and because of the fact that girls must marry out of their descent group and thus are a part of the household only until middle adolescence. As the domestic cycle progresses, so does the status of the mother advance with age. Leadership among women, however, is largely situational, depending on the ability to organize efficiently and to allocate tasks in preparing food for redistribution at ritual feasts.

Foster parentage is a means of providing for labor allocation in households without children. Household heads with no children of their own cannot be refused when they beg their more fortunate relatives to provide them with a foster child. The labor of these children constitutes an important contribution to household production in the form of gathering firewood and keeping cattle, in the case of boys, and assistance by girls in cooking and cleaning activities. Adults without such youthful assistants are at a definite disadvantage in the subsistence process. Therefore, categories of foster parents include both maternal and paternal relatives, very often grandparents, but also childless sisters and brothers of the paternal generation. A child is never given to a stranger and usually continues to live in the same hamlet as the parents. Furthermore, foster children are more often male than female because boys are likely to provide labor support for a longer period than girls, who, in adolescence, usually marry out of the community. A natural parent usually arranges marriage for a daughter who has been a foster child and shares the bridewealth with the foster parent(s). On the other hand, boys continue to belong to their father's clan and when they marry expect to receive a share of the father's land, which may be supplemented by a gift of property from the foster parent.

The roles of other relatives of the parental generation, including mother's brothers (*abo*), mother's sisters (*tat-lāma*), and father's sisters (*adā-da*), are essentially nurturant. Though a mother's brother may join his sister's husband in imposing ostracism on a recalcitrant older son, his relationship to ego is usually one of generosity and protection. A youth in trouble, whether with his father or with other paternal relatives, will usually seek refuge in his household. The mother's brother will attempt to mediate the disagreement unless he finds fault with the behavior of his sister's son, in which case he will join the father in imposing sanctions. If a sister's child becomes a foster son or is especially helpful in running errands, gardening, or watching cattle, a mother's brother may show his generosity by giving a cow and sometimes land. In return, a sister's son is expected to assist his maternal uncle whenever called upon and, even if separated by great physical distance, to visit the latter at least annually. The paternal and maternal female relatives are also expected to nurture ego in much the same fashion as a mother. Sisters will aid one another when their children are born, but their husband's sisters will not participate in such activity. A major role for the latter is as a substitute mother in the event that a brother's wife should leave or if he should die and his wife need help in rearing the children.

Grandparents whose daughters are married and who are left only with their youngest sons to support them in subsistence activities are most in need of foster children. Indeed, a survey of four hamlets in the research area revealed that, of all foster children, twenty-four (67 percent) were living in the households of paternal or maternal grandparents. All grandparents have the same terms, ahā-ho for males and ahā-he for females, and there is some of the closeness between them and ego that is universally associated with alternate generations. On the other hand, the relationship between males involves as much respect as required between father and son, for the oldest males are the final authority in all decisions involving members of the community. These old men do not usually punish their grandchildren physically, but their admonishments are considered particularly important because of the wisdom associated with their advanced years. By comparison, grandmothers have a nurturance role analogous to that of the mother.

The most productive segment of the population includes the young men and women. As noted at the beginning of this section, it is the youth, under the direction of the elders, who provide communal labor. Indeed, once a man is promoted to elderhood he directs but no longer performs the arduous manual labor involved in house building, clearing trails, cleaning ponds, digging graves, and other community tasks. Therefore it is appropriate to examine the relationships between youths, which may be characterized as brotherhood and sisterhood.

Seniority is as important within as between generations, so older brothers (bīra rōdo) exercise authority over younger brothers. This relation continues throughout life, though on the basis of field observations it is often a matter of a younger man helping an aging or debilitated older brother by taking his coffee to market, bringing his ensete seedlings from the highlands, or assisting in other activities requiring strength and high expenditure of energy. When they are young, however, the delegation by an older brother of activities originally assigned him by the father (for example, weeding, looking after cattle, running errands) is often resented by a younger brother and leads to quarrels. Parents will intervene, but they usually support the older brother on the basis of the seniority principle that younger brothers are expected to respect and obey their elders. As they grow older, brothers are expected to—and do—work together in helping each other to clear and plant their gardens, in addition to cooperating in other farming activities. Finally, it is the older brother who will direct his younger brothers—especially the youngest, who has the greatest responsibility—in caring for aging parents and who will instruct them in feeding the dead father's spirit.

Relationships between brothers (rōdo) have probably never been, nor are they in the present, as cooperative as the norms imply. The mythology portraying the establishment and territorial acquisition of important clans discussed earlier in the chapter shows these events to have been based on quarrels between brothers. This is not, however, simply a historical phenomenon, for examples of rivalry and conflict between brothers were recorded in the fieldwork situation. Perhaps the most dramatic was a pathological case involving a prolonged history of bizarre behavior. A young man attempted to stab himself when his father refused to answer his question as to whether he would consider him as superior in demeanor and achievement to his brothers. Though initially prevented from harming himself, the aggrieved son later committed suicide.

A dozen cases were recorded involving conflict between brothers or resentment over the exercise of authority and expertise within and between generations. Conflict situations concerned quarrels about responsibility for aged parents, rights to access to land belonging to a common paternal ancestor, and use of civil as compared with traditional land law. Half-brothers quarreled over hereditary rights in a polygynous situation, as did siblings over control of land held by a widowed mother. And in one case brothers quarreled over grazing property that their father had intended them to hold in common. Further, an instance was recorded where a dispute between two brothers over a boundary remained unresolved and was carried on by their sons in the following generation. A younger cousin, contrary to the seniority norms, responded with antagonism to an older paternal cousin who sought to advise him on how to improve his woefully inept dealings with relatives and other members of the community. Also in this category belong examples of resentment and disrespect for paternal authority, for instance, a case of an intoxicated son who assaulted his father and a case of an older brother who quarreled with his younger brother over his failure to provide sufficient care for their senile father.

The tension between prescribed cooperation and sometimes open rivalry can be traced to certain elements in the socialization of respect for authority. As previously discussed, parents tend to pick favorites among their children on the basis of the one who is most obedient and enthusiastic in serving an elder.[13] This encourages sibling rivalry. But at the same time that siblings are competing for the favor of their elders, they are also being subjected to a teasing technique to develop their ability to resist temptation. A child will be jokingly encouraged to be disobedient and then punished if he or she gives way to temptation. For example, an older child will offer a younger one a desirable piece of food, then withdraw it and wait to see if the child has a temper tantrum. If a tantrum occurs, the older youngster laughs uproariously. Occasionally a mother will tease an angry child by encouraging him or her to strike her or another adult. If the child loses control and strikes the adult, punishment ensues.

Adding to this socialization of rivalry are the problems of equality, competitive individualism, and sense of inadequacy that have come with the advent of a cash economy. Cash has provided a means of leveling wealth symbols, with the result that, as some informants suggest, "everyone has become equal." In effect, acquisition of money has made it easier to acquire such status symbols as articles of clothing, tools, cattle, food luxuries, and other items formerly available only to a few. As a consequence, people become more competitive by working to maximize individual gains from trade and to increase the amount of land planted in coffee. They are not unwilling to work with others, but cooperative ventures are increasingly directed toward individual profit rather than toward ritual or political endeavors for benefit of the whole community.

Among the Sadāma, as in other kinship-based societies, the descent group unity that comes with marriage and with dealing with members of other clans holds brothers together and helps to balance internal rivalries with an "externally oriented solidarity."[14] Other positive forces are the long-term reciprocities that can be taken for granted among closely related kin. This "generalized reciprocity" constitutes a reserve of support unlike the "balanced reciprocity" between distant relatives or strangers, which always requires a quid pro quo.[15] Some of these vaguely defined long-term reciprocities involve transfer of responsibility, generational replacement, ritual performance, and small-scale labor activities. These are activities that a male ego associates primarily with his siblings, father, father's brothers, mother's brothers, and father's brother's sons.

Transfer of responsibility refers to the expectation that a father's brother will be generous to ego when ego's father dies, by helping provide bridewealth and assisting in the acquisition of land. A similar function devolves on the older brother in helping to arrange marriages and in dividing bridewealth among younger brothers in the event of the father's demise. In return, ego has a vague obligation of deference and can be called upon to run errands for these older agnatic kin.

Generational replacement refers to the previously discussed expectation that in old age the youngest son should provide care for aged parents. This form of reversing nurturant roles in the declining years of parents is also vaguely defined, to the extent that failure by the last-born son should lead the older sons to assume these responsibilities.

Finally, brothers are expected to cooperate in performing rituals, but specific responsibilities for providing sacrificial animals, establishing an appropriate time, and calling others together are left undefined. In like manner, siblings and paternal parallel cousins are expected to help each other in small-scale labor activities, but the occasions and timing are unspecified.

There is much in the role of sisters *(rod-ōte)* that is analogous to brothers. Authority of older over younger siblings leads to a similar form of bickering that gives way after marriage to a sense of solidarity perpetuated by frequent visiting and gift exchange. If they live in close physical proximity, sisters are expected to assist one another when called upon.

The role of sisters vis-à-vis brothers is of ritual and economic significance. At elderhood promotion rites, the oldest sister should bring her brother a bull to support his stay in seclusion and should pay the fee of the specialist *(orgāsse)* who performs the circumcision.[16] In the event of her death, payment for the operation and the giving of a bull devolves upon her eldest son. Actually it is her husband who provides these resources, and in so doing he further legitimates the bonds linking the families by marriage. The youngest sister also has a role for she is expected to provide food for the boy (jāla) who attends her brother during his ceremonial confinement. All other sisters, with the support of their husbands, are expected to bring bulls and other foodstuffs during the seclusion period. Finally, after her brother's death, the eldest sister will assume the honorific role of ceremonially sprinkling water on his mourning pole to mark the end of the three-day death ritual. Reciprocally, all brothers and sisters will be expected to attend each other's mourning rites and to shave their heads.

Cousin terminology is Hawaiian, with both paternal and maternal cousins classed as siblings, distinguishable only as to sex (rōdo/rōdote). Effective interaction is limited by spatial proximity, but brothers do inherit some or all of their land in adjoining plots and their sons—also for a time their daughters—have the best opportunity to play and later to work together. Cooperation in gardening, house repairs, and other work activities is not as close as among brothers, but male cousins should respond when called upon to provide assistance. And most of these male relatives will be expected to help one another reciprocally, with contributions from their sisters, by presenting bulls and other foodstuffs during the ceremonies prior to elderhood promotion. Cross cousins, as well as maternal parallel cousins, will contribute as separate family groups by bringing these gifts to the secluded initiates. Cousins should also honor one another in death by attending each other's mourning ceremonies and should signify their respect by shaving their heads. Thus these relatives provide a reserve of labor support and assistance in the expensive elderhood promotion rites, the most important ritual in a man's life cycle, and they continue their respect for these linkages in symbolic activities after death.

So far in this chapter, clan structure has been suggested as establishing the boundaries for kinship relations, with neighborhoods and hamlets providing the limits for mutuality in labor exchange. It has also been shown how kinship shapes the allocation of land, the principal resource of production. A further emphasis has been on the kinship relations of production as providing a form of complementary indebtedness between generations. The redistribution of wealth and knowledge by elders in return for service and deference by youth generates a structural reciprocity that provides for authority without exploitation. Nevertheless, there is much room for variation in conformity to the rules of reciprocity. Individualism and rivalry in the pursuit of wealth are actually encouraged, though prestige is acquired only when wealth is redistributed. More significant is the fact that reciprocity between closely related kinsmen is limited by being taken for granted. It is of a long-term nature hence vague in application, instead of immediate and specific as in short-term quid pro quo exchanges.

Thus there is ample opportunity for conflict between self-interest and affiliative obligation, which leads to the question of what prevents interpersonal rivalry and conflict from being extended to clan and lineage relations? One possibility would be a structure of inequality between clans, giving some clans control over others. In the next section I examine this issue of social disparity between descent groups.

## Hierarchy and Inequality

The Sadāma are divided into two major groupings: cultivators and artisans. The cultivators are referred to as *wallabīčo*, while the artisans are divided into the three categories of ironworkers (*tuntīča*), leatherworkers (*hawāčo*), and potters (*hadīčo*). Also, certain divisions among the *wallabīčo* lead to status inequality, including possession of anga, especially heroic qualities of certain apical ancestors and priority origins.

It will be remembered that anga signifies purity of descent, continuity of land occupation, and the avoidance of "impure" foods consisting primarily of undomesticated animals. It also involves varying degrees of avoidance of the artisan groups that are associated with these unclean foods. The Āletā people in their struggle for land south of the Gidabo incorporated persons from other ethnic groups; as a consequence, they lack the descent homogeneity maintained by the Bushēans and by other descendants of Maldea, like the Havēla and Kēvennā. Thus the Āletā, lacking anga, are symbolically stigmatized. The descendants of Bushē, as well as Kēvennā and Havēla, will eat meat with the Āletā, but only when it has been slaughtered by a man with anga.

Furthermore, there are degrees of purity in regard to food taboos among those with anga. Members of the Holō clan are the most fastidious in this concern to avoid pollution. This relates to the fact that Abo, the father of the founder of the Holō, is generally recognized by Sadāma as the most noble in the pantheon of apical ancestors. His grave is the ultimate sacred site and inspires the most elaborate rituals performed by any of the clans.[17] The principal participants in these rites are the descendants of Abo, who compose the Holō and Gārbičo clans. But because of ecological and seniority differences, the Holō elders must annually cleanse the Gārbičo elders for their polluting dietary practices. This ritual is based on the legend that Abo originally directed his sons to plant only ensete, barley, and wheat. It happened that the founder of the Gārbičo moved some distance from his brothers and half-brothers to his mother's brother's residence, where he began to grow maize and millet. Thus in order for his descendants—who continue to plant and eat this food that grows so well in their homeland—to participate in rituals honoring Abo, they must be purified by the Holō. The seniority of the Holō and their closer adherence to the dietary restrictions of the heroic founder give them greater purity than the Gārbičo.

Though the artisans are clearly distinguished from the wallabīčo, there is a question as to whether they can legitimately be categorized as members of caste groups. This term has been widely, if loosely, applied to artisan groups in southern Ethiopia.[18] The problems with using caste as a concept derived from India have to do with patron-clientage relations, divinely ordained status, and hierarchical ranking on the basis of purity.[19]

Patron-clientage involves the issue of whether the disjunction between cultivators and artisans is simply a matter of the relationship between a set of aristocratic patrons and subservient clients. This is the situation between the minority cattle-holding Tutsi warriors and the majority of Hutu cultivators in east central Africa. The Tutsi patrons provide protection in return for the tribute in foodstuffs rendered by the Hutu. This is clearly a case of a twofold division in which a privileged aristocracy is able to exact tribute from the majority of subsistence food producers.

The second issue is whether the group differences have been divinely ordained, so that certain labor tasks are stigmatized as being unclean and polluting of other tasks, or whether it is simply a matter of differences in status and dignity. An example of divinely appointed status is provided by the Dime of southern Ethiopia. The Dime are divided into three categories, consisting of priests and chiefs who are considered "pure," commoners defined as "nonpure," and artisans considered as "impure." Only the pure may make sacrifice to the principal deities, the commoners provide the offerings for these rites, and the impure cannot participate.[20] Also, the priests and chiefs are committed to an elaborate set of food and cleanliness taboos and must avoid pollution by contacts with the artisans.

Finally, the matter of whether the groups are ranked in a hierarchy or divided into two contrasting occupational blocs is relevant. For instance, the Dime are ranked in seven categories based on purity, access to land and cattle, desirability of residence, occupational specialization, and ritual participation. By contrast, the Gurage and Konso, two other southern Ethiopian societies, are unranked and simply divided as cultivators and craftsmen.[21]

On the basis of these three determinants of caste (that is, hierarchical ranking, divinely ordained status, and the extent to which the stigmatized craftsmen control their means of production), I propose to examine the relations between the cultivators and craftsmen among the Sadāma. To begin with, it is difficult to establish that the members of cultivator clans show any consensus of a divinely ordained system of rank superiority of one clan over another. As previously indicated, there are claims to prestige by those who possess anga, but members of those clans without it deny that anga is important. All Sadāma tend to admire the mythical power of Abo, the apical ancestor of the Holō and Gārbičo clans. Nevertheless, none would consider Abo's descendants to be anything other than their equals. Furthermore, all the wallabīčo work the land, and clan members have relatively equal access to land, though some areas are more fertile and favorable for pasture than others. And every clan has its own ritual leader, who, along with the elders, officiates at sacred rites in which all may participate.

The situation for the clans of craftsmen is somewhat different from that of the cultivators. Just as among the Dime, the smiths, tanners, and potters are considered impure. Their ancestry is questionable, they eat the most polluted foods, they may traditionally have lacked access to land, and they practice occupations necessary to the cultivators, but restricted to artisan clans. These artisan groups are even distinguished from the cultivators in an olfactory way, as they are said to smell of the objects of their occupational status. Though all of these attributes are considered to have been ordained by the creator god Magāno, there are both mythologically defined and behavioral differences among these groups and in their positions vis-à-vis the cultivators.

The potters are the least impure. They are related to Bushē through his nephew Nāyā (see figure 1). Nevertheless, the antecedents of Nāyā are not untarnished. His father Hādi is alleged to be descended from a union between Silēmma and a donkey, and he was reared as if he were a brother to Bushē and Setāmmi. There is the familiar tale of jealousy between brothers, in which Hādi is tricked by the others into a form of self-destruction, leaving his son Nāyā as the only survivor. Nāyā's descendants could not receive anga and are said to have been landless until sent by the elders to outflank and harass the Āletā on their southern border. Before this event, Nāyā's descendants hunted wild animals instead of cultivating gardens. Then as game became scarce, their wives were forced to make pottery in exchange for food from the cultivators.

In return for their service in harassing the Āletā, the descendants of Bushē agreed to help the potters settle well into the interior, at a safe distance south of the Āletā. To reciprocate, the potters agreed to accept their patrons as lords and the Bushēans in turn accepted these artisans as their people. But once the potters had land, they acquired their own ritual leader and appropriate elders' councils, just like other wallabīčo clans.

Much less is known about the origins of the tanners and the smiths that is indicative of a status lower than that of the pottery makers. There is no distinction between tanners and smiths, and it is not unusual to find the same person practicing both occupations. Unlike the potters, however, these skills are both practiced by men. Their ancestors are sometimes vaguely related as brothers to Abo, the founder of the Holō and Gārbičō clans, but no genealogical connections are ever provided. According to some informants, Abo sent them away without land for eating the umbilical cord of a newborn infant, which forced them to work with hides and iron in exchange for food.

The pollution of tanners and smiths, despite their production of necessities for the cultivators, is greater than that of the pottery makers. This is to be seen in the fact that persons with anga will not partake of food in their presence but will eat with the potters. So great is the concern about pollution from the presence of a tanner that even indirect contact requires ritual cleansing. For example, during the period of field research an old elder of Holō clan died, and to honor his spirit the men of his hamlet slaughtered a bull on his grave. Much to their chagrin, they discovered after performing these rites that before the death, his wife had left a skin for preparation with a tanner. Consequently, the elders had to cleanse the corpse by slaughtering a sheep over the grave.

On the other hand, the Āletā, while observing the taboos on eating wild animals, will eat with the craftsmen. They will not, however, partake of meat slaughtered by them. Nor, like those with anga, will they permit artisans to be present at the circumcision rites preceding promotion to elderhood. Nevertheless, potters are given the sacrificial calf at the close of the three-day mourning rites. Also, they are permitted to dispose of surplus meat at Abo's grave when the Holō and Gārbičo clans honor this notable, but they are not permitted to enter the elaborate compound surrounding the grave. The lesser status of the tanners and blacksmiths is indicated by the fact that they are excluded from the vicinity where these rites are performed.

Craftsmen's clans, unlike those of the cultivators, are endogamous, the restrictions being only that individuals must marry outside of their paternal and maternal lineages. For a cultivator to marry an artisan is to lose status. As a result, the bulk of the potters are members of several large lineages occupying the land south of the Āletā, but there are potter households scattered among all the clans in Sidā-moland. The tanners and smiths are in a somewhat different situation: they have several lineages, but they lack clan land and are scattered throughout all clan areas.

To what extent does this information provide evidence for the existence of castes? Among the cultivator clans there are simply status differences based on the prestige of descent purity or kinship ties to an especially notable, apical ancestor. It is difficult, however, to discern any hierarchy of ranking based upon functional differences in authority or upon the performance of rituals. Even the previously discussed cleansing of Gārbičo clan elders by their Holō counterparts is primarily a means of demonstrating genealogical seniority, as well as spatial and descent group separation. Also, at least one of the four assistants to the ritual leader from Holō for the rites honoring the revered Abo must be a Gārbičo.[22]

For the craftsmen there are differences in status based upon pedigree, but there are also restrictions on marriage and exclusion from rituals performed by the cultivators. The potters have a somewhat higher position than the other two artisan groups because of a less-tarnished pedigree. Nevertheless, to suggest that one group has been divinely ordained above all others among the craftsmen, as well as for the cultivators, would be a distortion of the facts, for all the clans in Sidāmoland have their own ritual leaders who make sacrifice to the creator deity in addition to apical clan ancestors.

Most important is the fact that none of the clans, cultivators, or craftsmen is involved in patron-clientage relationships. No single descent group or cluster of groups is able to appropriate a surplus in the form of tribute from the production of the others. And though the artisans may have originally been without resources, early in their history they acquired both cattle and gardens. Such possession of property makes the tanners, smiths, and potters so different from their counterparts among the Dime of Ethiopia, who never acquired land. The Dime have only their skills as craftsmen, which makes them totally dependent upon the cultivators. The Sadāma, on the other hand, have resources of production other than their divinely stigmatized artisan skills.

It cannot be said that the Sadāma have a caste system without a ranked hierarchy, uniformly applied standards of purity, or dependency of some on the control of resources by others. Rather, the Sadāma have a twofold system in which cultivators are esteemed and craftsmen demeaned. This divinely ordained distinction is a convenient means for separating the desirable occupations of gardening and herding from the less-desirable practices of artisanship.

## Summary

It is evident from my discussion of the relationship of kinship to the allocation of resources that patrilineal clans set limits for acquisition and identity with the land. Within the clan framework, neighborhoods, hamlets, and households structure the organization for gardening and herding activities. Labor is organized on the principle of seniority, in which elders direct the youth in the production process. This is not, however, an exploitative authority but one of mutual indebtedness, for the elders are as obligated to support the interests of the youth as the youth are required to give of their labor in increasing the productivity of the gardens and herds of their elders. Nevertheless, like all social systems, it is far from harmonious and conflicts arise within and between generations. Moreover, clan mythologies indicate that in the past there has also been conflict between clans. This is to be expected, given the lack of hierarchical ordering of clan relations and, with the exception of the status division between cultivators and artisans, the relative equality in allocation of land and cattle. Despite this conflict and autonomy in control of resources, clans must cooperate in order for their members to reproduce themselves and in order to provide the necessary labor. The next chapter explains how marriage provides the necessary linkage between clans for furthering these vital functions.

5 Marriage and the
Sexual Division
of Labor

For the Sadāma, marriage provides a linkage between different descent groups, which expands the potential for mutual support of the household economy and performance of rituals vital to the preservation of elderhood authority. A man is not limited, however, to the enterprise of a single household, but he may expand his wealth and authority through several households by engaging in polygyny. In each case the wife is pivotal in contributing her labor, reproducing additional workers, as well as supervising and protecting the property in the absence of her husband. Furthermore, she often provides a valuable linkage of the household to the cash economy through her marketing activities.

## Marriage and Linkages between Clans

In recent years there have been numerous attempts to show that, between African corporate descent groups, marital relations across generations can provide an important "interconnectedness" that in effect constitutes an alliance system.[1] These alliances are generally formed not on the basis of direct or asymmetrical marriage exchange but through a complex system that stipulates only whom one may not marry.[2] There are no rules, as in direct and asymmetrical exchange, stipulating whom one must, or should, marry.

Nevertheless, there are aspects of linkages by marriage that constitute alliances between families in different descent groups. These include the mutuality between mothers and sons, the mediatory role of the mother's brother, and the ritual support from maternal cross cousins. The mother-son mutuality is based upon ties of nurture that are reciprocated by the son in providing support for his mother in her old age. Also, a mother's brother is expected to support his sister's household in sanctioning her children, as well as in showing nurture and mediating disputes between his sister's husband and their sons. In return the nephews are expected to visit and render assistance whenever requested by a mother's brother. Finally, mutual support is given by maternal cousins in the important and expensive promotion and death rituals. These relationships thus bind families of different descent groups together, but there is no prescribed exchange where one group must give women to a certain other group and take women from another, creating permanent alliances between clans and lineages. The family linkages do, however, serve to reproduce clans and to provide important sources of labor. Consequently, negotiation and maintenance of marriage ties are critical for production and marketing exchange.

Among the Sadāma, overt demonstrativeness between the sexes is unacceptable. Indeed, a husband and wife are said to "hide" their love, to keep it inside themselves, and in the presence of others to feign indifference toward one another. This restraint begins early in life when girls at approximately eight years of age are encouraged to stop playing with boys. The reason is that before marriage there is great emphasis on protecting virginity, and should a woman conceive earlier, her family is greatly shamed. Though in the past marriage is said to have been much later (some even say in the mid to late twenties), it is not uncommon today for a girl to be considered ready to marry at fourteen or fifteen and for boys at seventeen or eighteen. Ideally, the only unsupervised contact between the sexes in adolescence is at ritual dances marking the new year and elderhood promotion. Nevertheless, on such occasions young women must be escorted and closely observed by their older brothers. An unmarried older brother has a vested interest in protecting the virginity of a sister in order to maximize her bridewealth, some of which may be used to obtain his own bride. Adolescents, however, often meet surreptitiously in the marketplace, at funerals and mourning ceremonies in their neighborhood, and while performing household chores such as gathering firewood and fetching water.

In the past, infant betrothal was one alternative in marriage exchange between families. In this situation, considered unusual by informants, two friends in different clans would pledge their infant son and daughter for future marriage. The prevailing practice, however, was for parents to pick brides for their sons on the basis of information provided by married women relatives. The choice was made without consulting the potential bride and groom, on the basis of parental knowledge about a young woman's character, her estimated skill as a housekeeper, her health, and often her beauty.

Today the potential spouses are usually consulted prior to the negotiations, but the other criteria remain the same. For example, the attribute of desirable character refers to loyalty and obedience. A young woman should not be suspected of promiscuity or have a reputation for being flirtatious. Another aspect of character, perhaps mentioned less because it is taken for granted, is the importance of avoiding linkage with a family stigmatized by *buda*, the evil eye. Beauty in terms of tallness and symmetry of facial features is said to have been a more important criterion in the past as a means of enhancing a husband's prestige. In the present situation of a developing cash economy, however, there is much more concern for loyalty, health, and housekeeping skills. These are the most frequently discussed items when informants are asked what they look for in choosing wives for their sons.

The basic rules that marriage partners must not be members of one's own clan or of one's mother's lineage are accepted implicitly. Marriage with any cousin is also proscribed. A further implicit assumption is that it is desirable to create linkages in marriage with wealthy families. From the standpoint of the bride's family, this means a marriage in which the groom has plenty of land, a large herd of cattle, and the ability to provide a well-built house for his bride. This will ensure that their daughter's sons will have a substantial inheritance and will be able to provide well for their mother in her old age. Another anticipated advantage, since the advent of cash payments, is that bridewealth from a wealthy family will be greater than the average and the shares to the bride's brothers, father's brothers, and mother will be correspondingly higher. Furthermore, the son-in-law will be expected to serve his wife's father like a son when needed, and they will support each other, exchanging gifts during the lengthy, expensive ceremonials leading to their respective promotions to elderhood. In turn, the bridegroom and his family will receive more than the household and reproductive services of a wife. Indeed, if proximity permits, he will be able to call upon his wife's brothers for assistance in gardening and other tasks, and they will

*add'l labor force — exchanged care.*

*all about the money*

support him with tangible gifts in the elderhood promotion process. He will be expected to reciprocate in assisting his brother-in-law both when in need of labor and in promotion rituals.

The gift-giving and protective role of a wife's brothers to their sister's sons has already been described. Also, as indicated, in the event of a married sister's death, her eldest son is responsible for providing support and for performing certain rites when mother's brother is promoted to elderhood. As Fox has shown, marriage does more for a man than provide for the continuity of his descent group.[3] A family alliance is established between himself and his wife's father and brothers in which his sons constitute an extension of the relationship. It is more than an alliance of friendship or potential political support; rather, it is one of tangible economic benefit in terms of providing additional labor and financial assistance to that provided by one's agnatic kin. This economic aspect will become more apparent in the discussion to follow regarding postmarital relations between in-laws.

A father will decide to negotiate a marriage, either on his own or at the urging of a son enamored with a girl he has seen in the marketplace. Though the services of a broker are not considered necessary, on the basis of observation this is often the practice when the families are unacquainted. For example, a Hitāla man wishes to arrange the marriage of his son with a young woman from the distant Gārbičo clan who has recently been visiting relatives in his hamlet. Since the Hitāla father is not acquainted with her father, he goes to the head of the household where she is staying and requests his assistance. This man, as it happens, has a close Gārbičo friend who is well acquainted with the father of the potential bride. Through a friendship network in this indirect manner, the two families are brought together to negotiate the marriage. In another instance a Hitāla man wishes to take a Lamalla woman whom he has seen in the market as a second wife. He does not know the father of this woman, and his own father is dead. Consequently, he goes to a cousin of his whose daughter is married to a Lamalla man acquainted with the father of the potential bride. The suitor then makes arrangements to go with his father's brother, his cousin, and the cousin's son-in-law to open negotiations. This procedure is in keeping with the rule that the principal negotiators should be fathers, or father surrogates, of the prospective bride and groom. Thus once again the seniority rule becomes the basis for authoritative decision making.

Before the turn of the century, bridewealth payments were made
in the form of iron bars called *womāša*. Informants stressed that, since
the Sadāma had to trade with other ethnic groups to obtain the iron
to make this money, it was scarce and highly valued. As a consequence there was a general consensus that bridewealth negotiations
were more protracted than at present. But early in this century Eu-
ropean-style money in the form of silver coins gradually began to
replace iron bars in bridewealth payments. Then after World War II,
as cash cropping in coffee became important, the use of Ethiopian
currency became common. This was easier to obtain than iron bars
and was associated with a previously unavailable assortment of consumer goods such as manufactured clothing, blankets, transistor radios, bicycles, and sundry other items. In effect, people have come
to value Ethiopian currency far more than iron money, and this had
led to a shortening of bridewealth negotiations. Also, in the past a
prospective bride was given a cow that was to become a part of her
household herd when she took up residence in the groom's hamlet.

Traditionally it could take as long as six months to complete bridewealth negotiations because of the customary etiquette that a family
should not appear eager to give up a daughter, the aforementioned
scarcity of iron money, and the often great distance between the
households of the families involved. Presently, with the use of cash
and the relative ease of travel, the negotiation time has been greatly
reduced. Despite these changes, it is considered correct manners for
the suitor's negotiators to make at least three visits to the prospective
bride's household. The first visit is to open proceedings, the second
to introduce the suitor, and the third to settle the bridewealth payment. According to informants, contemporary bridewealth payments
range from $60 to $150 Ethiopian.[4] Older men suggest that before
World War II the range in payment was between three and four
dollars.

The following is an example of proceedings taken from the previously mentioned Hitāla-Gārbičo negotiations:

> An old stepfather and a cousin were the principal spokesmen for the
> Hitāla suitor. They had been led to believe, by the man who helped
> bring the two families together, that the bride's family anticipated a
> payment of $90, but they set their goal as a limit of $75. So after arrival
> in the bride's hamlet, a suitable exchange of greetings, and everyone
> being comfortably seated under a shade tree, the suitor's cousin stepped

forward and placed $60 on the hem of the cloak of the bride's father. The latter, with a gesture of contempt, pushed the money to one side. This led the cousin to remark that establishing a relationship of love between relatives was more important than money. The argument failed, however, to impress the bride's relatives, and the Hitāla men withdrew from the little circle of negotiators to reconsider their original offer. Shortly they returned and added $9 to the small stack of bills, and the cousin began again to urge the superior value of amicable relations over money. The bride's relatives continued to feign indifference. At this point the man who had brought the two families together sat down beside the cousin and engaged him in a whispered conversation, reminding him that the bride's relatives were thinking of $90. After this the cousin arose, deposited $6 more on the pile of money, all the while begging the bride's father to be generous and accept. Once again the supplication failed to impress the father. At this juncture another Gārbičo relative arrived and, after inquiring about the preceding course of negotiations, admonished the bride's father for seeming to be too hasty in accepting money, as if he needed cash more than his daughter. The suitor's cousin followed with an impassioned harangue, the gist of which was that present-day people talked too much, ate too much, and always wanted more money, but they were never satisfied. Such dissatisfaction was not in keeping with traditions. The audience seemed impressed and the bride's father remarked that it almost made him want to reduce the bridewealth. He then got up with his relatives to leave the main group and discuss the matter in private. Meanwhile the go-between intimated to the suitor's relatives that he thought the bride's family was still intent on receiving $90. The cousin indicated he believed that if they begged and held firm they could arrange the marriage for less. Shortly the bride's kinsmen returned and rejected the offer. There followed several more conferences interspersed with speeches from both sides proclaiming the great skills and fine character of the prospective bride and groom. In the course of these events the pool of money was increased to $84.

Finally the Gārbičo negotiators announced that the women were ready to serve food. The suitor's relatives then assumed that the offer had been accepted, as the offering of food after prolonged negotiations was customarily a sign of agreement. But after eating, the bride's relatives complained that the bridewealth offer was not enough and that clothing should be purchased for her mother. Following consultation with his Hitāla relatives, the cousin came forward with six more dollars but adamantly refused to buy clothing for the mother. After a few rather feeble arguments over the clothing issue, the $90 was formally accepted.[5]

Later the man who brought the two families together for negotiations indicated to the ethnographer that the bride's relatives had hoped to obtain a bridewealth of $105. On the other hand, the spokesman cousin of the suitor suggested, in private, that they had expected to give no more than their goal of $75. This spokesman also confided that he was disappointed in the poor speaking ability of the bride's father, as well as his discourtesy in reopening negotiations after the visitors had been fed. Nevertheless, satisfaction was expressed that this poor performance enabled the suitor's kin to complete final negotiations in only one day.

The Sadāma are realistic about the enmity between clans and seek to overcome the potential for conflict by an elaborate series of exchanges between the relatives of the bride and groom. Traditionally the enmity was acted out in a ritual leading to the symbolic uniting of the two families. The rites began with a simulation of taking the bride by force from her father's household. It will be recalled that brides of the past usually married in their early to middle twenties. And at this advanced age they underwent the clitoridectomy performed by the women of their father's hamlet. This occurred several months after completion of the bridewealth negotiations. Then several more months would elapse before the younger relatives and friends of the groom took part in the mock assault upon the bride's household. They were verbally abused and pelted with pepper and dirt by women of the hamlet. Then the leader of the groom's relatives broke down the door of the house, rushed in, and captured the bride. Wrapped in a large shawl (šām-ma), she was then triumphantly carried back to the groom's community, where the women opposed her entry into her new household. With the aid of her escort, she entered safely inside, and all the members of the groom's neighborhood were invited to participate in a period of feasting and dancing. The ceremonies ended with a blessing by the elders for fertility of the couple and their cattle.

Informants maintain that because of the expense of the feast in the past, only persons of wealth could afford to carry out these elaborate rites. Then and now most marriages are celebrated by a much simpler process. The groom and a few relatives and friends go to the household of the bride, where her father formally hands her over after admonishing the new husband to cherish his daughter, treat her with justice, and not punish her in any way that may result in bodily injury. (The latter admonishment refers to the universal use of corporal punishment for misbehaving wives.) The clitoridectomy and subsequent period of seclusion then take place in the husband's community. First the bride will be examined for virginity by the old women, and then the specialist *(aforšēsa)* will perform the operation.

There is much concern about virginity, which indirectly has economic implications. For a girl to menstruate before marriage is considered unusual, and given the early age of present-day marriages (fourteen to fifteen), this normally does not happen.[6] It is also in keeping with informants' observations that while many begin to menstruate after beginning sexual intercourse, there are those who do not commence the cycle for one or two years after marriage. In any event, girls who do menstruate before marriage are suspected of having lost their virginity, since the Sadāma assume a connection between menstruation and sexual intercourse. At the same time it is admitted that the connection need not be absolute. This seems to mean that a young woman suspected of promiscuity who does in fact begin the female cycle before marriage is very likely to have her virginity called into question. Such question will have a negative effect upon bridewealth negotiations, which may indirectly affect the amount of cash available to offer in obtaining a bride for her brother(s).

A suitor can gain an economic advantage by marrying a divorced woman, for whom he will not have to give bridewealth. Alternatively, he could simply reduce his bridewealth payment by marrying a woman who is alleged to have lost her virginity. Most young and older men, however, are reluctant to follow either course of action, since it would lower their prestige in the community; to avoid paying the full bridewealth for a virgin is a sure indicator of poverty.

Following clitoridectomy, the groom's family must also assume the expense of the seclusion period. This involves a considerable outlay, since during the early stages of the preferred two months of sequestration the bride should be fed buttermilk and meat to hasten the healing process and to help her regain strength. Nevertheless, despite the costs, clitoridectomy is still universally supported by men and women. Men believe that sexual satisfaction cannot be properly obtained unless a woman has had the operation. Women agree that, regardless of the pain, a marriage cannot be properly consummated without this surgical experience. The depth of this belief, however, is open to question, given two examples from the field notes of Christian women who married without undergoing the clitoridectomy. As a consequence, they were shunned by the other women in their respective communities. Thus there is indication that one who violates the norm constitutes a threat to the esteem of those who have demonstrated that they can surmount the pain and discomfort of ritual mutilation. This pressure to conform is rationalized by the assumption that without the operation a woman throughout her married life will experience dissatisfaction with everything and with all persons in her household. Moreover, this attitude will be transmitted to her children, who will never have enough land, cattle, or money.

It is appropriate to mention two alternative forms of marriage. One involves elopement, in which a young woman agrees to go to the household of a young man, without the formality of bridewealth negotiations. The young man's father must then negotiate bridewealth with the girl's father. This means that the compensation is usually greater than normal, as the father will argue, often falsely, that he has already been offered a high bridewealth for his daughter. Even so, in the opinion of several old informants, elopement is increasing as young people meet in school and elsewhere more frequently and informally than in the past.

By contrast, dē-rō, or taking a bride by force, is said to be a declining practice. When a youth engages in this activity he will initially be fined by the elders' council. Then his father will be asked to give bridewealth. In the event it is refused, the girl must be returned to her father's household, with compensation provided for any injuries incurred in the abduction.

Once a new wife is under the tutelage of her mother-in-law, she must show respect and obedience. But when she has learned something of the idiosyncrasies that make her husband's hamlet different from her own and has settled into her own household, she assumes full responsibility for the work load. She must, however, practice strict avoidance of her father-in-law until and if, usually years after the marriage, they mutually agree to end the procedure. Furthermore, a wife should avoid mentioning her husband's name or the names of his agnatic kin.

A new husband and his relatives must reinforce the alliance with the wife's kinsmen by a formal visit to her father's hamlet. The visit, known as *feetōma*, normally takes place by the end of the first year of marriage. Feetōma is considered a means by which the husband and his relatives show respect and appreciation for the virtues of his new wife by presenting gifts of food and money to her kin. It is a sign to the wife that her services are appreciated, and if it is not performed she may leave and return to her parents' household, until the husband and his relatives come with gifts and beg her to return. At the same time, son-in-law and father-in-law mutuality, though less compelling, should have all the attributes of the father-son dyad. The son-in-law should perform labor in gardening, caring for cattle, or any other activities in which the wife's father may need assistance. When appropriate, in terms of age and position in the elderhood-promotion cycle, they should attend each other's circumcision and exchange bulls. In a final act of respect, the one should attend the other's mourning rites.

Just as a wife must show respect for her father-in-law, so a husband must reciprocate with avoidance of his mother-in-law, her sisters, and his wife's eldest sister, who takes the place of the mother-in-law in the event of her death. In turn, the wife's mother will symbolize the linkage with her in-laws by bringing a feast of ensete smothered in butter. This feast should take place after the birth of the first child, but it may be as long as five years after the marriage because of the time involved in accumulating sufficient cash to purchase the butter. A mother-in-law must do this on her own by selling some of her husband's coffee cherries, often taken without his permission, and/or by selling some garden produce in the market. The butter must be specially prepared by boiling, adding spices to remove all impurities, and boiling again.

When presented in his hamlet, the feast is consumed by the son-in-law and his agnates. The recipients should respond to this honor by presenting the mother-in-law with a cash gift, ranging from twelve to fifteen dollars. In addition to strengthening the bonds between two different sets of kin, this festive exchange is believed to enhance the prestige of the mother-in-law. Whether or not she decides after the feast to end avoidance is entirely her option. Frequently she does opt for continuation of avoidance, unless there is a crisis situation such as the need of a son-in-law's labor, or marital discord that may be successfully mediated by a mother-in-law.

A mother-in-law should also visit and bring food when her son-in-law begins seclusion prior to elderhood promotion. If she has reason to believe that her son-in-law is an especially brave man, she may once again bring ensete covered with so much butter that "it runs down the outside of the bowl like water." In the middle of the bowl of porridge is placed a large, horn spoon. When all the men of her son-in-law's hamlet are assembled, she will ask who will remove this spoon. This is the signal for a son-in-law or any man who feels he has demonstrated courage or prowess in killing the enemy or wild animals to come forward and narrate his deeds.[7] If this recitation can then be verified and if there are no successful challenges, the hero removes the spoon and the assembled men consume the feast. Thus the mother-in-law succeeds in honoring the bravery of her son-in-law or another of his relatives and strengthens the alliance between ordinarily opposing sets of kin.

The importance of linkage between a woman's eldest brother and her sons has been mentioned. Her younger brothers also have a special relationship to her husband in that they should combine their resources to provide him with a bull, money, butter, and/or milk at his circumcision rites and they should honor him in death by mourning for him. The husband and his siblings are reciprocally obligated. Wives' sisters have no obligations beyond respect to her husband. Finally, though it is considered unusual, a husband may call upon a wife's brothers for labor assistance when in need.

The economic importance of siblings-in-law, as well as cousins by marriage, is no small matter when one considers their potential contribution to elderhood promotion, that most important and expensive of all events in a man's life cycle. During the period of seclusion his agnates will care for his garden and cattle, but he must provide most of the resources, which today involve cash expenditures for entertaining the guests who come to honor and congratulate him. For example, in 1964 one man who had been only a week in seclusion (*barcima desse*) spent $50 Ethiopian for *arike*, butter, ensete, milk, and three sheep.[8] To obtain this money he sold the bull (for approximately $100) his brother brought on the day he was circumcised, and he was counting on gifts from in-laws and cousins to provide further support. With this help he expected to get through the two months of seclusion with $150 he had been saving. Another man who completed the seclusion period spent at least $300 of his money entertaining guests, a large sum considering the average annual income of a household head in 1964–65 was $266.[9]

## Polygyny

If a man has sufficient land and cattle, it is recognized that he will need to have more than one wife. This expectation is based on the symbiotic connection between cattle and ensete, necessitating a household virtually in the center of a garden in which manure may conveniently be accumulated and easily carried by basket to the surrounding plants. To have widely separated parcels of land or an unusually large, concentrated holding requires a labor force of wives and their children. When questioned as to the importance of polygyny, the invariable response of men was that they needed several wives and their children to assist in production, if they ever hoped to acquire wealth. Under these circumstances the extra expenditure of bridewealth to acquire a second wife produces a far higher benefit relative to cost, providing the expenditure can be justified in terms of available land and cattle. Moreover, polygyny means an additional reserve of in-laws for support in ceremonials and labor, though it also adds to the recipient's reciprocal responsibilities.

One indication that not many men have enough resources to warrant polygyny is the relatively small number of household heads with multiple wives. In three communities surveyed in 1964-65, eight of the fifty-nine householders (14 percent) had more than one wife, and of this number only two had as many as three wives. Nevertheless, informants insisted that polygyny is not a sign of wealth, possibly because they think of wealth in terms of persons having many or large plots of land and more than one hundred head of cattle. In Āletā few men have resources on this scale; informants could name no more than five or six. A man must have enough land to justify separate gardens and enough cattle to provide at least three or four head per household. In polygynous arrangements, multiple wives and their offspring provide an essential labor force. Furthermore, contemporary cash cropping in coffee requires persons to keep watch over this valuable commodity as a protection against theft and to see that neighbors do not encroach by planting beyond the boundary. Therefore, insofar as the three communities are representative, it is evident that most men lack sufficient resources in land and cattle to justify a second wife even though they could manage the bridewealth.[10]

One qualification, however, involves the fact that Christian converts are permitted only one wife, and twenty-one of the fifty-nine men are in this category. Nevertheless, when a man converts to Christianity and can have only one wife, he is expected to continue supporting his former wives with land and cattle. The wives in turn continue to provide labor, and their offspring remain legitimate heirs.

Also, in the sample area only one household head is known to have given up a second wife through conversion to Christianity.

Informants believe that the only way in which polygyny enhances a man's prestige is by enabling him to provide more food for redistribution on ritual occasions than monogamously married men can. There are other advantages, such as the assurance when one wife is indisposed, through illness or childbirth, of always having someone to prepare food for family and guests. There is as well a continuity in sexual relations. In return a husband is expected to follow a cyclical rotation of living five days in the household of each wife. Indeed, the most frequently mentioned drawback to polygyny arises out of showing partiality to one wife over the other(s) in terms of sexual preference or division of property. Nevertheless, even with the present-day land scarcity, multiple wives are considered an asset. For if a man lacks sufficient land to transmit to his heirs, he hopes to educate them for jobs in the wage sector, with a view to receiving assistance as they acquire income. In the case of daughters, the returns from their bridewealth will assure the father of sufficient cash resources to assist his sons in marrying.

## Marriage Dissolution

The ideal wife keeps the household in order, shows obedience to her husband, consistently performs her task of manuring and occasionally assisting in weeding the garden, carefully supervises young children, and, when the husband is away, sees that the children keep careful watch over the grazing cattle. Clearly all of these attributes focus directly or indirectly on the production efficiency of the household and the important role of the wife in furthering this goal. Wives seldom measure up to the standards of the ideal.

Most husbands, however, accept the fact that no one is perfect, and they are likely to admonish and exercise punitive sanctions only in cases of flagrant disregard of these norms. Actions that threaten the mutuality of a husband's relationships with his agnates and friends seem to bring severe reprimands and harsh punishment. Specifically, these actions include the failure of a wife to feed guests who arrive when a husband is absent and negligence or delay in feeding men who are working with him. This lack of proper hospitality of course endangers his ability to obtain labor for subsistence gardening activ-, ities and picking coffee cherries. Supplementing the household labor force is especially important once the coffee berries are ripe if a man is to minimize the danger of theft and sudden hailstorms that could jeopardize his main source of income.

In the early days of marriage, most men do beat their wives in the hopes this will cause them to conform. Since, however, they admit that beating seldom leads to the desired ends, one must conclude that wife beating is primarily a result of frustration and anger, rather than of reasoned control. Moreover, these acts of physical violence are viewed ambivalently within the community. On the one hand, young men are recognized as lacking the control of their emotions that is expected of elders; nevertheless, such behavior is considered detrimental to community harmony. Consequently, wife beating is tolerated only within limits, so that one who consistently beats a wife becomes subject to gossip and ultimate admonishment by the hamlet elders.

In situations of marital conflict, the last resort for a husband is to send his wife away. Friction between spouses resulting from failure to conform to ideal wifely attributes, if cumulative, is likely to result in this ultimate action. There is, however, another cause of dissolution that is attributable to the relatively recent advent of a cash economy and is not yet expressed as a part of the norms. It has to do with alleged carelessness of wives in spending money. Though husbands claim they provide money for market purchase of condiments and other articles of domestic consumption, they maintain that spouses take the money and buy clothing for themselves. Wives deny this allegation, asserting that they are forced to resort to subterfuge by selling their husband's coffee cherries to acquire sufficient cash for household necessities. Regardless of how the money is spent, it is generally agreed that this petty pilfering of coffee has become almost customary behavior. Nevertheless, men so resent the practice that it has become a sufficient reason for sending wives away.

Wives, on the other hand, leave husbands whom they consider to be tyrannical in demanding obedience. Other reasons for leaving include inadequate or remote housing, failure of husbands to provide new clothing, and resentment over having to give up land and cattle, if and when a husband acquires a second wife. A wife may also leave if quarreling develops over a husband's failure to show her relatives proper respect by taking the previously mentioned gifts of feetōma.

What, then, is the magnitude of wives leaving and being sent away, and does this constitute actual dissolution of marriage? In a total of 119 instances of leaving and sending away of wives from a 1965 sampling of three communities, the percentage leaving (56 percent) is somewhat higher than the percentage being sent away (44 percent).

Considering the 1965 marital histories of the sixty-seven wives of all household heads, twenty-nine (43 percent) have left or have been sent away by their present or previous spouses.

Notwithstanding these high figures of marital disharmony, it does not necessarily follow that they reflect marriage dissolution. Indeed, informants insist that there is a great deal of coming and going in the early years of marriage. Once a child is born, however, a woman is unlikely to leave or to be sent away. For example, statistics from one hamlet show that fifteen of twenty wives (75 percent) leaving or being sent away left before the birth of a child.

Regardless of whether a marriage is monogamous or polygynous, childbirth is as important as the marriage itself. Ideally the mother and infant should remain in confinement for two months. This special treatment is more than a means of honoring the event, for it is an interval in which the mother regains her strength; she is fed rich food and devotes all her attention to the infant. The actual time of seclusion depends on cooperation from women of the hamlet, who should take turns bringing daily bowls of ensete porridge covered with butter. In addition, the husband seeks to enhance the health and honor of his wife by slaughtering a cow to feed her and to provide a feast for the hamlet elders, who then bless the mother and child. Since this is an act of mutuality in which all householders will share at some point in the domestic cycle, there is always an effort to participate. Nevertheless, it is very difficult at the height of the dry season (January, February, and March), when milk yield is low and coffee cherries are being withheld for the higher prices of the June marketing period.

Whether a woman leaves before this important event of childbirth depends upon her initial adjustment to and acceptance by her husband's community. Furthermore, the early age of marriage may mean a lengthy delay before fertility and the birth of the first child. These factors provide sufficient time and reasons for conflict to develop between the newly married. When there is controversy, a favorite technique of a wife who feels she has been wronged is to return to her father's household. To go back to her old home is a sign that she does not want a complete break with her husband.

Alternatively, she hopes that her husband will come and beg for her return, or after a reasonable interval she will return with her father and ask the elders of her husband's hamlet to negotiate a settlement. And even though he may have sent his wife away, a husband must accept the elders' decision. When, however, a wife does not return to a father's household but goes instead to another relative, this is a sign that she wishes to end the marriage.

There are several factors that serve to deter the dissolution of a marriage. First, a viable garden and household have been established, and both spouses have an interest in the reproduction function that will provide an increase in labor support and security in old age. Furthermore, for a woman to leave and then to seek remarriage leads to a situation fraught with ambiguity. Since bridewealth is nonreturnable, the husband always retains rights that he may press over any children she may bear.[11] This will be a deterrent to a new suitor. Moreover, if the woman has been married for several years without reproducing, he may be skeptical of her fertility. Finally, should a woman with children leave, it is permissible to take only a nursing infant, which will be claimed at weaning by the father. At the same time, she has reason to fear that unless older children are reared by her husband's mother, they will be given to a co-wife or to a husband's brother's wife. Because such children will become rival heirs to their children, these persons are reluctant to become surrogate mothers. Indeed, children's tales (māto) are full of themes concerning the "evil stepmother." So all of these factors, though they do not prevent, militate against divorce once children are born.

In sum, marriage entails an extension of relations to other descent groups, which, in addition to increasing kinship obligations, provides advantages in the form of additional labor support for production and ritual. As well as nurturing children and provisioning the household, the labor of the wife complements that of the husband in his gardening and herding activities. Furthermore, wives can supplement household resources by their trading activities in local markets.

Though there is much emphasis on the authority of husbands and obedience of wives, the division of labor between spouses cannot be maintained unless based on mutuality. Thus wives leave husbands who are too heavy handed, and husbands send away those whose self-centeredness interferes with fulfilling their household responsibilities. Nevertheless, mutual interests in the reproduction process have a way of aiding the accommodation to authority and responsibility once children are born to further and perpetuate the production/ reproduction cycle.

## Marketing

> As she dressed hurriedly in the damp chill of the predawn, Dančilli thought of the bright red kerchief she might purchase if she were lucky in selling all of her ensete at the market. Then as she bolted a snack from the previous evening's meal, she wondered if she would be on time to meet the Gārbičo trader from whom she would buy ensete to sell in Kavelēnko market. In the past two weeks she had made a fifty-cent profit each time she had sold a muleload of ensete, purchased from the trader for $2.50 a load. If she could only be so fortunate today, she would be able to buy the kerchief as well as some sugar and salt, which she badly needed to replenish household stocks.

This extract from my field notes portrays Dančilli, who in her thoughts and actions is typical of hundreds of women who engage in small trade to provide for personal adornment and for small household needs. Traditionally, opportunity has existed for both men and women to engage in such trade, primarily with the Darasa, Walamo, Arussi, and Gugi. Before Emperor Menelik's conquest in the 1890s, the women exchanged coffee cherries with Arussi women for butter and ensete with their Gugi and Darasa counterparts for milk and butter. The Walamo brought textiles to local markets, as they continue to do, in the form of large cotton cloaks (sēmma) and trousers (gūmfa). They also brought slaves to be purchased as an additional labor force to assist in gardening, house building, and herding.[12] The Darasa were the major source of salt, and it is possible that, as in so many other areas of Ethiopia, salt bars were at one time a form of money.[13]

Nevertheless, there is much more knowledge and interest among Sadāma concerning the use of iron bars in trading among themselves and with surrounding peoples. From all accounts they gained access to iron through Alaba and Borana traders who occasionally visited their markets. As there are no known ore deposits in Sidāmoland, iron ore smelting was unknown, which made iron a scarce commodity and an ideal medium of exchange. So by the latter part of the nineteenth century there were in circulation the angle irons of the Walamo called *mārša*, straight iron bars fashioned by local smiths with a loop in the end known as *womāša*, and *masāni* from the Darasa consisting of an iron bar hafted to a wooden axe handle. A womāša was the equivalent of four mārša or two masāni, and in exchanges when an object was less in value than a mārša, varying amounts of butter, ensete, and honey would be used in the transaction.

Before the latter part of the nineteenth century, for example, a ball of butter six inches in diameter was worth one mārša and could be divided for smaller transactions. A pot of honey and a package of prepared ensete (wrapped in ensete leaves) a foot square were each reckoned as the equivalent of one mārša. Important items of trade (for instance, a pregnant heifer or a large bull) were worth several womāša. Iron bars were also made available on loan, at one hundred percent interest, for use as bridewealth or payment for labor. Then, after Menelik's conquest in the 1890s, the Maria Theresa thaler became available, having been used in Ethiopia since the beginning of the nineteenth century.[14]

Markets are held in all clan areas. *Dālla, Dīko, Kawāda*, and *Kavelenko* as the names of the four-day week also designate regional markets, two of which are now held in administrative towns. In addition, numerous smaller markets in the countryside service several neighborhoods, independent of regional markets or town centers. In fact there are so many markets, large or small, that one is always available within at most a few hours' walking distance of any community.

A regional market like Kavalēnko is a large affair, attracting in the course of the day at least several thousand persons of all ages. It is held in a large pasture of at least two hundred acres, and the only structures are a few stalls of mud and thatch where food and drink are sold on market days. Most of the sellers congregate in small groups with their produce spread out before them on old sacks or shawls.

In the past it is said that women predominated in marketing, but with the advent of a cash economy many more men have become involved in the process. Thus on the day Kavalēnko market was surveyed by the anthropologist there were, other than the persons purveying food and drink in the stalls, 562 persons selling commodities and services. Of this number 36 percent were women and 64 percent were men. Women predominated in the sale of items asso-

Kavelenko, One of the Four Major Regional Markets

ciated with their allocated household tasks such as prepared ensete, milk, barley beer, and vegetables. Men, on the other hand, controlled the sale of livestock, European manufactured commodities such as clothing and sundries, along with the cash crops of coffee, teff, corn meal, tobacco, and barley. And, since men have historically controlled wealth in land and cattle, it is not surprising to find that they have completely taken over the marketing of cash crops. There also were members of the artisan groups selling hides, iron tools, jewelry, and pottery.

As is the case for most such gatherings, marketing is more than an occasion for exchanging goods. It is a convivial social event furnishing an opportunity for adults to gossip, young people to engage in courtship, and some to gamble at cards and other games of chance or to indulge in drink. Other than the visiting of relatives or (in the case of Christians) attendance at church services, this is the only opportunity for women to leave their communities and to interact with people from more-distant places. So visits to the market are eagerly looked forward to by Sadāma of all ages. Indeed, as cash cropping has become an important adjunct to subsistence farming, government officials and technicians have begun to complain that the amount of time spent in marketing is a great waste of labor time, leading to low productivity.

Furthermore, even though outside of the household the market-place is the principal locus of distribution, there is always a sufficient production surplus to support ceremonial redistribution. Periodic contributions are made on ritual occasions such as funerals, mourning ceremonies, and circumcision rites, to which all the members of a neighborhood contribute in order to feed the hundreds of participants.

In brief, it is clear that the network of relationships created by marriage provide the Sadāma with a reserve of persons who can be called upon for economic and ritual assistance. Though the household is the main production unit, when labor is in short supply or there are long and expensive elderhood promotion rites, in-laws can be expected to provide support. Within the household the husband clearly has authority, but it must be tempered by the need for loyalty and commitment from his wife or wives. Wives are critical in reproducing the labor force, managing food processing, disciplining and nurturing children, and contributing their own labor to the cultivation of the garden. By nature of their contribution they must be involved in the decisions affecting the running of the household economy. For a husband to become despotic in the exercise of authority is to break the bonds of mutuality with his spouse(s) and in-laws. In this event he would bankrupt the domestic economy and even have difficulty obtaining sustenance, given the exclusive role of women in processing food. On the other hand, there is an advantage for a wife in remaining loyal and committed to an ambitious husband, since she will have more resources for her children and be secure in her old age. Finally, there is the importance of the marketplace, which once was dominated by women bartering local commodities. But women still make an important contribution to the household economy by selling small amounts of their husbands' coffee cherries, prepared food, and vegetables.

6                  Beliefs, Ritual,
and Authority

To understand how social control is maintained within clans and how conflicts between clans are reconciled, it is necessary to examine how the Sadāma conceptualize authority. Such an examination leads to consideration of fundamental beliefs about the establishment and maintenance of order in the universe, beliefs that provide people with a model for social control. I begin this chapter with a discussion of the pantheon of deities, the mystical origins of the people, the conceptualization of time as it relates to the life cycle, beliefs about "good" and "evil," and the rituals that, properly performed, are expected to preserve harmony and bounty in the universe. Then, having analyzed the underlying ideas and rites supporting authority, it is appropriate in the following chapter to consider the concrete, social expressions in the form of the generational class system, leadership roles, and elders' councils.

## Deities, Mystical Origins, and Time

The Sadāma believe in a pantheon of deities ranked in order of esteem, consisting of sky gods, dead elders, and spirit beings. The sky deities are associated with creation and power, while the principal role of the dead elders is to sanction the authority of their living counterparts. By contrast, spirit beings, consisting of possession spirits and tricksters, are regarded with ambivalence, because of their varying ability to influence people's lives for good or evil.

Magāno, the creator, began his activities by fashioning man out of earth and then created woman by taking a rib from the earthman. After that, the creator lived in close association with the people, instructing them on how to conduct their daily lives and on avoiding incestuous relationships. Later he quarreled with the people, either over their refusal to accept the inevitability of death or over their selfishness, and then he returned to the sky. And where previously there had been only darkness, he created the sun, moon, and stars to provide light. But before leaving earth the creator admonished the people, saying: "I created you out of the soil and you will return to the soil. You will work the soil and gain your sustenance from it. If you must grieve so much, I cannot live with you. From now on you must help yourselves."

The sun is said to be the creator's eye and the moon is the husband of the sun. The moon not only provides the basis for a calendar but is also the regulator of the timing between conception and birth for women and cows. The stars are spoken of by some as the sky god's cattle and by others as fireflies that live on earth during the day and return to the sky at night.

The other ethereal element is Bānko, the deity of thunder and lightning. Like the creator, he is said to have lived on earth for a time, but with a member of a specific clan, the Wiāno. But unlike the supreme being, whose substance is never described, Bānko is portrayed as being part fire, water, and iron. In the description of his relationship with the Wiāno man, much emphasis is placed on the importance of the service and hospitality provided by the man. Therefore, before returning to the sky, the deity made a pact with the man, agreeing to assist his descendants if they would observe certain food taboos, such as the avoidance of goats. In return Bānko gave these people the power to protect their land by enabling them to destroy their enemies.

The clans have a form of totem known as a *tārre*, consisting of a forked stick on which a special type of plant or part of an animal is impaled. These totems are used to protect property, since it is believed that anyone crossing a boundary protected by a tārre will experience dire consequences, such as pernicious vomiting or diarrhea. The totem of the Wiāno clan is protected by Bānko and is the most powerful of all, because it involves the killing of a trespasser with a bolt of lightning. Other clans may use this tārre, but it can be emplaced and removed only by a member of the Wiāno.

Basic to an understanding of the importance of dead elders is the process of dreaming and the concept of *halōli*. The term *halōli* is often heard in elders' councils and may be broadly interpreted as "the true way of life." The specific truth referred to depends upon the situational context and may concern veracity in giving evidence, faithfulness to the norms of mutuality in everyday activities, generosity, and avoidance of jealousy. Since this concept was established from the very beginning, it is the dead elders who are believed to be closer to this ideal condition than the living elders. Consequently, they are in a position to use dreams to inform the living elders of deviations from the "true way." Indeed, dreaming is important to the Sadāma precisely because it is the principal means of communicating with the spirit world, especially when there are ambiguities concerning halōli. The following episode recorded in the author's field notes exemplifies this process:

An old man opened the meeting of a neighborhood council of elders by announcing that D, a recently deceased relative, had before his death dreamed that he should pay a fine to the council. Indeed his mother, wives, and several other close relatives were standing on the periphery of the circle of seated elders waiting to present the payment. A long discussion followed as to whether the elders should first inquire as to why the deceased's relatives were paying the fine. Eventually this led to the listing of several wrongs committed by D, such as his failure to attend mourning rituals, lack of cooperation in housebuilding, and the destruction of a tree under which clan sacrifices had traditionally been offered.

One of the leading spokesmen for the elders then related a long moralistic tale about creation of a mutual protection arrangement between a lion and a ram.[1] The substantive meaning of the tale was that without recompense for violation of the rules of mutuality, one could not predict the consequences of supernatural punishment that might be inflicted on one's descendants. Therefore the elders should accept the money as recompense, in order to protect D's children.[2]

The relatives then came forward and placed $1.50 on an ensete leaf in front of the oldest elder. The old relative then said: "We are giving this money because D ignored halōli." Further discussion followed in which they were warned not to attend the mourning ritual for D because of his life-long violations of halōli. The content of the dreams followed a similar format, in which the oldest man in the council was seen carrying by himself the heavy mourning pole, usually carried by dozens of young men. In one case an elder had dreamed that he should purchase a sheep in a particular market, slaughter it, and cleanse himself with the blood before attending D's mourning rites. The assembled elders agreed that this man should follow the dictates of his dream, but since D's relatives had paid the fine, he and his descendants should be released from any potential punishment for his violation of the rules, and they should all attend his mourning rites.

Though all men receive dream visits from their dead fathers, reminding them of their obligations to honor the elders and to live according to the dictates of the true way, only men who are noted for living according to the concept are able to receive dream communications from ancestral notables, other apical clan ancestors, and the creator sky god.

Such persons are also considered to have iyāni, in the sense of being blessed with good fortune. The term *iyāni* may be variously translated according to the situation; for example, it can mean a father's spirit (in the phrase *ānu iyāni*), good fortune (when used in connection with the most favorable days in the calendar), or a very powerful possession state. *Iyāni* is also used in different contexts by the Oromo, a people widespread throughout southern and central Ethiopia, to mean divine being, guardian spirit, good fortune, and favorable day in their lunar calendar.[3] Among the Sadāma it is very unusual for a person to be possessed by an iyāni. To have this spirit is to have great power for doing good, because it is an essence sent directly by the creator sky god, it is always predictable, and it is associated with the truth. In recent times, iyāni spirits have been present in the *Wando Magāno* movement, in which the hosts have attracted large followings because of the belief that they have ability to resolve disputes connected with cash indebtedness, theft, and marital disputes.[4] It is significant that these spirits appeared at a time of crisis in the years just prior to the 1974 Ethiopian Revolution, when the Sadāma were beginning to experience all the problems of a cash economy and there was great political uncertainty.

By contrast, *šatāna*, the principal form of possession spirits, are considered to be less powerful and to be fickle liars. Possession is an alternative for obtaining desirable status by those who fail through their own efforts to conform to the ideals.[5] These spirits may be transmitted from a parent to a favorite child or may be acquired following a long period of illness. The original possession spirits are said to have taken the form of a conjugal family whose abode was near the southern border of Sidāmoland around Lake Abaya. It is clear, however, that over the years spirits from the Arussi and the Amhara have been added to the indigenous family group.[6] In the possession process, an individual host may acquire one or more of these spirits, but the first one to appear is considered the leader and spokesman for all.

Informants were generally of the opinion that many more people were possessed in the past than in the present, primarily because Emperor Menelik's conquest and later the Italian occupation are said to have caused people to lose faith in their power. Since World War II, Christian missionaries from Europe have made further contributions to the decline, in addition to providing a powerful supernatural alternative. In the past, an individual possessed by a spirit could not relinquish it until death, but today many people who for one reason or another are dissatisfied with their spirits may escape from them by becoming Christians. Nevertheless, there are still many Sadāma possessed by šatāna. The hosts are about equally divided between men and women and are recognized as having low status in their respective communities.[7]

Unless the possession experience is inherited from the previous generation, the presence of spirits is usually suspected when an individual acquires an illness that is difficult to diagnose. To confirm their presence, a specialist *(kilānčo)* must be consulted, who is adept at identifying possession cases and at determining the procedures necessary for calling the spirits.

The procedure invariably involves assembling all the adult members of the hamlet at night, when spirits are abroad. They gather in the household of the possessed and call the spirits by singing and drumming, according to the rules laid down by the specialist. The spirits respond by entering the head of the host, causing it to shake gently at first, but the tremors gradually increase in intensity until the whole body has begun to vibrate. People say that the spirits are riding the individual as they would a horse or a mule.[8] Then the spokesman for the community asks the spirit leader its name and whether it is responsible for the host's illness. The spirit usually admits that it has caused the illness because the possessed refused to recognize it and its followers. Bargaining then follows, with the spirit ultimately agreeing to protect the host and his or her conjugal family and cattle from illness, in return for recognition and service. The service aspect involves a large annual feast to "feed" the spirits, one that all the adult male members of the village are expected to attend. This process is repeated whenever an illness occurs within the family.

Often there is an avowed desire on the part of the host that his or her spirit will be powerful enough to make the person clairvoyant and thus able to attract others who will come to serve and bring gifts.[9] There are many stories told of people originally living in poverty who acquired a powerful spirit and then became famous and wealthy because of all who came to provide service. This is in fact a hoped-for but seldom-obtained goal. In most instances, the host and members of the conjugal family live in fear that they will fail to serve the spirit adequately by not providing enough food or gifts. The spirits, for example, often request rare or difficult-to-obtain jewelry and charms, for which the family of the possessed must search in the various country markets. But instead of receiving protection and power, the possessed usually suffers continued ill health or even death.

Despite these dangers, low-status people with spirits do attract more than the usual amount of attention from their kinsmen and other members of the community. This is especially true for married women who, under the aegis of their spirits, can make demands on their husbands, as well as the men of his clan who are resident in the village.

There are other kinds of amorphous spirits, such as the tricksters known as *radāna* and those associated with certain prominent natural phenomena. Radāna are most noted for taking the form of a human in order to play tricks on other people. It is not unknown for them to strike individuals, without warning, with such blows to the head that the victim suffers deafness or even insanity. They are also said to like to milk cows and smoke the water pipe. When engaged in such activities, radāna should never be disturbed by a human for fear of encouraging bodily assault leading to the aforementioned debilities.

On the other hand, nature spirits are less aggressive and destructive and those of especial importance are associated with several mountain peaks where clan sacrifice may be performed. The deity of the mountain is simply addressed, for example, as the spirit of Halu Tulu and is asked to respond to the sacrifice by ending the drought or poor health that may be afflicting clan members.

Thus the sky deities provide a charter setting out the finiteness of human existence, the importance of mutuality, and the destiny of man to cultivate the soil. The dead elders have a more specific role to support the living elders in upholding the true way of life as it pertains to the situational requirements of generosity, truth, and the rules of social exchange. These deities are guardians of a cooperative, productive community where individuals must work together in harmony to make the land produce. But, with the exception of the iyāni spirits, the possession spirits are concerned with the strivings of

individuals for power, health, and wealth. And because of their demands for the accumulation of food and treasure to honor themselves
and their hosts, they represent a force for wasting resources and
creating fear and disruption within the community.

The smaller units of time and their relationship to important events
in the life cycle are described by a lunar calendar. This involves a
twenty-eight-day cycle, with the beginning and end dependent on
the position of a constellation of seven stars in close proximity to the
moon. When the stars, which are called cows following one another,
are in front of the moon as it proceeds west in its orbit, the cycle will
begin again the next day, but if they are behind the moon, the cycle
will not start until the second day. In the event the heavens are
obscured by clouds, there is an elaborate procedure of adding additional days before the beginning of the next cycle. The men who make
the observations and know the names and significance for each of
the twenty-eight days are specialists given the title *īyānto*.

To be born on certain days of the cycle is to acquire wealth; birth
on other days leads to poverty. Likewise, character attributes are
based on day of birth, including bravery or cowardice, a pleasant
versus a quarrelsome or dissatisfied disposition.[10] Only a few designated days are acceptable for the performance of rituals involving
sacrifice, the beginning and ending of mourning ceremonies, housewarmings, and circumcision rites. Certain days are designated as
propitious for the older but not for the younger generation to perform
animal sacrifice. Moreover, children born on a given day will be
considered a menace to their parents, while those born at another
time in the cycle will be expected to bring great blessings to their
mother and father. There are favorable and unfavorable days for travel
and the performance of economic transactions like borrowing and
lending money. Even different climatological predictions can be
made on the basis of whether the rains begin on one or the other of
two days in the cycle. Also, a favorable time exists for the activities
of artisan groups, and during this period the activities of all other
groups will be adversely affected. Five days are considered neutral,
in the sense that they are neither favorable nor unfavorable for the
previously enumerated events. Finally, days with completely negative connotations occur three times, with one actually designated as
*bītta*, a term that also means "sorcery."

The celestial calendar indicates the chance aspects in the cosmos
such as climate, wealth, poverty, economic transactions, and certain

personality attributes. Even the cultivator/craftsman duality is recognized, with certain time frames favorable for one or the other group. But the calendar is intended to introduce a sense of order and predictability into these events. The people are quite aware that positive or negative aspects of the passage of time cannot be separated from individual initiative.

## Good and Evil

The Sadāma, like peoples elsewhere, recognize the ambiguities of "good" and "evil." They accept these values as polar concepts and recognize a certain circularity between them in the sense that one can develop out of the other. An example of this ambivalence was provided by some informants, who suggested that the decisions of the elders arising out of deliberations in council are supposed to be "good" for the people, but if they quarrel or postpone action too long, their decisions may have "evil" consequences. Thus an organization that is highly valued may produce negative results. There is also an element of fate involved, as in the case of the distinction between "acceptable" and "nonacceptable" behavior. Normally the two are easily distinguishable, but if a man is constantly being punished by the elders for violating the norms and there is no change in his behavior, then they conclude that it was his destiny to be continually in trouble.

There is a definite belief in an afterlife above the sky, called *imihēšo*. All people, regardless of their deeds, go to this land after death. Some informants believed that those who had been notable for their evil acts were punished in various ways, while those whose behavior had been in conformity with the norms were rewarded by living in the style of wealthy men. Evil deeds are defined as stealing, telling lies, borrowing money without repayment, violating property boundaries, ignoring incest taboos, and failing to render assistance to kinsmen. There are messengers (*solcōnčos*) who serve the creator deity and who are aware of the life histories of all the dead. They escort evildoers to one of the three places of punishment: a thorn bush, fire, or a bottomless pit. The latter two are considered the severest form of punishment.

There is a recognition in these concepts that rightness and wrongness are not absolutes and that, regardless of effort, some individuals will be ill starred and incapable of conformity. Flexibility in regard to values thus implies a possibility for negotiation and compromise according to the situation, which is so much a part of the authority exercised by the elders. Furthermore, there is evidence that the esteemed behavior is cooperation in fulfilling obligations that preserve the integrity of land use, indebtedness, and mutual assistance.

## Rituals and Symbolism

The emphasis in the previous sections has been on beliefs about the cosmos and the passage of time, and on how these aspects structure the concepts of authority and mutuality in the relations of production. This section will focus upon the social relationships and symbols of ritual. In this context, "ritual" refers to those ceremonies in which people acting and thinking in concert, according to a prescribed set of rules, seek to obtain desirable goals. Practices considered will be honoring of the dead, generational class promotion rites, and domestic ceremonies.

Reference has already been made to the life-long relationships between sons and fathers that continue after death through dream visitations. The Sadāma speak of "feeding" their dead fathers in using the phrase *ānnu-worāmo*, meaning "a bull for father," which is quite distinct from the concept of giving animal sacrifice, for which the term *kakōllo* is used. A father's ghost may appear in a dream at any time and ask to be fed a bull at a designated place, but if it appears without speaking, it is permissible to substitute honey for a bull. Moreover, if there is a shortage of bulls or if the price is high, a son will often plead poverty, regardless of the ghost's instructions, and provide only honey. Some action must be taken, however, or it is believed that the son will die.

All the clans have rites to honor their apical ancestors. Most elaborate are those of the Holō and Gārbičo for their esteemed founder Abo. Indeed, Abo is considered by many to rank next to the sky deities in terms of controlling supernatural power. People are more likely to appeal to Abo than the sky deities because of the fact that he is among the most powerful of ancestor spirits and because he was once of this world and therefore has a greater understanding of human problems. When Abo died, it is said that his spirit hovered about the grave and continued to direct his descendants in the proper conduct of their affairs. Today this grave site, located in a sacred forest on the side of a mountain, continues to be one of the most important ritual centers for all the Sadāma.[11] Every seventh year the elders in the various Holō and Gārbičo lineages are expected to bring to the grave a sacrificial bull in honor of Abo. Following this ritual the men proceed to honor the graves of their respective forefathers. At each grave a man will pour out a small amount of consecrated honey, having previously prepared by purifying himself through sprinkling blood from a slaughtered lamb over his body. As he proceeds on his way, he must be able to identify a number of widely dispersed grave sites, some of which are easily distinguished by the characteristic burial mound surrounded by a rotting bamboo fence. Other sites are marked only by trees planted generations ago. In this pilgrimage he is accompanied by his eldest son, so that he too will learn the location of the graves and in turn be able to transmit the information to his brothers and sons.

Death rituals, in terms of interest and numbers of participants, are among the most important of all communal activities. Burial (*medāša*) mobilizes the efforts of the neighborhood, as well as friends and kinsmen from distant clans. The participants in the five-day burial rites of a distinguished old man can number in the thousands.

When an old patriarch is near death, he should be attended and cared for by his wife (or wives), sons, and brothers, who are also responsible for washing and dressing his corpse when he dies. As in most phases of the life cycle, age distinctions continue to be important after death. If it is a young man who has died, the men of the neighborhood will be called immediately to prepare the grave, while close relatives sit by the body and weep. In the case of an old man, the body is sprinkled with spices and honey and is kept for three to five days as a sign of respect for his age.

The corpse is then placed near the homestead in a tomb consisting of a tunnel under the earth. It is made by digging two shafts to a depth of five to six feet and then joining them by the tunnel, which is large enough to contain the bodies of two men. This tomb prevents the body from being fouled with earth, a taboo that has to do with status considerations. People curse others by likening them to the dirt under their feet or by throwing dirt on their persons. Consequently, to honor the dead, every effort must be made to protect the corpse from such a negative status symbol. Then the shafts must be filled and grass planted on the top of the grave to signify the continuity between life and death.

For five days following the burial, guests come to express their condolences and to receive the hospitality of the neighborhood of the deceased. Afterward a fence is built around the grave, the structure and decor of which is dependent on the age, sex, wealth, and fame of the dead person. Elaborate bamboo fences are constructed for old men; old women are entitled to a smaller version of similar design. By contrast, the structure for young men is of boards, while young women having the lowest adult status receive only a fence built of sticks. If the deceased acquired fame by killing an enemy warrior or a dangerous animal such as a lion, his kinsmen may arrange to have an effigy wood carving of himself or the animal he killed placed near the grave.

Like the burial rites, the period of mourning *(kayĭčo-witla)* lasts five days and usually takes place one to two months after interment, because of the need for accumulation of enough food to feed all the participants from visiting clans. Informants attributed the origins of these rites to a desire to cheer up the survivors of the deceased. Indeed, as in the burial ceremonies, it is the neighborhood led by the elders that provides the food and accommodation for the large number of visitors.

The procedure begins with expressions of condolences to the close relatives of the dead person: "Why did this man who was so wealthy, brave, friendly, and famous have to die?" This is followed by a listing of his friends, perhaps a short poem about the valor of men in his generational class, and occasionally a description of the cattle he captured from enemy tribesmen after his initiation. Since so many people are involved, most of the rites take place in a large open space, such as the neighborhood pasture.

After these preliminaries the *dore* pole, a tree twenty-five to thirty feet in length from which the bark has been stripped, is emplaced in the center of the crowd of mourners. If the dead man has killed a fierce animal or an enemy warrior, the pole is painted red; otherwise it is left in a natural state. Then the mourners gather to one side to begin the singing and dancing as the female relatives of the deceased parade around the pole carrying their kinsman's personal possessions, including his cloth belt, lanyard, milk gourd, and rifle. In their midst are two or three women drummers who are close relatives, and a man recognized for his song-leading ability. The songs that follow pertain to the valor of famous warriors, interspersed with verses of how much the deceased will be missed. This singing accompanies the dancing, along with the reenactment of a mock battle with spears

The Grave of a Distinguished Elder

The Dore Pole and the Ritual Dancing for Mourning the Dead

and shields, additional ways of honoring the departed. As a sign of grief, close female relatives weep and mutilate their faces to induce the flow of blood.

Periodically the ceremony is interrupted in order to serve food to the visitors and to provide them with tobacco. This activity not only is of considerable expense, but it generates a great deal of concern, for failure to serve and feed guests properly is a sign of social indifference or rejection, which may result in gossip and a poor reputation for members of the neighborhood. In some cases it may lead to disputes in which guests complain to the elders that they have been improperly treated.

The pattern of rites on the following two days is similar to the first, except that the themes of the songs are changed. There is less emphasis on honoring the dead and more on the importance of halōli (the "true way of life"). Those who would violate the norms, such as women who spend their husband's money foolishly or old men who marry young girls, are subject to ridicule. These activities come to an end on the third day, and the pole is lowered to the ground. At this point the negative and abnormal aspects of death are symbolized. Rather than a bull or an ox (the ordinary forms of animal sacrifice), a calf belonging to the deceased is sacrificed at the foot of the pole. The animal is placed on its left or evil side, as opposed to the right side, which is associated with a good omen on normal occasions.[12] Instead of the meat being divided among the participants, as is ordinarily the practice at a sacrifice, the carcass is given to members of the potter's clan. A woman instead of a man performs the purificatory rites by sprinkling water on the pole, as she holds shields and drums with a bundle of leaves in her left hand. Then in-laws and close agnatic kin of the deceased shave their heads. The last two days are for "cooling off" and are used by the members of the neighborhood to console and help the surviving wives and children plan for the future.

The mourning rites for women are arranged differently, with the focal point of the ritual being four sharpened sticks, rather than a pole driven into the ground. These are draped with clothing and the utensils appropriate to the role of the deceased. In keeping with the different but complementary role of the female, the three days of dances and songs vary considerably from those provided for men.

These rituals dramatize the emotional concerns about the finiteness of life revealed in the narrative accounts about the origins of death at the beginning of the chapter. Yet the idealized properties of the living, as to the sexual division of labor and status differences connected with aging, are played out as having continuity. The norms are symbolized in the songs honoring the dead as if they represent an influence of the will of the latter upon the living.

If death and mourning rites provide a link between the sanctioning power of the dead and living elders, it is the initiation and promotion ceremonies of the generational class system that validate the changing authority status of men. These activities provide for the induction of men and boys into the system, as well as, years later, their promotion to elderhood.

Preinitiates first gather at a traditional clan camp site under their class leader.[13] Feeding and tree symbolism are of obvious importance in this procedure, as they are in burial and mourning. Feeding symbolizes the complementary role relationship between the authority of the older generation and the service role allocated to the younger generation. Thus the initiates first plant a tree as emblematic of their particular class, and each member places a handful of grass beneath the young seedling. The grass stands for the peace and harmony that is supposed to prevail between the preinitiates. Then during the following two months, the young men travel about the countryside visiting and being fed by members of their father's class who are now elders and by their foster fathers of another class who have been responsible for them prior to initiation. Each father will contribute a bull to the group, which is reciprocated on the part of the sons when their fathers die.

After this interval of feasting, the initiates once again assemble in their camp. This time they sacrifice a bull and leave the camp boasting of the cattle they will capture from enemy warriors. At the edge of the camp they fight a mock battle with initiates of the preceding class who are of approximately the same generation. Fathers and foster fathers of both groups prevent the fighting from getting out of hand. In effect this conflict and its control is a symbolic expression of the authority of the older to resolve conflicts between members of the younger generation, as well as the acceptability of intragenerational rivalry. This is much the way that relationships between males are structured in everyday life.

Some twenty-eight years later it will be the turn of these initiates in the promotion cycle to become elders. The ceremony involves circumcision, followed by a two-month period of seclusion. During this time, they are served by their agnatic and affinal kin, who care for their garden(s) and bring them gifts of cattle, butter, and milk. The candidates' prestige will depend on the amount of support their kin provide in contributing their labor and gifts, so as to ensure the full two months in seclusion.

Social withdrawal comes to an end with an elaborate ritual of cleansing, feasting, and dancing, in which all the members of the neighborhood participate in honoring the candidates. Elders from previous promotion cycles engage in elaborate recitations of the deeds performed by notables of the past. Young men visiting from different clans take their cue from this relatively peaceful, poetic banter to boast and threaten each other while dancing. Just as in the heated exchanges of the mock battle following initiation, the new and old elders intervene to prevent violence.

Community maintains other rituals, such as the new year's feast, called *fiče*. Though this feast is gradually disappearing in some areas where people have begun to follow the Amhara calendar, it is still proclaimed by the head of each clan and his delegated elders in every neighborhood. The activities involve members of the conjugal family symbolically washing away the old year, followed by the reciprocal exchange of meals between all the households in a hamlet. Young men and young women then gather in the marketplaces to sing and dance. For those clans in which the elders maintain the concept of purity of descent (anga), the celebration is of especial importance. To these men, the feast marks the conclusion of a significant unit in the time span extending from the clan founder to the present. Elders believe that failure to celebrate the new year would break the continuity and would destroy their anga, as well as their authority status.

Other rituals are important for the hamlet and household. For example, *wo-wāte* is a form of conditional vow for women that serves to reinforce the importance of their child-bearing role. This involves a childless woman committing herself to give a feast for the other women in the hamlet to honor a designated deity, on condition the latter enables her to bear a child. Regardless of the lapse of time, if and when a child is born, the woman will prepare ensete, and the husband will slaughter a bull to feed all the women. Then on their way to the feast, from which men are excluded, the women will harangue and insult all unwary males they happen to meet. Indeed, after the feast the participants engage in sexually seductive songs and dances ridiculing men. But the women conclude the festivities by blessing all the members of the household.

In this ceremony there is a reversal of roles, in which women temporarily exercise authority over men. This transposition underscores their critical reproductive role in the production process, which is at odds with their day-to-day subordination to male authority. And as Gluckman has suggested for ritual license in general, the blessing of the wife and husband together immediately following ridicule of him by the older women is indicative that cooperative endeavors of the family take moral precedence over individual roles.[14]

A much more frequently occurring community and household ritual is the sexually segregated housewarming. It occurs as a consequence of house construction being based on a reciprocal exchange of labor of men of the neighborhood. The recipient is required to feed the builders during the five- to seven-day construction period, as well as to provide a feast when the house is finished. So on the evening of the last day, when the thatch roofing is in place, the workers gather inside the new house for the repast. When the meal is over, the elders, followed by the young men, raise and lower their outstretched arms and hands several times, calling in unison for the blessing of the household by various supernatural agents. The creator deity is called upon first, followed in rapid succession by lesser spirits, including ancestors and those associated with important sacrificial spots such as prominent mountain peaks. After this, dancing and singing continue well into the night. And within a few days of the completion of construction, the women of the neighborhood perform a similar ceremony of feasting, blessing, and dancing.

Finally, there is the conditional vow called *tāno*, consisting of a compact between an individual and a supernatural being hoped to be a benefactor. The compact may involve any of the pantheon of deities, though in practice possession spirits and those of dead elders are seldom used, because of previously existing arrangements that may exist between hosts and possession spirits and the perpetual reciprocal obligations between fathers and sons. But regardless of the deity, the vow is usually made to improve one's health, to acquire wealth, or to overcome a condition of childlessness. A supplicant will promise to give a bull in return for so important a gift. Nevertheless, there are lesser concerns that may lead to a compact, such as safety on a journey or success in marketing. Women in particular are likely to make such minor compacts by rubbing butter on the sacred trees under which ritual sacrifice is conducted and by pouring milk in streams that must be crossed. All this is done in hopes that the spirits of these natural objects will protect them in their travels and market dealings.

Just as the beliefs about order in the cosmos show different levels of inclusiveness and status values, so do the rituals. Death and mourning rites, for example, as well as those connected with the generational class system, indicate extensive horizontal and vertical links. These connections include horizontal ties between clans and lineages because of affinal obligations to participate in obsequies and to honor promotion to elderhood. The same is true of initiation, with initiates of a new class coming from all descent groups. Vertical linkages are shown through the symbolic values attached to aging, such as observing a longer burial period for the elderly dead, providing more elaborate fencing for their graves, and giving elders precedence in seating and feeding arrangements on ceremonial occasions. The authority of the elders is dramatized by their preventing the initiates' mock battle from getting out of hand, indicating that gerontocratic edict should take precedent over the horizontal divisions of class loyalties. By contrast, new year's rituals, compacts with deities, and housewarmings are more exclusive, involving the clan, neighborhood, hamlet, or individuals.

The importance of gerontocratic authority is demonstrated by the tree symbolism found in so many activities and rituals. Animal sacrifice, meetings of elders' councils, and the rubbing of butter on bark for protection in travel and marketing take place under the spreading branches of huge podocarpus trees. In the rituals, trees are used to mark old grave sites, the dore pole is the focal point of mourning rites, and each class of initiates acquires a special tree to mark their existence as a group. Because elders meet in their cooling shade to make policy, resolve disputes, and call upon deities to provide health and welfare for the people, trees symbolize cooperation. On the other hand, they are also the abode of certain possession spirits that are associated with ill health, power, and individualism. Consequently, the stately podocarpus becomes an icon for the Sadāma, standing for the fundamental problem of balancing individual self-interest with community obligation.

Finally, these rituals have important economic implications. They are indeed expensive, as can be seen from the fact that it usually takes two months for people in neighborhoods to accumulate the necessary food to perform the mourning rites. Also, the time that a man spends in seclusion prior to promotion to elderhood is dependent upon the size and dependability of the labor force he can muster to care for his garden, as well as the number of kinsmen likely to bring him gifts for support of the feasts and feeding of guests.

The household head must produce more than is necessary to feed his family, so as to fulfill his obligations to contribute to communal feasts. This surplus is appropriated by the community to be redistributed in honor of the deities or at the transition of an individual from lower to higher status. At the same time, these festivals are also a means of showing respect and concern for persons outside the household who are important in providing their labor and other forms of assistance in crisis situations.

Authority and
Social Control

From the very beginning, the people quarreled with the creator over human longevity, and he left them to return to the sky. Thus it was given to the apical ancestral heroes and succeeding generations of elders to elaborate the true way of life (halōli) in terms of the importance of truth, mutuality, and generosity. In this role they have been sanctified by the various tree and burial symbols, as well as the death and promotion rituals. The Sadāma recognize all these matters as a part of their cosmos, but they also know, as is indicated in the structure of the celestial calendar, that chance can turn individuals away from this true way of life. Spirits promoting self-aggrandizement, such as the šatāna, can disrupt the life of the community.

The potential built into the cosmos for injustice and wrongdoing must be dealt with by the living elders. They are the ones who must confront the mundane aspects of these problems by making community policy on a consensual basis and by settling disputes so as to reestablish a modicum of harmony between disputants. Since it is the elders who have authority and are the principal instruments of social control, it is necessary to consider the elderhood recruitment process and the way leaders are chosen in order to understand how the Sadāma perceive and institutionalize authority. Much of this procedure takes place within the framework of the generational class system, known as the lua.[1]

## The Generational Class System

The lua is not an age-set system as that term is usually understood. For example, the following is a widely used definition: "persons who have been initiated during successive annual ceremonies of a single initiation period; this may be divided into sub-sets consisting of those who have gone through the same ceremony together."[2] Further, these sets normally pass through a succession of age grades that are allocated differing responsibilities. In southern Ethiopia, however, there are a number of societies in which people do not pass through a series of grades with explicit differentiated functions but are grouped as "classes based on time."[3] People may or may not be grouped in classes according to chronological age.

There is such a class system among the Sadāma, in which the critical differentiating factor is generational rather than chronological age differences. This system involves five classes, in which a hypothetical ego will throughout his life cycle be categorized in some form of adjacent generational relationship with all the others. Thus, to begin with, a son is always initiated in the class following that of his father. These five classes rotate in a clockwise, circular fashion, changing every seven years as indicated in figure 3. The process begins when ego is born. He then commences the preinitiation cycle

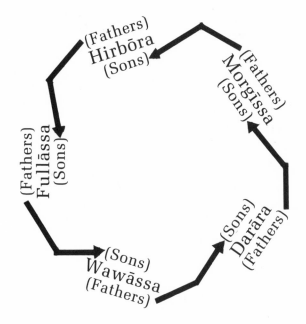

**Figure 3.** Counterclockwise Order of Lua Membership: Fathers to Sons. *Source:* Author.

and is placed in the class just behind that in which his father was installed at birth. He will be considered a foster son of the members of this class until initiated into a permanent group following in sequence that of his father. This event can occur only after his father's class has begun their elderhood cycle, which comes twenty-eight years after they complete their initiation rituals.

For illustrative purposes it is convenient to postulate a situation in which a hypothetical father has just been initiated into Morgīssa at the end of a seven-year interval and to trace the consequences for other classes in the cycle. It will further be assumed that a son, ego, is born shortly before or after his father's induction ceremony. Table 1 lists the social position at this point in time of ego's relatives in the respective classes. The sequence will continue with sons of the pre-

**Table 1.** Social Correlates of Class Changes in the *Lua*

| | |
|---|---|
| **Hirbōra** | Elders of this *lua* complete their fourteenth year of elderhood. Initiates, sons of elders of Morgīssa, complete their seven years of cattle raiding and military exploits following the commencement of their initiation cycle. |
| **Morgīssa** | Ego's father along with other men who are sons of the Darāra complete their initiation ritual marking the beginning of their initiation cycle. The Morgīssa elders, members of the preceding cycle, complete their first seven years as elders. |
| **Darāra** | Ego's grandfather completes the first class interval of elderhood as his group finishes their circumcision rites. |
| **Wawāssa** | Ego's great-grandfather's class has seven years left before completing their second cycle and being retired from the *lua*. The sons of the Fullāssa have now finished their initiation cycle and are ready to begin the elderhood cycle. At the completion of the first interval of this cycle they will replace ego's great-grandfather's class as Wawāssa elders. Ego becomes a foster son of these men and will be under their tutelage until his initiation into Hirbōra twenty-eight years hence. |
| **Fullāssa** | The fathers of ego's foster fathers begin the twenty-first year of their elderhood, with two more intervals remaining before retirement from the *lua*. |

*Source:* Author.

ceding class entering succeeding lua classes of their fathers and being junior to the elders of a previous cycle in their respective classes.

Ego will be replaced by the sons of the men in the next class of his cycle as initiates thirty-five years after his own induction, and twenty-eight years later as elders, upon the retirement of his class. Though the Sadāma conceptualize class and generational differences, they do not have a term for cycle, which is a construct introduced by the author. Based on a listing of all the class leaders, of which there have been twenty since the establishment of the lua among the Āletā, it can be estimated that the system is at least 140 years old. Consequently, not enough time has elapsed for the development of the cycle concept, but should the lua continue, it is possible that a term will develop for ease in classifying the temporal sequences.

At various points in time, ego will be linked to all of the classes in differing cycles of development. The hypothetical case in which ego is an initiate in Hirbōra is illustrative of this situation. Thus when he becomes an initiate in Hirbōra, his sons will be foster sons of Darāra elders and his father will be a Morgīssa elder. Ego during his initiation rituals will have been fed by his foster fathers, the elders of Wawāssa. When he is promoted to elderhood, he will reciprocate as a foster father for the preinitiate sons of the Wawāssa, and his sons will leave Darāra and be initiated into Fullāssa. Meanwhile, his grandfather's class of Darāra elders will be nearing retirement from the lua. This shows the structural basis for the horizontal and vertical class linkages indicated in the elders' ritual feeding and mediation of mock battles, described in the last chapter.

Unlike the *gada* system of the Oromo, marriage and the establishment of a family is unrelated to one's status in the class intervals. And though there is no analogous generational class system for women, in the past when there was marital separation, the woman was expected to observe certain marital restrictions. She was forbidden to marry a man from the class of her husband's father or of her husband's foster fathers, though it was permissible to remarry into any of the other classes.

Finally, the lua provides the structural basis for complementary relations between generations, for it is the initiates who provide the labor, defer to the elders, and, in the past, demonstrated their courage by obtaining cattle during raids on neighboring ethnic groups. This labor and deference is rendered in return for the elders' redistributing land, providing bridewealth, and training the initiates in the principles of truth, generosity, and mutuality that constitute the true way of life.

The cattle raids were carried out during the first seven-year interval of the initiation cycle and provided an opportunity for initiates to demonstrate skill in taking large numbers of cattle under dangerous conditions. Though the animals were divided equally among the men, the extent to which they could boast about their exploits to the succeeding class was dependent on the total captured during this time. Also, it was possible for a man to win a reputation for bravery through a daring act, such as stealing into a cattle pen and removing all of the animals before the owner was aware of his presence. This form of skill was considered more important than killing the enemy, though a man could attain fame and acquire the right to special honors at his funerary rites by killing an enemy under circumstances requiring unusual courage. These exploits provided the material for poetic boasting that has been kept alive for generations and that continues to be used at mourning ceremonies and on the occasion of circumcision feasts.

In terms of providing labor, initiates continue to work under the supervision of the elders building houses in the neighborhoods, clearing streams, maintaining trails, digging graves, and erecting funerary fences. Their labor is supplemented by the deference that younger must show toward older men, as symbolized by the practice of following class seniority in the order in which men receive food at public gatherings, the sequence they follow in expressing condolence to a deceased's relatives at a mourning ceremony, and in the presentation of the traditional nonfermented horn of honey during the circumcision feast.[4]

During the initiation cycle a young man will seek to demonstrate his ability to acquire wealth and to speak well in the council of elders. Though he may not make decisions, he is encouraged to participate in policy debates and to discuss evidence in various disputes. But only after promotion to elderhood will he be permitted to participate in the actual decision making of the council.

So it is promotion to elderhood that represents the culmination of the individual's efforts to demonstrate wisdom and courage and to develop a reputation for having wealth. The reputation he has established will be indicated by the manner in which he entertains visitors during the seclusion ritual, the number of people who volunteer to help his sons care for his gardens and cattle, as well as the assemblage of relatives and friends in attendance at his circumcision hut. These are indications of a neophyte elder who will henceforth be reckoned as a leader in the community and in the councils.

Regardless of whether one becomes a notable, all elders acquire certain perquisites as signs of their new status. Most important is the fact that his new authority as a decision maker is based not on his position in the clan but on his elderhood status in the generational class system. Consequently, elders who are outsiders can participate in council deliberations and decision making anywhere in Sidāmo-land. Furthermore, elders are exempt from communal labor, they have the right to slaughter sacrificial animals, and they are assigned seats of honor at burial and mourning ceremonies. But an elder is also expected, as a guardian of the principles of the true way of life (halōli), to acquire a disciplined circumspection of demeanor not found among initiates. He must become, in effect, a living representative of the ideals of the ancestral deities. Moreover, an elder needs patience, rectitude, and an ability to appreciate the broad matters of policy, if he is to contribute successfully to council deliberations.

## Leadership

There are three leadership positions that provide for dispute mediation and officiants for the performance of ritual sacrifice. These include clan and class leaders, as well as the position of distinguished elder. The clan leader, or mote, has only a perfunctory role in regard to the working of the class system. Nevertheless, it is his job to signal the onset of each seven-year interval for initiation. To do this he must determine that all disputes involving the shedding of blood within or between clans have been resolved. This is considered the principal indication that peace and harmony exist among the people.

The Āletā mote signals the advent of this condition of social tranquillity by calling for all the initiates to assemble for his blessing and the appropriate animal sacrifices. He then leads in the sacrifice of three bulls, one on the hill of Golāmā overlooking the plateau where the Āletā won an important victory over the Gugi, another at Birā, the original home of the Āletā clans, and a final one at the initiates' camp in Goida (see map 1). Aside from ritual leadership, his only other function in connection with the generational classes is to dispatch class leaders to settle disputes unresolved by elders' councils.

Every set of class initiates has its own leader called a *gaden* and an assistant known as the *jet-lāwa*. Eight of the most distinguished elders of a retiring class select eight initiates to choose these two class leaders. They base their decision on dreams and consultations with shamen (kilānčo) in selecting a list of candidates. In reality there are always several candidates known to all for their speaking ability, wisdom, and congenial relations with others. Because dreams are considered messages from the deities and shamen have especially powerful possession spirits, this divine intervention provides a means for testing consensus among the selectors. In effect this approach gives a sense of objectivity in support of personal opinion, to which one may then assent without fear of losing face by being unduly influenced by another. The final candidates are the ones deemed to best exemplify the aforementioned character traits.

As the embodiment of peace and well-being, a gaden can never participate in cattle raids or other aggressive actions of a military nature. So, once selected, he becomes the officiant at ritual sacrifice performed for the members of his class, as well as one of the most important mediators for settling disputes. When one of the class members dreams that the gaden should sacrifice for the welfare and health of the group, he will call the members together at the place designated in the dream and obtain a sacrificial bull of the designated shape and color.

The third and oldest form of authority is that of the *wōma*. A wōma is the epitome of elderhood and is considered by many informants to have existed before the advent of generational classes. This view would tend to be supported by the fact that the Holō and Gārbičo always have had such a leader, often a young man, as the principal ritual functionary in the rites occurring at their apical ancestor's grave.[5] He is selected by rules similar to those used in the recruitment of a class leader. Though necessarily young, because of the great amount of time and energy required in ritual officiation, he is treated with all the deference reserved for a very old man and is expected to behave with the decorum associated with such a personage.

In Āletā and in other clans of the Sadāma, however, the wōma position is connected with the generational classes. For example, the first wōma in Āletā was a member of the Hoyē clan. So elders from this clan are always privileged to select the candidate from those who have survived more than two cycles of the class system. Once chosen, this distinguished elder must continually be available for consultation, so that other elders may meet daily at his homestead to enjoy the satisfaction of association, as well as to constitute a perpetual council for resolving disputes.

The wōma and gaden are clearly ritual and mediatory figures, whose influence in policy making and settling disputes is contingent on their revered status in the generational class system. But what of the role of the mote? Does his position constitute that of a clan chief? And how does it relate to the elders? The issue is whether these clan leaders are essentially "petty chieftains" with hereditary positions, serving as spokesmen for their respective groups and as masters of ceremonies without any sanctioning power.[6] Or do these persons constitute leaders of what Service has characterized as the "classical chiefdom," consisting of hierarchically ranked descent groups, theocratic chieftainships, redistribution, and lavish display distinguishing the ruler from commoners?[7]

Outside of the Āletā, every clan and lineage has a mote, but for the Āletā there is one such leader for the twelve clans. There was no Āletā mote among the various clans that originally crossed the Gidabo River with Locke. Though Locke was the leader in the fight with the Yamarĭčo clans, he preferred the status of a warrior to the peacekeeping role of a mote. It was only after they had established themselves in Āletā that Locke is said to have asked a man from the Gissa clan to be mote.

The position is based on primogeniture and, outside of Āletā, the occupant must always come from the senior lineages. Indeed, the original Āletā mote was from a junior branch of three related lineages. Later when these groups became three separate clans, the elders of the other two insisted on having their own leader because Gissa was the junior. Nevertheless, the Gissa leader has continued to be mote of all Āletā.

So the position does involve succession by hereditary right, but the sanctioning power linked to this authority is less obvious. His actions in settling disputes are circumscribed by the elders, and as a peacemaker he cannot take part in any activities likely to inflict force or violence on others. Thus for the Āletā leader, unsettled disputes from clans and occasionally even neighborhoods may be appealed to him, but he must call together elders from the various clans near his residence at Birā to debate the issues and must abide by their consensual decision. Moreover, should he in any way fail to adhere to traditional norms, these same elders will punish him with a fine. For example, a few years ago the mote extended the fence around his house so that it blocked part of a pathway leading to the marketplace. For this inconvenience to passersby, the Birā council of elders threatened him with a heavy fine unless the fence was removed. The mote eventually dismantled the fence. In effect he does not have superordinate authority over anyone, including the class leader, whom he may send to mediate a difficult dispute. The mote has no part in the class or distinguished elder selection process and has no power of removal should he be dissatisfied with the performance of any of these notables.

The real power of such a leader is spiritual rather than secular. He gives sacrifice to the creator for all Āletā or, as elsewhere in Sidāmoland, for the members of his clan. Sacrifice is made primarily on occasions when it is believed possible that all may be threatened by disease or famine. The rites are performed to forestall such events, usually when an elder dreams that the creator or an apical clan ancestor appears and warns of impending doom. These dream apparitions appear in the form of a man painted red or black, and after giving warning they inform the dreamer that disaster can be avoided by offering a bull with distinctive markings at a given sacred locale.

A mote acts as a master of ceremonies in proclaiming the new year's festival and in blessing the initiates before they begin their induction cycle. In this connection he has the power to bless or curse, hence a form of supernatural sanction. Nevertheless, in regard to the sanctity of his person, informants often observed that a class leader is almost as important as a mote, because of the way in which people are expected to show him honor and respect. And a distinguished wōma elder is frequently considered more important than either the mote or a class leader.

Accumulation and redistribution of wealth is a critical attribute for the development and maintenance of the secular power of a chief. The ability to give largess and provide services are the most important means by which a mote may be able to obligate others and obtain their political support. There are five ways in which he may accumulate resources for redistribution. One is through receipt of *gumātta*, a form of tribute given at installation from initiates of each new generational class. Another is from the gifts received in conditional vow compacts. A third has to do with the rights to labor from initiates in the class system. He also has a priority right to use of vacant land. And finally, he will occasionally receive gifts from people who dream they should give a bull or other form of tribute in return for his blessing.

The reasons for giving gumātta are made explicit in the legend surrounding the origins of the Āletā mote. At a time when the Āletā were expanding their control of land well beyond the confines of Birā at the expense of the Gugi, they wanted a man who would always be located in one place so as to be available to officiate at rituals and to help in mediating disputes. Since this first mote was poor and needed to be on the move in order to expand his land holdings and obtain better pasture for his cattle, the elders told him they would provide the necessary resources to enable him to remain at Birā. So the people were requested to bring him firewood, tobacco, and iron money, with the members of each clan taking turns in bringing these objects annually. Later the provision of gumātta was limited to tribute at installation and the periodic presentations made by class initiates, who are expected to provide the mote with clothing and a new house. Also, at installation, members of each clan bring a small iron bar, called an *abāya*, as well as a horn filled with honey, and they ask the mote to bless them by calling on the creator to bring them health, wealth, and a prosperous harvest.[8]

By the beginning of this century, every clan had begun to contribute a small amount of Ethiopian currency at these installation ceremonies. Given the great value of iron, the large quantities of honey, and the periodic renewal of housing and clothing, it would appear that gumātta in the past served to provide the Āletā mote with substantially more wealth than the average person. For example, one old informant indicated that each clan was expected to bring him four pieces of iron money, which would amount to forty-eight iron bars from the twelve Āletā clans. Furthermore, gifts of bulls or heifers in return for his blessing should have provided substantial increments to his herd. He also had first rights to vacant land, and while he could not force people to work, the Birā elders have usually requested young class initiates to perform any labor he has requested. The rationale for this arrangement has always been that he lacks time to labor for himself, since a mote should be continuously available to settle disputes and to bless and provide solace for the people.

With all of the largess provided the Āletā mote, he has the means to feed numerous disputants and the continuous flow of visitors seeking to honor him and receive his aid. He also has an advantage in not having to compete for tribute with the mote of lineages, as is the case elsewhere in Sidāmoland. Moreover, there is no rival distinguished elder (wōma) with his own ritual officiants, as exists among the Holō and Gārbičo.

Thus the Āletā mote clearly has a favorable situation in receipt of tribute, as compared with other clan leaders. Among the Yānāssi, each class gives a heifer and clothing at installation, but the mote has no rights to vacant land or labor and does not receive a new dwelling at each class initiation. Only a lineage mote has priority access to unoccupied land. And the Shabādino likewise have given only clothing to the mote at the time of his installation. Today, however, every new initiate class gives him money and clothing, and people bring him gifts when seeking his blessing. In the case of the Holō and Gārbičo, when they install a mote they bring him only a large pot of honey, the position brings no entitlement to land or housing. Indeed, his main perquisite is the help his neighbors are expected to provide annually in planting his ensete, maize, and coffee.

A comparison of these various positions shows that the Āletā mote has traditionally had more and a greater variety of tribute and services. In the past, iron bars and quantities of honey from each clan, as well as new housing every seven years, were all advantages unavailable to the mote elsewhere. Perhaps of even greater importance was the possibility of increasing his wealth through access to vacant land and a supply of labor to exploit it. Despite these advantages in accumulating wealth, the mote was required to redistribute much of it in providing succor for those in need and hospitality for a continuous stream of visitors. Nevertheless, the scale of accumulation and redistribution was not at the level of classical chiefdom. Service has suggested that large-scale redistribution requiring sizable stores of goods to mobilize labor in agriculture, craft production, and war was the most important activity in a chiefdom.[9] But the clan leaders in Sidāmoland, as men of peace, never participated in war, had no lavish supplies of food or goods stored in warehouses, and received labor support periodically only by agreement from the elders.

It is evident that clan leaders are much closer to being petty chieftains, in the sense of being descent-group spokesmen and acting as masters of ceremony without sanctions, than they are to being the leaders of classical chiefdoms. The position of mote is hereditary within a given descent group, but there is no hierarchy of leadership in clans or lineages that he can control by allocating goods or forming alliances. A mote does, however, provide theocratic leadership by uniting descent groups for the performance of sacrificial rites in times of crisis. And he does receive and redistribute a limited amount of tribute, but not with sumptuous display and consumption on a lavish scale that would set him and his kinsmen apart from others.

The inequality and accumulation necessary for the development of chiefdoms did not occur among the Sadāma for reasons of ideology, ecology, and predatory expansion. Ideologically, for example, there is continual reference by informants from clans descendant from Bushē to an unwillingness to give tribute to the mote, because they are all relatives and hence equal. Further, all their elders have anga, which means that they all have power, so there is no necessity for giving any more to an individual. Even the Āletā, despite their lack of anga, have an equalitarian ideology that encourages them to explain away the limited power of their mote as a matter of historical accident. For the position was originally rejected by a warrior leader and accepted by an old man, only on condition that his wealth be supplemented by others. There are also several legends regarding the tragic demise of leaders that became tyrants.

The equalitarian political system is in keeping with the ecological adaptation of the Sadāma to the mixed ensete and cattle economy. Until the last generation, there has been sufficient land, relative to the size of population, to accommodate the expansive interests of individual cultivators. Plentiful land resources were assured by expansion into territory only partially exploited by herding people like the Gugi. Indeed, one theory concerning the rise of chiefdoms is that competition for limited agricultural land leads to one group vanquishing others and creating a hierarchical system of controls.[10] But most of the Gugi simply moved out, and the few that remained adopted the life style of the Sadāma and continued to live as strangers in their communities.

Evans-Pritchard long ago suggested that the advent of prophets as leaders among the Nuer established these men as "pivots of federation" in uniting various descent groups.[11] Segmentary lineages under these prophet war leaders were united as never before in opposition to the "Arab European menace." In like fashion, Āletā lineages became coalesced, but under war leaders in opposition to the Yamarīčo and Gugi and not under the mote. And it is possible that before incorporation into the Ethiopian Empire, the Āletā were evolving into the initial stages of a chiefdom. If so, it was not through military leadership, for the mote remained a man of peace. His receipt and redistribution of tribute, along with his ability to unite Āletā descent groups in ritual, made this chief's position unique among all those in Sidāmoland. But whether wealth and ritual leadership would have been sufficient to overcome the controls of the elders in the process of creating hegemony of the chief remains one of history's unanswered riddles.

Having demonstrated that chiefdoms did not develop among the Sadāma and that the mote are clan chiefs, it is now possible to examine the question regarding their connection with the authority of the elders. An overall evaluation of the life style of the Sadāma indicates that beliefs, rituals, the juridical-political system, and the economic base converge in this relationship. The differences between the two types of leadership reflect the fact that one is associated with clans that are genealogical and territorial and the other with classes that are cyclical-generational and conceptual.

Clans provide the structure for land acquisition and marriage relations, which underpin household production and reproduction of the labor force. The clan chief is the intermediary between the people and the creator deity in crisis situations. Ideologically the role of the clan was established by the dicta of the creator proscribing incest, requiring the cultivation of the soil, and designating the movement of celestial bodies as determining the timing of birth in women and cattle. The genealogical network of the clan and its representative, the clan chief, is the social structure for carrying out these directives. As such, the clan provides the form for the production and reproduction of the household.

Classes structure juridical-political relations between generations and link together the household-producing units in hamlet and neighborhood. The elders periodically mobilize the labor from the households in the processes of house building and maintaining trails and streams. This form of community cooperation helps to maintain the social interconnectedness of households in support of subsistence and the small surplus of production necessary for ritual redistribution. Moreover, the elders intervene in settling conflicts that arise between households, by effecting a compromise between domestic self-interest and community obligation. In this connection clan chiefs have no authority until they have been promoted in the elderhood cycle. Even then they are subject in their decisions to the consensual agreement of the other elders.

Living elders, including clan chiefs and class leaders, are supported by the beliefs and rituals deifying the dead elders. For it is these dead who may communicate through dreams with the living, regarding especially flagrant violations of the true way of life. These violations of mutuality, generosity, and the dictum against jealousy threaten the maintenance of cooperation in the hamlets and neighborhoods. Therefore, it is not surprising that elderhood authority is so lavishly and elaborately sanctified in the death, mourning, and generational linkage rituals. And it is no accident that these are the most costly rituals in terms of the food contributions that must be made by all the households in a neighborhood. Yet this is not an appropriation in which individual household producers are exploited by the elders, living or dead, for every adult contributor is a receiver of such tribute at his or her own rites. The authority of elderhood is also demonstrated in initiation and promotion ceremonies, in which distribution of wealth, knowledge, and justice is dramatized in return for service and respect by the youth.

These same elaborate rituals of death symbolize the ideology of the sexual division of labor. The key issue for the men is authority, as portrayed by the mourning pole, around which the singing and dancing takes place, glorifying the deeds of the deceased and notables of his class and also the importance of the principles of the true way of life. In the case of the women, their role as producers is stressed, in which the tools of their work become the focal point of the songs and dances honoring their labor.

## Elders' Councils

We have seen the process, as a result of the generational class cycles, by which all men ultimately become decision makers. They are guided by leaders noted for their mediatory skills and privileged to represent their constituents in ceremonies that link all people with the deities. It remains, then, to consider the actual procedures by which the elders settle disputes and make policy in implementing the principles of halōli (the "true way of life").

Elders' councils are referred to by the term sōngo. They constitute the formal organizations for making policy and settling the disputes that arise within and between hamlet, neighborhoods, and descent groups. It is in the day-to-day functioning of these groups that quarrels are resolved and policies devised for avoiding autarky at the household level and for preserving community cooperation in maintaining production.

In most clans there are four levels of sōngo, while in Āletā there is a fifth. For the hamlet with its small cluster of kinsmen and resident strangers, relatively simple matters are dealt with such as marital problems, quarrels over garden boundaries, and altercations between residents concerning destruction of property by livestock. This is a frequently used level of negotiation, in which public sanctions are not involved. Formal matters of policy affecting the whole community are seldom discussed in the hamlet elders' council. Instead it is the neighborhood council (or, if it is a large neighborhood, it will be subdivided into smaller units) that is most frequently involved in settling cases of theft, land disputes, and assault. Policy matters usually concern the direction and administration of rituals, control of grazing practices, allocation of unused land, and collection of taxes.

The lineage council is not as frequently involved in disputes and policy considerations as the neighborhood councils. Nevertheless, because of the threat of kinship solidarity and the initial responsibility for direct negotiations concerning compensation, Āletā lineages have been primarily involved in settling homicide cases.[12] On the other hand, clan councils receive appeals from dissatisfied claimants whose cases were originally considered by elders of the neighborhood, settle land disputes between lineages and neighborhoods, and administer ritual sacrifice in crisis situations, usually under the leadership of the clan chief. Then in Āletā there is a fifth and most inclusive level of council operation for the settlement of disputes between clans and as an appeals council for dissatisfied claimants from the various clan councils.

As informants defined the positions of one level of council vis-à-vis others, they considered them as arranged hierarchically in terms of the importance of matters to be discussed and the number of great orators who would be influential in making decisions and settling disputes. Thus there is a continuum in regard to content and influence, extending from the least important council at the hamlet level to the opposite pole, the Āletā council.

A quorum for a neighborhood council exists when an elder is present from every hamlet, while at the clan level it is necessary to have a representative from all the neighborhoods; for an Āletā council to take place, each clan must have a delegate. Women and children are excluded from participation at any level. When women are concerned in matters before a council, they must be represented by a male spokesman.

Once a quorum is present, a council is begun by the oldest member intoning the phrase "Do you hear?" Persons with policy issues or disputes for settlement then state the substance of their business. If a man wishes to speak or bring evidence before the members, he simply asks permission of the previous speaker when he feels it necessary to interject relevant information or when the latter seems to have finished his presentation. Ideally, the procedure requires careful adherence to this form of etiquette, along with an oratorical style placing emphasis on the succinct statement of facts. Moreover, if the presentation is to be influential and win the respect of the assembled elders, it must be interspersed with metaphors and moralistic, sometimes humorous, stories. These are important in reducing tensions when it is difficult to gain consensus among the members or when tempers flare over the refusal of a defendant, despite damning evidence, to admit guilt. Speakers who possess this story-telling ability and an impressive, oratorical style of delivery become well known throughout the countryside and are obligated to present the cases of less-competent speakers whenever their aid is requested.

First it is necessary to establish the jurisdictional relevance of a quarrel or policy issue. Since it is considered that clan and Āletā councils deal with "more important matters" and have more influential spokesmen than the average neighborhood council, there is a tendency for disputants to want to take their concerns directly to these bodies of higher authority. Though the case is likely to be sent back to the neighborhood, initial deliberations at a higher level may win the assistance of a prominent elder to expedite a settlement in the neighborhood. Another factor limiting the use of the clan council in Āletā is the checkerboard pattern of clan territory, the great distance between segments making it difficult to convene the elders on a regular basis.

Once the jurisdictional issue has been settled (for example, in a dispute between two persons), the plaintiff is asked to state the facts of his complaint while the defendant listens. The oldest man present then formally asks the defendant to reply, by saying, "Do you hear what he has said?" When both sides have been heard, each man will be questioned separately in order to get at more of the facts than have been revealed in the previous discussion. Then both disputants are

One of the Notable Spokesmen at an Elders' Council

sent away, and the case is discussed by the entire council. After these deliberations, the elders seek to obtain a consensus among themselves as to which disputant is in the wrong and, having decided, they call the guilty party before them and say, "We want to tell you that you are wrong for the following reasons . . . " The guilty one is asked to confess his wrongdoing, give up the dispute, and consider what compensation to provide for his actions. When it is impossible to reach a consensus and a suspect cannot be persuaded to confess, the elders will declare that the creator will pass judgment. This is tantamount to a curse upon the suspect if he has lied about his innocence. Regardless of the outcome, a dissatisfied disputant may appeal to a higher level of council. Because of its implications for social disruption, an appeals case takes on a degree of urgency and complexity that may lead to the mediatory intervention of a clan chief or a class leader.

There are four kinds of sanctions applied by the elders: fines, ostracism, oaths, and cursing. All of these penalties may be imposed only on men, though they apply indirectly to women and children involved in delicts, since husbands and fathers are responsible for their conduct. After accepting a guilty verdict, a wrongdoer requests the elders to specify what he must do in recompense. Invariably they demand that he pay a fine. He usually responds by going forward and placing a small sum of money on the hem of the cloak of the oldest man present. The first payment is usually rejected and the demand is made that the sum be increased. Increments are then added until the individual begins to plead that the council is reducing him to a state of poverty. When this happens the elders must respond to his plea and reduce the amount to a token payment, for the purpose of the fine is not punitive but is a means of demonstrating publicly that the wrongdoer is appropriately remorseful for his offense. For whenever a person commits a delict, he is considered to have placed himself temporarily beyond the pale of the community, and he must seek to gain reentrance by showing proper respect for the elders, who are the guardians of the true way of life. Also, in cases where individuals experience loss or property damage, the guilty person must make restitution.

When the evidence against a man is clear-cut but he refuses to accept the verdict, or if he acknowledges his guilt and refuses to pay a fine, the elders may impose the form of ostracism called sīra. The imposition of sīra requires other members of the community to avoid eating, touching (in greeting), working with, or entering the home of the guilty party. It is a condition that can be removed only if the clan chief dies or if the person agrees to pay a fine and to beg forgiveness of the elders. A more rigorous form of this sanction is known as sīra wolēm benātti, in which the culprit must be excused by both the elders and the creator. To remove it, one must beg forgiveness of the elders and the creator, then pay a fine consisting of a cattle horn full of honey, eight dollars in silver coins (in the past, iron bars), and enough barley to feed the council. All of this must be presented to the clan chief. This form of ostracism is also imposed when a person has knowingly violated the norms, has shown contempt for the clan chief, or refuses to stop in the name of the chief when caught in the act of violating custom.

There are also elaborate oath-taking rituals. The oaths are most frequently used in regard to theft, when the thief cannot be identified. Household heads are required to swear an oath of innocence over a fire, stone, or blade, with the admonition that they will be killed by one of these objects if they have lied.

To appreciate the frequency and kinds of disputes that must be settled publicly, it is necessary to examine what are considered to be offenses affecting the community and the penalties applied. There are indeed several of these offenses that constitute serious violations of the true way of life, that may be categorized as disturbing the peace and violations of property. The former have to do with murder and actions leading to bodily injury.

Because homicide constitutes a disruption and threat to the genealogical network, it has traditionally been resolved by the leaders and elders' councils of the clans and lineages. If, for example, a homicide involves men from two different clans, there is a danger that the resulting animosity will escalate into a blood feud between the two groups. Therefore, in Āletā the mote will seek to negotiate a settlement, while elsewhere the elders of a third clan will attempt to restore peace. Traditionally, peace could be restored only when the murderer's clan had presented a sēmma (a large cloak) and several sheep to the eldest brother of the mother of the deceased. This procedure was followed by presentations, called *gumamōrra*, of eight cows or a combination of cattle and iron bars to the deceased's clan. But his immediate family could not receive this payment, as it was considered a form of bloodwealth and as a consequence was awarded to the elders of his clan directly involved in the negotiations. If, however, a homicide involved two different lineages within a clan, then the clan council would arrange a settlement following bloodwealth payment procedures similar to those for interclan homicides.

The process was the same, only involving a more limited population, when the homicide occurred within a lineage and the principal parties were the households of the accused murderer and the deceased. In all instances, witnesses would be called by the appropriate elders' council to ascertain the circumstances of the homicide. Once the compensatory aspects of the negotiations had been completed, it was necessary to perform a ritual for restoring harmony between the disputants. This ceremony involved the elders who had mediated the dispute sprinkling on the disputants either blood from a sheep or a mixture of water from the water pipe, butter, and juice from the stem of an ensete plant.[13] At the same time they were admonished not to spill blood again and to maintain peace between their households.

These procedures began to change following the Ethiopian conquest at the turn of the century, as the Maria Theresa silver thalers came into use and the Ethiopian government instituted a system of tribute and taxation. As a result, the bloodwealth payment came to be set at one hundred of these silver coins, given to the family of the deceased to be used only in the payment of taxes. A murderer was turned over to the police and, if witnesses were willing to testify, was eventually brought to trial. Bribery [gočīsa] was practiced by both sides in attempting to influence witnesses as well as police and court officials. And if a case actually went to trial and the defendant was found guilty, the judge would ask the relatives of the deceased whether they wished mercy or the death penalty for the convicted murderer. Afterward, elaborate negotiations took place between the elders, at appropriate levels of the lineage or clan, usually resulting in a bloodwealth payment in Ethiopian dollars and a request for mercy. Then if the defendant was granted mercy by the court, he received a short prison sentence of several months.

During the two periods of field research, one instance of homicide was recorded and followed in detail. In this case Borassa, a Gārbičo clansman, in a drunken brawl allegedly struck and killed Mutu, a Hitāla.[14] Both the victim and his assailant resided in a predominantly Hitāla hamlet.

Shortly after the death, Mutu's wife and other close relatives went to a nearby police post and accused the assailant of murder. Though he was arrested, he was shortly released, presumably because of a lack of witnesses. In fact his relatives had convinced the elders of the Gārbičo clan council that Borassa was innocent, and they collected money to bribe witnesses and court officials to prevent the case from coming to trial. This was not enough, however, to prevent murmuring among his neighbors that Borassa was a murderer. Consequently, the Gārbičo elders sought to negotiate a settlement with their counterparts in Hitāla clan, so that amity between households could be restored. Five notable elders from four neutral clans were asked to mediate a settlement. For more than a year, meeting once or twice a month with the lineage elders in the area where Borassa and the deceased had resided, they sought without success to reach a settlement.

For several months it was difficult to make headway because of procedural matters, such as the lack of a quorum and concerns about the neutrality of the mediators. These obstacles could be dealt with, but two others were never overcome. One involved the jurisdictional propriety of the inquiry. At the outset the spokesman for the lineage elders, a man called Adisso, brought this to the attention of all the participants. The correct procedure should have been for elders from the deceased's neighborhood, those from the neighborhood in which the homicide occurred, and a neutral neighborhood council to meet together and resolve the dispute. They should have obtained witnesses, taken them with the accused to the police, and arranged a settlement with the estranged households. The second problem was that many of the lineage elders, including Adisso, were Christians and refused to collect funds to counter the bribe money collected by the Gārbičo clan. Bribery, they claimed, was against Christian principles.

It was against this background that the relatives of the deceased began to despair of a settlement and finally appealed to the Hitāla clan council. When the council met, Adisso and the others were admonished and urged to press on toward a reconciliation to end the contentiousness between relatives, before the approaching class initiation ritual.[15]

More meetings were held throughout the spring of 1965. But the most that Adisso and the others could do was uncover two more witnesses to the assault. In the presence of the police, however, one witness was uncertain about the identity of Borassa. So the elders concluded that he had been bribed by one of Borassa's relatives. In desperation they now confronted the mediators from the Gārbičo clan with the demand that they admit Borassa's guilt before arranging a settlement. The latter claimed they were instructed to restore amity between Borassa's household and his neighbors, not to discuss guilt or innocence.

And so it seemed by the middle of the summer of 1965 that negotiations had reached an impasse. At this point the relatives of the deceased approached Adisso and the other elders. They requested them to collect money from the Hitāla to bribe witnesses and court officials to reopen the case. After lengthy discussion, the Christian elders, led by Adisso, refused to participate in such a blatant violation of their religious principles. The traditionalists felt they could not take action without the Christians, since they were the most senior elders and leading spokesmen in the council.

Eight years later I learned that the case had never been resolved. One previously unknown factor was revealed by informants, namely, that the victim Mutu was the descendant of a former slave. Nevertheless, it was agreed that the clan and lineage elders were required to do everything in their power to settle the case. But Adisso had the last word when he indicated that since the witnesses had been bribed once, "we wouldn't want to bribe them again, so we said the creator will be the judge and left it at that."

Though this case remained unresolved it illustrates the importance of clan and lineage councils in settling matters threatening the genealogical integrity of the descent groups. Hearing such cases and receiving difficult appeals cases from neighborhood councils are their principal functions. Had the office of Āletā chief been occupied during this time, it is likely that the victim's relatives would have appealed to him and the Āletā council. He in turn could have urged—not forced—the Hitāla elders to expedite an amicable settlement. But he could not have had any influence on the Gārbičo clan council, which was beyond his jurisdiction.

Several aspects of the case have important implications for changes in the juridical-political system. One was the questionable procedure of involving two clan councils in a case that should have been resolved within the lineage territory where the affair took place. Possibly this is indicative of a traditional problem for resident strangers. So even though the assailant's relatives had resided in the Hitāla neighborhood for several generations, they felt compelled in a crisis to seek help from their agnatic Gārbičo kin. The situation may have been complicated further by the recent introduction of cash cropping. The customary bribery, which used cattle and other goods, was now made much easier with money. Thus Borassa was able to use money in conjunction with traditional clan loyalties to circumvent the government court system. At the same time, Adisso's commitment to Western-style Christian ideology prevented him from utilizing Hitāla clan loyalty in raising the necessary cash to counter Gārbičo bribery, which might ultimately have led to a negotiated settlement.

Somewhat different from homicide as a form of violence are bodily injury and sexual abuse. The latter include such matters as incest, adultery, and seduction. Incest is defined simply as sexual relations between members of one's own and one's mother's clan. The jurisdiction for this delict lies with the clan council, since it is considered a violation of the marriage exogamy rule. It is a subject that informants spoke of in lowered voices, considering it to be a heinous crime, but they admitted that it occurred occasionally in all clans. Nevertheless, the intentions of the persons involved are important in determining the sanctions. If it can be shown that the participants were unaware of a blood relationship, there is no penalty. When, however, the practice is intentional, the elders fine the man and ostracize him if the fine is not immediately forthcoming. They then slaughter a sheep and as the blood flows they say to both parties, "We have poured blood on the ground and through this blood you are once again members of the clan." This blood is then sprinkled on the guilty pair. Alternatively, the elders cut the breasts of both offenders and mix the blood to symbolize that it is the same and that they are of one clan.

If a man commits adultery, a husband—should he catch him in the act—may beat him to death.[16] Such cases leading to homicide are unusual, but if there are witnesses to the act and the husband does not assault the culprit, the offender may be taken before the clan council and fined.

The clan elders must also have jurisdiction over seduction and rape cases. In the event of seduction, they will fine the man and admonish the mother for allowing her daughter to stray too far from her supervision. In the past, infanticide was practiced when a child resulted from such a union. By contrast, when rape is committed and proven, the fine is usually so high that the man is unable to make immediate payment and ostracism is imposed.

The most frequent form of assault occurs when quarrels exceed the bounds of verbal animosity and lead to bodily injury. These disputes frequently concern intended or unintended violation of property rights and often are the result of a quarrel between two different household heads within the same clan, threatening cooperation within the neighborhood. Consequently it falls within the jurisdiction of the neighborhood council. The man who committed the injury will be required to provide sustenance for the injured person, and if he was in the wrong he will be fined by the council. Should the fight be across clan boundaries, then the clan councils will be involved. A third clan will mediate a settlement requiring the person committing the injury to provide sustenance for the injured man until the latter has recovered from his wounds.

The following case that occurred during the period of field research is a frequent occurrence of this type of delict. It is an example of negligence by a member of one household leading to damage of the garden of another, followed by a retaliatory act threatening cooperation between neighbors.

At the outset, Kifile, the son of Gonsamo, admonished and beat Adella, the son of Borka. Adella had neglected his duties as a herdsman, and his father's cattle had gotten into their neighbor's garden. Being older, Kifile had a right to punish the younger boy for neglecting his duties. But Adella complained to his father Borka, who then threatened and tried to beat Kifile with his stick. Kifile in turn threw several stones, striking Borka and his mother, who was standing in the crowd attracted by the commotion. Though the men in the crowd managed to quell the disturbance, Borka went to the hamlet elders and formally complained about Kifile's behavior.

It was coffee harvesting season, however, and several attempts to convene the elders resulted in postponements for lack of a quorum. This angered Gonsamo, who complained that they were wasting time that could be better spent working in their gardens. Nevertheless, the elders persisted in calling meetings, insisting it was important to resolve disputes that could lead to enmity among relatives.

When finally the council did convene, Gonsamo answered the complaint by insisting that his son had a right to discipline the younger boy. After hearing witnesses and consulting among themselves, the elders informed Borka that he had been wrong to threaten Kifile. Kifile had been correct in punishing Adella for his negligence. Therefore, they initially imposed a heavy fine on Borka. But when he admitted his error, the fine was reduced to a minimum and his wrongdoing was excused. Kifile then admitted to the elders that in his anger he had sought to retaliate by harming Borka, though he had not meant to hit the old lady. As a consequence, he was reprimanded for this disrespectful behavior, and several elders wanted to impose a heavy fine on his father. But Gonsamo agreed to vouch for his son's future good behavior, so the imposed fine was minimal.

Though the dispute was seemingly trivial, the elders used it to uphold the principle of older persons having the right to direct the labor of younger ones in tasks that affect the well-being of all households in the community. Moreover, they were concerned to control animosity between households, which otherwise could hinder cooperation. On the other hand, Gonsamo was more concerned with disruption of his gardening activities than with community harmony. It is noteworthy that he was one of the leading Christian elders in the hamlet. As such, he was perhaps less dependent than traditionalists on local economic assistance and social interaction.

In any public delict involving killing livestock, damage to property, or theft, the matter of intent is of crucial importance. If a man accidentally kills an animal belonging to another, there is considered to be no breach of the peace or recovery for the loss. Should the animal have been intentionally destroyed, however, the owner must be compensated and a fine paid to the elders for disturbing the peace. Also, to take someone else's property, even though not in use, entails a fine. Since such an act is very near to theft, the most abhorred of public delicts, it is a disruption of the peace. In the past when a theft occurred, it was customary to bind the captured thief hand and foot until his case could be heard by the elders. Then he would be admonished for his irresponsible conduct, fined, and required to pay compensation. Nowadays all household heads in a hamlet are required to undergo an oath when a theft is suspected. Then when the thief is captured, he is turned over to the police.

The disputes coming most frequently before all levels of councils during 1964–65 were those concerning land rights (see table 2). This high frequency is probably a recent development connected with the advent of a cash economy, increasing population, and land shortage. Indeed, all informants were of the opinion that control of land is the

**Table 2.** Sampling of Agenda Content from All Levels of the Sōngo in Āletā, 1964–65

| Topic | Frequency | Percentage of Total |
|---|---|---|
| Discussions of policy and ritual | 21 | 37 |
| Cursing of sorcerers | 6 | 11 |
| Disputes | | |
|   Murder | 1 | 2 |
|   Theft | 5 | 9 |
|   Land | 11 | 19 |
|   Over women | 1 | 2 |
|   Verbal | 3 | 5 |
|   Fighting[a] | 5 | 9 |
|   Money | 4 | 7 |
| Combined policy and cursing ritual | 27 | 47 |
| Total disputes | 30 | 53 |

[a]Between groups or between individuals.
*Source:* Author.

greatest source of contention among the present-day Sadāma. Nevertheless, quarrels over land are not entirely new, as illustrated in the mythological origins of the people. Generally the disputes are over boundaries and land transfer, they tend to be between two men, and they are less likely than the previously discussed cases to endanger the peace of the community.

A most interesting example of a land case, occurring during the early period of fieldwork, was one that had remained unresolved for more than a year. It had originally been brought before the neighborhood council, but failure to resolve the matter led local elders to appeal to the clan notables for aid in bringing about a settlement. The dispute involved a wealthy old man named Hami who had a large garden next to the disputed territory. His protagonist, Barti, was a young man who had been given rights by a third party to plant a garden on the land in question. Years before, Hami had given this third party the right to use the land as a resident stranger. Then when this person left to find better pasture for his cattle, he turned the garden over to Barti. Barti had been paying the land tax directly to the government for several years. The controversy developed when Hami suggested that Barti should give him the land tax. This was ostensibly to ensure recognition of Hami's rights to control allocation of use. Barti refused and challenged Hami's claim to the property. Consequently Hami spent one hundred dollars to open an action in the district court for regaining possession. But close relatives and elders urged him to give up this costly alternative and to bring the dispute before the neighborhood council.

During a year of negotiation, the elders of the neighborhood council had managed to persuade Hami to renounce his claim to the use of half the disputed territory. Barti was holding the remainder in reserve, in the event that the stranger returned. But since he claimed usufruct rights to all the land, Hami maintained that he should control this land. Barti would not agree.

In their preliminary discussion of the case, the clan elders agreed that it was unseemly for such a prominent, wealthy elder as Hami to quarrel with a young man over a small piece of land. And when the disputants appeared before the council, Hami indicated his agreement with this assessment. He magnanimously agreed to give usufruct rights to most of the land to Barti, with the exception of a small parcel adjoining his garden. Further, he would not expect Barti to contribute to the costs of the abortive court action. Initially Barti accepted this proposal and requested that the elders draw a new boundary incorporating a small piece of the property with Hami's garden.

The elders then proceeded to set apart a small triangle of the disputed property for Hami. When they showed it to Barti, however, he rejected the compromise because the land contained some of his recently planted ensete and coffee seedlings. Despite all appeals and the added incentive of rights to harvest from the seedlings, Barti was vehement in his rejection. But when an old man finally took him aside and pleaded with him to accept for sake of community harmony, he finally relented. He apologized to the elders for his obstinacy and accepted the compromise.

Much the same sequence of events followed when Hami was shown the plot. He, too, initially rejected it, but on the grounds of a procedural error by the council.[17] Following profuse apologies by the oldest council member, Hami was satisfied and accepted the agreement.

In this case both men did a great deal of posturing, threatening each other with further court actions and initially feigning indifference to the pleas of the elders. Though this was a means of saving face by avoiding unseemly haste in accepting compromise, it later surfaced that neither disputant wanted the other to think he was afraid of going to court. In the end there was a written agreement, in which Hami received the small piece of property and was recognized as holding rights in perpetuity to all the land below the triangle. Both men agreed to split payment of the annual land tax. And the case, which had taken two days to resolve, ended with a feast for the council, served by the two former disputants.

This dispute should have been settled by the neighborhood elders, yet since they could not reach agreement and it was a matter of land rights, appeal to the clan elders was appropriate. Furthermore, there was an important underlying conflict not made explicit in the course of deliberations. Why should Hami, a renowned speaker with large gardens and cattle herds be concerned about a small piece of land he ignored for many years? One reason is the importance of cash cropping in coffee, which has led men like Hami to recognize that coffee will in the future be a measure of wealth. Another is the slowly changing concept of land tenure. For as the government tends to recognize and encourage individual title in land for tax purposes, arguments in support of traditional tenure rights become difficult to sustain in a court of law.

Consequently, it would seem that much of Hami's overt concern about the boundary was a ploy to obtain official recognition of his rights to ownership. In this effort he was only partially successful, because the compromise recognized Barti and his descendants' continuous rights to use most of the disputed property. This unsatisfactory state of affairs became evident several months later when the two men quarreled over who should have possession of the tax receipt for the land. This was important, because precedent has been established by government courts in recent years to attribute property ownership to the person or persons whose name(s) appear on the tax receipt.

Another form of potential conflict has to do with accusations of sorcery, which if unresolved will sooner or later disturb the community peace. Sorcery, as explained by informants, is always traceable to jealousy and is the ultimate destructive force in the society. It turns the individual and the household inward away from the community and for this reason is socially disruptive. As such, sorcery is appropriately and invariably settled by an oath-taking ritual administered by the neighborhood council.

Sorcery usually comes to the attention of the community when individuals interrupt council proceedings with a request for all those assembled to curse sorcerers. The petitioner then relates how certain unmistakable signs in his garden or household have led him to suspect that some unnamed person is seeking his destruction. As it happens, sorcerers may be of either sex, but they can practice their machinations only against their own sex and can be sanctioned for this behavior only by males. But regardless of how this form of magic is used, it is defined as evil and provides a means for rallying public support against the practitioner. For example, if a man acquires concomitantly with great wealth a reputation for hoarding, he may be suspected of being a sorcerer. Should he noticeably seek to increase his wealth at the expense of his kinsmen and if any individual living in close physical proximity dies under mysterious circumstances, the suspicion will be considered as confirmed.

Stigmatizing persons as sorcerers is, at best, a process fraught with uncertainty. Informants are usually unwilling to categorize specific individuals as sorcerers for fear that those named will possess unusual powers to harm others. When, however, there develops a consensus that an individual shows an excessive amount of greed or a willingness to promote individual gain at the expense of others, or when there are unexplainable misfortunes connected with his presence, there is often gossip to the effect that the person is a sorcerer.

Such a man was observed by the author during the two periods of field research. The man, whom I will refer to as B, was a very successful farmer and was superficially friendly and ingratiating. Nevertheless, informants indicated that though he accumulated large amounts of money from the sale of coffee and had a highly productive garden, B was miserly in redistributing his largess. He sought to postpone the marriage of his son in order to avoid bridewealth payments, and he found it difficult to keep a wife because of an unwillingness to provide her with clothing and other amenities that he could well afford. Though B was an elder, he often violated the rule against discussing deliberations outside of council meetings by gossiping about these affairs with others. He antagonized his neighbors by extending the boundary of his garden into a public pathway. So when two old men in neighboring households died of unexplained illnesses, it was rumored that B sought their death in hopes of gaining part of their land. In short, he showed an excessive self-centeredness that led him to horde rather than redistribute his wealth, he inconvenienced his neighbors and relatives, and to compensate for the resulting resentment, he attempted to ingratiate himself with anyone willing to respond. Consequently, people began to whisper among themselves that B might be a sorcerer.

When there is a consensus that someone in the community is a sorcerer, then the elders assemble all the young men and household heads in the neighborhood for the oath-taking ceremony. It is presumed that a true practitioner of evil magic will be unable to swear such an oath, but in the event that a suspect does take the oath and suspicion remains unabated, an ordeal is provided to resolve the uncertainty. The suspect is forced to eat a mouthful of soil and salt.[18] If he is innocent, nothing will happen, but should he be guilty, it is believed that death will follow. The basis for this reasoning is that man, having been made out of earth by the creator, can be destroyed by the same substance for behaving contrary to the laws of nature by practicing evil magic.

The quantitative division of deliberations at all levels of the sōngo in table 2 provides some indication of the importance of disputes in comparison with policy and ritual matters. Land disputes involved nearly 20 percent of sōngo activities, with only policy and ritual matters being a more frequent subject of deliberation. Informants in fact frequently commented on the importance of land disputes. Violence was also relatively high at 11 percent, but there was only one homicide.

## Discussion

In this chapter it has been shown how beliefs and ritual support both the broad rules that govern order in the universe and the authority of clan chiefs and elders, and how these leaders apply the rules to conflict situations. Elderhood is essentially an abstraction, being based on ranking according to position in class cycles. Clans, on the other hand, are more tangible because of their corporateness; that is, clans are associated with specific territories and have ritual chiefs to intervene with the deities on appropriate occasions. Clan affiliation gives individuals access to the land, which is the principal factor in subsistence production. But it is the elders with their authority and the youth with their community labor, both the result of the brotherhood of generational classes, that establish and maintain cooperation within and between communities, regardless of kinship affiliation.

Whether the issue involves the elders at the clan level in rectifying the consequences of a homicide or marriage rule violation, or at the neighborhood and hamlet levels in directing labor and maintaining cooperation between households, the elders are always concerned to reconcile self-interest with affiliative obligation. Bringing these elements together usually involves conflict between individual pursuit of wealth or excessive use of authority and between what is fair to others in preserving the network of mutual exchange between households. The elders show respect for the individual by avoiding the full imposition of their power with its limited sanctions. Instead, they seek to effect a compromise that will not result in loss of dignity to a disputant or rule violator. Nevertheless, the dicta of the creator, the cult of the dead elders in support of the living elders, and the broad principles of the true way of life support the predominance of community obligations. Though it is possible for an individual to gain power through spirit possession, such occurrences are viewed with ambivalence. For more often than not, the power is fleeting and is gained at the expense of other members of the household and hamlet.

Terray has suggested that varying forms of cooperation determine different modes of production.[19] This claim would predict the presence of two such modes among the Sadāma: one is associated with the clan and household, where agnatic kin, affinal relatives, and friends cooperate to make the land productive; the second mode is the neighborhood work group, bringing together distant kin or nonrelatives for large-scale cooperation in providing for rituals and capital improvements linking together hamlets and households.

I have shown how the beliefs about the relation of man to the land, marriage rules, death, and influence of the dead upon the living in preserving customs are dramatized in elaborate rituals. These beliefs and ceremonies provide the ideological charter for the elders' authority in establishing the two modes of production. The case examples illustrate the process of situationally defining the rules and of dealing with threats to cooperation between individuals and groups.

These disputes also provide the hint of a third mode of production, as a result of a recent articulation with the international economy. Thus the land dispute case indicates the importance of cash income, leading to a contradiction between traditional and government concepts of land tenure. In the homicide example, money was used to enhance the traditional form of bribery. And new religious affiliations were used to circumvent the rules of responsibility in both the homicide and the bodily injury cases. The process of relating the traditional modes of production, the authority of the elders, and traditional beliefs to a cash-oriented economy, along with the development of a new form of labor cooperation, forms the subject matter of the next two chapters.

8           The Process of
Change

In the previous chapter, I indicated changes developing in juridical-political, economic, and ideological institutions as a result of contradictory rules of land tenure, the effect of money in modifying values of production, and the existence of conflicting religious beliefs. To appreciate the significance of these modifications it will be necessary to examine their historical background, as a prelude to considering the response of the Sadāma in developing self-help associations. I shall do so by considering the incorporation of the Sadāma into the state system, the influence of government administration and legal codes, the impact of the cash economy, and the effect of religious proselytism in changing beliefs.

I do not mean to imply that there were no important historical changes in Sidāmoland prior to these recent happenings. Indeed, it has been impossible to discuss origins, mythology, economy, and the like without referring to various points in time when the ancestors were strangers to the land, held genealogical ties with the Gugi and Borana, experienced despotic rulers, and shared trade relations with surrounding peoples. To be sure, there are certain general aspects of their culture, such as the generational class system, mourning rituals, beliefs about the cosmos, and other traits resembling those of nearby Ethiopian cultures.[1] Nevertheless, the Sadāma have lived apart from other groups for a sufficient period of time to develop distinctly different traditions of kinship, production, ideology, and authority. Furthermore, they see themselves as being different from others, and the conquerors from the north also consider them as different. But it was this conquest by the armies of Emperor Menelik II in the late nineteenth century that constituted the root cause for many contemporary conflicts and institutional contradictions.

130

## Conquest and Incorporation into the Ethiopian State

There were apparently several motives for a southern advance out of Shewa Province by Emperor Menelik's armies in the 1890s, including the reestablishment of domination over the loose congeries of kingdoms and groups that had been interrupted by the massive movements of the Oromo peoples in the sixteenth century; an interest in acquiring control over the valuable trade resources of the south, such as gold, ivory, coffee, spices, and slaves; a concern for acquiring more land for an expanding northern population that had suffered from severe famine during 1889–92; and a fear of the increasing pressures from French, British, and Italian imperialism.[2] This invasion was different from those of the past, which were more in the form of raiding expeditions. Menelik's armies were the first Ethiopians to be extensively equipped with modern European weapons, enabling them to establish permanent garrison enclaves among southerners like the Sadāma who lacked this form of technology.[3] Indeed, it is doubtful that the gabbar system of tribute and forced labor could have been imposed in the 1890s without this superiority in weapons.[4]

The few accounts by old men who were small children at the time of the invasion substantiate the historians' observations. As one informant explained, the Sadāma failed to unite against the invaders. At first the Āletā believed that the Yamarīčo would succeed in throwing back the enemy before they reached the Shabādino clan on their border (see map 1). Then for a time the Āletā succeeded in holding the invaders at bay near Golāmā, but after some months Menelik sent another general who drove them west to the Gidabo River. Here the Āletā built barricades at the important crossings, yet having only spears and swords they soon found that they were no match for Amhara guns. Their amazement was great when their previously impermeable hippopotamus-hide shields would not protect them against bullets. Nevertheless, during this period of the fighting the Hadičō and their traditional enemies the Darasa came to help, realizing that the invading armies would soon be attacking their communities.

It is said that the slaughter was great on both sides. Finally, a famous old man dreamed that it would not be possible to stop the Amhara and that it would be better for the Sadāma simply to accept them. So the Āletā chief made peace with the invaders, who left a small garrison and then proceeded further south and west to conquer the Konso and Walamo.

Shortly following the establishment of a garrison, every clan was required to provide annual tribute of two large oxen and a pot of honey to Emperor Menelik. Though this form of tribute was shortly discontinued, the gabbar system that was simultaneously imposed had more significant consequences and was of longer duration.

Gabbar, it must be stressed, gave Menelik's soldiers rights to the service of the Sadāma, but it did not give them control over their clients' land resources. Theoretically a given soldier received the right to collect taxes for his personal support from the Sadāma assigned to him, but since they seldom had access to cash, he in effect acquired their labor.[5] Furthermore, over the next twenty years, the garrison was supplemented by northern colonists who came to seek their fortunes by hunting elephants or taking low echelon bureaucratic jobs, for which they often received land in lieu of a salary. Like the soldiers before them, these people avoided intermarriage and religious proselytization in order, as they saw it, to avoid contamination of their culture by local people.[6] Moreover, prior to the 1920s they often purchased vacant land that could be bought for a relatively low price; in Āletā, according to informants, the land left by those who fled from gabbar was given to these outsiders by the chief as a means of courting favor. But from the standpoint of the Ethiopian government, the gabbar system and colonization was initially a success in that it helped to establish a buffer zone against the expanding European powers, as well as provided the emperor with a new source of political offices and tribute to reward his faithful followers.[7]

Given the equalitarian ideology and social system of the Sadāma, with no precedent for patron-client relations, it is not surprising that gabbar was so resented and that many left their land and fled to remote rorest and mountain areas. In some instances their vacant land was left in the care of friends or relatives or was virtually abandoned, creating the basis for future land disputes. Also, by the mid-1920s it was increasingly evident that gabbar was no longer an effective patronage system and, indeed, that it was a detriment to developing the productivity of the Ethiopian state.[8] The reason for this disenchantment with gabbar was that after the turn of the century there were no new frontiers where the government could seek resources for rewarding faithful servants of the state. At the same time, however, past and present members of the military were already taking up so much of the surplus production of the peasantry through tributary labor and high land rents (as much as one-third of a household crop) that the productive capacity in support of the nation was virtually nonexistent. As a consequence, the government was hard-pressed to acquire the necessary components of state infrastructures, such as roads, schools, and hospitals.

Furthermore, there were insufficient resources to establish effective centralized administration over the vast new territories of the conquered south. As a result, the government in Addis Ababa had to rely on a form of indirect rule by creating or working through traditional local authorities who were given the title of *balabat*.[9] Since these men were to collect tribute and settle local disputes, indirect rule tended either to reenforce existing hierarchies or to create them where none had previously existed. In the case of the Sadāma, as indicated in chapter 4, these titles were given to the chiefs of the various clans and to the Āletā chief. The reward for these officials was usually vacant land in lieu of salary. As many Sadāma had fled the gabbar system, however, hoping to return in better times, there developed a certain ambiguity regarding the status of vacant land. In time, respect for a chief with a government title came to depend on his willingness to protect the land rights of those who had fled.

A second reason for dissatisfaction with gabbar was the realization by the late 1920s that it was not conducive to promoting the increasing interest in coffee production. Though the government had begun as early as 1912 to survey and divide the land into gaša, the concern of northern settlers to become more involved in cash cropping of coffee led to the measurement and distribution of what the government considered to be unassigned land.[10] For it was recognized by those nonmilitary settlers who were ineligible for gabbar, that they were in effect being deprived of a cheap labor source that would be necessary if they were to expand their holdings in coffee. Since many of these people had mules, land, capital, and knowledge of the trade network, all they needed to succeed was a supply of cheap labor. Indeed, it was these Amhara men and their descendants who ultimately came to dominate the coffee trade and, as will be shown later, became an important element in the development of self-help associations. Nevertheless, the gabbar system remained in effect until the Italian occupation (1936–41) and was not formally abolished until after World War II.

In sum, the most significant aspect of the conquest and initial incorporation into the Ethiopian state was the imposition of gabbar and some disruption of control by the Sadāma over their land. In effect a tributary mode of production was created in which peasants retained access to the means of production, but tribute was exacted by military-political force.[11] Gabbar led to a decentralized power structure in which local notables temporarily gained control of important elements of production, primarily labor, by controlling the bulk of the local surplus.

At the same time, a household mode of production, based on the symbiotic bond between ensete and cattle, remained intact. Furthermore, because of the relatively small numbers and ethnocentrism of the conquerors, other cultural aspects such as kinship, ideology, and even social control were minimally affected by the initial phases of the occupation. The most important economic impact of the conquest was the development of an interest in the production and marketing of coffee. All of this was interrupted, however, by the Italo-Ethiopian war and the short stint of European colonialism, lasting from 1936 to 1941.

The goals of Italian colonialism, applicable to all Ethiopia, were to establish a modern infrastructure of highways, public buildings, telephone exchanges, and Western medical facilities, as well as to encourage the settlement of millions of Italian migrants.[12] There were some remarkable feats in the building of roads, bridges, and public buildings, but Italian farmers could not be persuaded to migrate to Ethiopia in large numbers; the few that did were interested less in farming than in acquiring positions as shopkeepers and skilled artisans in Ethiopian towns. In general, the Italian occupation was too short, and the resistance of Ethiopian patriots made matters too hectic for much Western-style modernization to occur.

Informants tended to support this conclusion. One old gaden explained how, following the Italian invasion, Amhara who had been leaders in using gabbar labor asked the Sadāma to support the war effort. When, however, the Ethiopian armies had been defeated, the Sadāma, along with the Gugi and Arussi, sought out these leaders and slaughtered them. Then, upon arrival of the Italian troops, many Sadāma fled, but the Italians asked them to return, pointing out that they were friends who had defeated their former "masters." Since they did not take the land and since they abolished gabbar, the newcomers were at first welcomed, and some individuals even joined the Italian military. But in time the people became disenchanted with rigid conservation measures and continual requisitioning of cattle to feed the garrisons. Also, as they were made known, there was resentment toward Italian proposals to colonize the land, though in the end the occupation was too short for these plans to be realized.

## Government Administration and Legal Codes

I do not intend to review in detail postwar institutional changes at the level of the Ethiopian state, but it is necessary to consider those developments that affected at least indirectly the structure of authority, the elders' councils, development of a cash economy, and ideology. It is perhaps sufficient to indicate that a new constitution was promulgated in 1955 that for the first time provided many of the trappings of a parliamentary democracy. In fact the document was largely a facade, since the emperor retained full power and control in terms of initiating and approving legislation.[13] There was no real change in the absolute power of the emperor from what it had been in prewar days, while at the provincial level of administration there was also the facade of bureaucratic controls and formal rules, circumscribed by personalized authority, individual opportunism, and control by the emperor.[14] The emperor was essentially working to overcome the decentralized tributary mode of production of the previous half century and to bring it under control of the central government. And for the Sadāma the presence of provincial administrative officials provided, as will be shown later, a convenient alternative to the authority of the descendants of the colonizers and soldiers of the prewar era.

From the standpoint of recruiting and maintaining traditional authority, generational class rituals and principles have remained largely intact. Sometimes Ethiopian governors at the district (*awraja*) and subdistrict (*wereda*) levels have sought to discourage initiation rituals because of raiding activities and the implications for strengthening ethnic nationalism in opposition to the state. Most government officials, however, have accepted the system as a harmless tradition, some even going so far as to contribute an animal for sacrificial purposes. Nevertheless, raiding is no longer permitted and a substitute practice has developed of purchasing cattle and placing them in the woods along the Arussi boundary. The initiates then conduct a token raid that on occasion may erupt into fighting with the neighboring Arussi.

In traditional cattle raids the initiates would divide the cattle among themselves, each one expecting to get at least one animal. Today the cattle from a token raid are given to the class leaders. The initiates are expected to contribute sufficient funds to purchase eight to twelve cows, four or five goats, as many sheep, and sometimes one or two donkeys. Such a windfall for the two leaders, based on current prices, constitutes a considerable increment to their capital resources.[15]

There have also been some highly criticized negative developments, such as the corrupting of the class leader selection process, in which it has been suggested that the eight selectors for a recent class were bribed to choose a particular man for the position. Moreover, shortly after Emperor Menelik's time the government attempted to persuade the Āletā chief to provide the class leader with the office and title of *koro*, as a means of adding to the chain of officialdom in the indirect rule process. The chief refused on the grounds that an administrative role would conflict with the traditional role of the class leader as mediator and peacemaker.

Also, the authority of the elders continues to be important, especially since they still play a key role in the distribution of property and bridewealth. They continue to provide most of the bridewealth money that enables their sons to marry and acquire their own labor force. Furthermore, the increasing shortage of land and the resulting quarrels over property make the elder's role in dispute settlement even more significant than in the past.

Since it was decided not to give class leaders government rank, the title of *koro* was given to the lineage chiefs among the Yamarīčo. But in Āletā the elders were asked to hold a council and appoint one of their number to the position. In both cases the office of koro, like that of balabat, became hereditary. His responsibilities were to ensure that the balačika (lowest ranking official in the government hierarchy) collected the land tax and enforced conservation regulations, that people patronized the rural small claims court in which he officiated, and that rulings of government courts were enforced. Examples of the latter were the frequent enforcement of property settlements in which a subdistrict court ordered the koro to confiscate the property of a defaulter. Only in the event there was resistance to his actions would the court send government police into the countryside. And in these activities the koro was assisted by the balačika, one for every gaša in a subdistrict and one of the four men holding a tax receipt for that area. In fact, the main job of the balačika was to allocate and collect a share of the assessed gaša tax from the various household heads residing on the land.

The major problems with this postconquest leadership structure have had to do with succession and corruption. In regard to succession, the problem was the contradiction between recruitment for the impersonal role of a government official by means of traditional, personalized descent. Thus, for example, an old koro told how he had decided to retire from office by giving the position to his son, but when he discovered the son was accepting bribes and failing to show proper respect for his father and the people, he decided to take back the office. The son, however, refused to recognize paternal authority and surrender the lucrative position, forcing the father to take him to court, where he succeeded in regaining the office.

The following is another example of a more complex succession problem that lasted over several generations. In figure 4, A was a chief and a government koro in a Yamarīčo lineage. His son B refused when his father wished him to succeed to the positions, because he did not like the idea of being a koro and having to work with the Amhara. Since his brother and his brother's son were already deceased, A passed the positions to C, his brother's grandson. Now, C held the titles for many years but in his old age decided to give them to his paternal cousin D, partly because the titles would have been rightfully his had the father B been willing to accept them and partly because his own children F and G were too young to assume such responsibilities. Nevertheless, after the death of C, his children F and G went to court to try to take the position away from D. The case

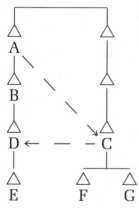

**Figure 4.** Lineage Mote and Koro Succession. *Source:* Author.

lasted for several years and at the time of field research was on appeal to the High Court in Addis Ababa. Meanwhile, D died and his son E continued the litigation, claiming rights to the titles.

In recent times the most notable of succession disputes has been that for the position of Āletā chief and balabat. It is important as an illustration of the contradictions involved in combining a traditional leadership role with that of a state administrator and the subsequent divisive impact upon the Āletā clans. Also, it shows how disunity was a potential convenience to the central government in controlling the Sadāma people.

The last chief, who died in 1961, had not followed the primogeniture role. His father had preferred him to his older brother because he had more formal education. And the father had assumed that this would enable his younger son to be more effective in carrying out the balabat functions. But when the father died before actually naming a successor, the two brothers quarreled over the position and went to court. Then, as the older brother concluded he would lose the case, he agreed to give up the two offices in return for some rifles, tools, and a small sum of money. As it happened, however, the new chief/balabat lived only a few years, and many elders attributed his early demise to violation of the primogeniture custom.

Though the dead chief had several wives and numerous sons, his senior wife had no male issue. So the eldest daughter of this wife claimed the position on the basis of Ethiopian inheritance law and was opposed by her eldest half-brother. He was supported by many elders who favored male primogeniture. But others in the chief's clan sought a compromise, giving the daughter and her husband[16] the balabat position and giving the ritual/mediatory role of the chief to the older brother of the deceased chief. In consequence, there followed four years of litigation between claimants.

During this time a majority of the Āletā became skeptical of the feasibility of compromise, believing the sister and her Amhara husband would in the end control both positions. Divisiveness increased in the summer of 1964 when the Ethiopian High Court ruled in favor of this couple. Nevertheless, the ruling induced a number of elders to appeal directly to Emperor Haile Selassie to overturn it and to support the young male contender. They argued that male primogeniture was the customary practice, and several months later the emperor supported their position.

Then all through 1965 the Āletā council of elders met frequently to raise money to pay for the previous litigation and to appoint a distinguished elder as adviser to the young chief-designate. Also, those who had supported the sister and her husband admitted their wrongdoing and sought to make compensation by paying fines to the council. The elders could not, however, reach a consensus on appointment of a regent adviser. And a year later, when the young chief was in the early stages of his generational class initiation, there was still no regent. Therefore, the government officials gave the balabat title to the half-sister and her husband.

Several years later, after the Āletā elders had complained vehemently about the despotism of the balabat, the government revoked the title. They requested the council to select a new heir for both positions, and the elders asked the older brother of the deceased chief to designate one of his sons. But the deposed balabat fought back by mobilizing the northern merchants and large landholders to aid in spreading a rumor that the Āletā council was plotting insurrection. And though this was soon shown to be false, the controversy prevented resolution of the succession crisis before the end of field research in 1973.

In anthropological theory two alternative forms of succession have been postulated: "determinant" and "indeterminant."[17] Potential heirs are either brothers or sons. Both alternatives have advantages and disadvantages.[18] Thus fraternal succession avoids the problem of a much younger person having to take responsibilities he may not be prepared to assume. On the other hand, there is always the danger that brothers will seek to subvert the system in favor of their sons. But these problems can be eliminated when sons have priority over brothers, providing the ruler is not without issue. Moreover, a rigid primogeniture system cannot flourish over a prolonged period because of the possibility of an incompetent person gaining power.

It is evident from the examples that the Sadāma have an "indeterminant" system, with a preference for primogeniture in choosing successors for the position of chief. There are, however, the above mentioned classic problems with this form of succession. In the first example, one sees the advantage of fraternal succession, in this situation a paternal cousin, because of the youthfulness of the chief's sons. Nevertheless, as those sons grew older and the father was deceased, they sought to subvert his decision. Also, the succession of the Āletā chief shows most of the problems of indeterminancy. There is evidence of contradictions arising out of sibling rivalry, resulting from paternal favoritism. Thus the eldest holds ascribed rights to authority on the basis of seniority, but the youngest tends to be favored because of his ascribed service to his parents. In the case of the Āletā chief, ostensibly it is formal education that gives the younger brother an advantage over his elder sibling. And there is also the problem of lack of issue from a senior wife, which contributes to an increase in sibling rivalry in the succeeding generation.

The most difficult succession problem, however, has been that of seeking to combine a personalized, ritual position with one that is impersonal and administrative. Such a position involves a contradiction between the traditional and modern concepts of succession. On the one hand, the importance of formal education became a means for circumventing traditional rules of succession, and the position acquired a monetary value. Nevertheless, leadership by the chief continued to convey many traditional overtones as a symbol of ethnic unity, so that tampering with succession could have dire consequences for the group and the individual. A case in point was the premature death of the last chief, who had, in the view of many elders, usurped the position.

The Āletā example also illustrates how the Ethiopian government controlled succession to forestall the development of political opposition by either the descendants of the northern settlers or the Sadāma. Thus the divisions created by the proposed compromise to separate the roles of chief and balabat were used effectively by the emperor to keep the two combined and to win favor with a majority of the Āletā. Then the divisions that had already developed between the clansmen of the chief and other Āletā clans could be ultimately exploited to give the balabat position to a northerner. But when the Āletā complained of exploitation by the balabat, the government could conveniently remove him to prevent the possible establishment of a political following among the northern merchants and landowners. The cycle could then be repeated with the development of disunity among Āletā factions in the struggle to name a new mote/balabat. In turn the former balabat aligned himself with the northern merchants in accusing the Āletā of plotting insurrection. This divide-and-rule policy was similar to that followed by the central government in other provinces prior to the revolution of 1974.[19]

Self-aggrandizement and corruption are the principal reasons for the intensity of recent struggles in Sidāmoland. Opportunities for individual gain have arisen as a result of the rights of balabats to receive vacant land and the potential for bribery in a developing cash economy. One of the perquisites in the original assignment to this position was a right to land not awarded by government title or already inhabited by the indigenous people.[20] Those persons who assumed the balabat position immediately following the conquest were thus well aware that much unoccupied land was vacated as a result of Sadāma having fled the gabbar system. In laying claim to this land, however, their descendants either failed to consider or completely ignored the return of these people or their descendants. Then as coffee production became more important after World War II, the land increased in value, and a chief/balabat with some formal education and a minimal amount of business acumen could hope to become wealthy and acquire prestige by farming the land and presenting small parcels to prominent government officials. As previously mentioned, not all traditional leaders who assumed the balabat position followed this goal of self-aggrandizement. In fact, some leaders and their descendants worked diligently to protect the customs and lands of their people.

The last two Āletā leaders, however, sought to further their own wealth and positions rather than promote the welfare of the people. Indeed, many Āletā believed that these men, the only ones to receive the Ethiopian title of kannazmač, acquired their honors by giving other people's lands as gifts to government officials.[21] It is said that the few elderly Sadāma without relatives who called upon the last chief to fulfill the traditional obligations of providing assistance to the aged were required to sign away their land rights before he would consent to help. Then he would violate this trust by giving their land to government officials.

Finally, as cash became the prevailing medium of exchange in obtaining official services or assistance in dealing with the government, it became necessary to bribe the balabat. In fact, this form of corruption to secure favors and advantages in the mediation of disputes even became widespread among koro officials. Although, from the government viewpoint, this was a convenient means of compensating low salaried or unpaid officials among the Sadāma, it served to promote fear and distrust of all persons associated with the central government. Furthermore, it encouraged people to rely on the elder's councils in making local policy decisions and in settling disputes.

Unlike the attempts at government cooptation of clan chiefs, there have been only infrequent efforts to interfere with the dispute-settlement and policy-making functions of elders' councils. This has been largely due to lack of sufficient government personnel to establish effective control in the countryside.[22] Nevertheless, establishment of a national court system and erosion of certain procedural aspects have had an impact on the effectiveness of the elders' councils.

After Menelik's conquest and prior to 1931, the Ethiopian Empire was divided into six regions, each with two judges who heard petitions from persons whose disputes could not be conciliated locally. At the same time, governors at various administrative levels held informal adjudicatory functions.[23] Further, there was the option of appeal from decisions by a judge to the emperor or his court chamberlain. In fact, the main role of the governors was to settle disputes among northern settlers in the conquered territories, and their contact with the indigenous inhabitants was minimal. Then in 1931 the Fetha Nagast (the traditional legal code of Amhara people) was officially recognized as the law of all the Ethiopian Empire.

Before the full implications of this proclamation could be realized, however, the Italian occupation occurred, and local customary law prevailed once again. Indeed, it has been suggested that during the Italian occupation traditional dispute-settlement and social-control procedures in the various regions were strongly supported by the colonial power.[24]

Following the occupation, the most significant development was the replacement of the 1931 code with the Penal Code of 1956, which contains many aspects of the legal systems of industrial states. There followed the Civil Code of 1960, which provided for the retention of certain aspects of customary law. Such a provision is absent from the Penal Code primarily because it is concerned with punitive sanctions, while the Civil Code is based on restitutive sanctions, which are presumably similar to those imposed under various forms of customary law. Thus title 20 of the Civil Code recognizes the validity of traditional forms of conciliation and arbitration, which are analogous to many of the procedures followed by the elders' councils.[25] A formal court system was also established with a subdistrict court, district court, and provincial court. Furthermore, this system retained the opportunity for appeal to the High Court in Addis Ababa and ultimately to the supreme imperial court of the emperor.

Just as important as the court system was the estabishment in 1947 of the *atbia dagnia* as a form of small claims court.[26] In Sidāmo Province the districts are divided into *atbia*, each containing 130 gaša under the jurisdiction of a koro. The koro became the *dagnia*, in effect a "marketplace judge,"[27] who could adjudicate civil cases limited to claims of not more than twenty-five dollars and minor criminal offenses in which fines could not exceed fifteen dollars. This rural, small claims judge was also expected to apprehend criminals wanted by the police, issue court summons, question witnesses with knowledge of an alleged offense, and conduct investigations prior to the arrest of an accused offender.[28] In these actions he was to be responsible to the district court, the governor, and the police. It was anticipated that the atbia dagnia would constitute a transitional link between traditional ways and the new legal norms of the state and that the procedures and values of the latter would gradually replace the former.[29]

As it happened, however, district officials were uninterested in supporting these small claims courts and showed more concern with the koro as a supervisor of tax collections in the countryside and as someone to issue court summons.[30] Furthermore, when judicial procedures were altered in 1965 to fit the new penal and civil codes, no mention was made of small claims courts. In order to account for the deletion, the minister of justice later issued a directive specifying that the atbia dagnia would retain his adjudication function in criminal matters, but he was to serve only as a conciliator in civil cases. Nevertheless, his role remained ambiguous in the sense that there was nothing to prevent him from ignoring the civil and criminal codes altogether and simply following the norms and procedures of local customary law. This was in fact the course of action taken by the two atbia dagnia known to the author.

In 1973 it was possible to interview and observe the court proceedings of a koro/atbia dagnia highly respected by the people in the countryside. He indicated that most of the cases coming before him involved cash indebtedness. If there were witnesses involved he would usually make a decision or refer the case to an elders' council. Furthermore, it was his view that most people preferred the elders' councils to the small claims and the higher courts; consequently (and perhaps because he was a leading elder in the Holō clan), he preferred to refer as many disputes as possible to them. Residing on the edge of clan territory, he held court once a week in a small marketplace near his home.

When sending disputes to an elders' council, the procedure was to allow the elders three or four weeks to negotiate a settlement. If by that time an agreement had not been arranged, the disputants were instructed to return to the small claims court. There they were charged a fee according to the complexity of the case, and messengers delivering summons had to be paid by the plaintiff. (These service charges increase, the higher the level of court used by a litigant.) It is important in this connection to recall that in the council there are no charges for the services of the elders.

Though it was rumored in 1973 that some koro/atbia dagnia became wealthy through bribes received from litigants, the nature of the cases involved makes this questionable. For example, in one session of the court under observation, fifteen cases were brought, all but one concerning small, unpaid debts. Of this number, only one dispute could be resolved, two were referred to the neighborhood council, and the rest (twelve) were postponed because one or more of the disputants or witnesses failed to appear.

Several generalizations emerge from limited participant observation and from the opinions of informants regarding these rural, small claims courts. In general, matters coming before them are primarily concerned with cash indebtedness and seldom involve the land, marriage, or bodily injury disputes that are so prevalent in the elders' councils discussed in the previous chapter. Also, there is only one of these courts to 130 gaša, while there is seldom a gaša in which there is not at least a hamlet and neighborhood council. Consequently, in using these small claims courts there is a definite drawback in having to travel long distances to settle minor disputes. Finally, it would seem that the people consider the small claims court more as a convenient alternative for coercing debtors when it is difficult to obtain payment than as a link with the laws and procedures of the Ethiopian state system. This has been confirmed elsewhere by a study among the Arussi, where individuals advance reasons similar to those of the Sadāma for preferring traditional norms and procedures to those of the small claims court.[31]

As for the functioning of Ethiopian courts at higher levels, there was a widespread opinion among Ethiopian peasants in general that scant justice was to be obtained from the judiciary, whose decisions usually favored persons with the largest cash resources.[32] Though Sadāma were using these courts in the sixties and seventies, their experience was almost universally negative because of the high costs, sometimes involving bribery, and—with one notable exception—their exclusion from participation as judges.[33]

In fact, most of the men who became court officials were the descendants of northern settlers and Menelik's soldiers. These were the same persons who in the postwar era came to dominate the coffee trade, who set prices, monopolized marketing procedures, and often cheated individuals in the use of weights and measures. Under the circumstances, it was not surprising that Sadāma began to see an analogy between the rules of the marketplace and the entrepreneurial-like operations of the courts. In effect, the merchant-buyer and the producer-seller roles were simply reversed, with peasants becoming the buyers of justice and the court officialdom constituting the sellers. Indeed, of the cases that came to the attention of the ethnographer, going to court was most likely to occur in litigation with non-Sadāma, as a means of maximizing one's advantage in ultimately resolving a dispute in the elders' council and as a way of showing power over another.

Four cases were collected involving land claims by Sadāma against Amhara. These were all disputes in which Sadāma were going to court to protect their land from alleged encroachment by northern settlers. In these instances an elders' council would have been inappropriate. For example, a Sadānčo had years ago given an Amhara some land in payment for help in a court case. The land was highly fertile, and because the boundaries of the parcel had never been clearly established, the new owner kept expanding his garden until a young man—his neighbor—complained. This neighbor took him to court when he claimed that the land on which the Amhara had allegedly encroached—nearly a hectare by the young man's estimate—was a part of the parcel. Though the young neighbor received financial help from his relatives, the case was very costly, and after eight years of litigation the end was not in sight. The dispute had gone all the way to the High Court in Addis Ababa, where the judges had found in favor of the defendant, and now the young man had made a final appeal to the court of the emperor. Meanwhile the Amhara defendant obtained a court order from his brother, the local subdistrict judge, evicting his neighbor from the disputed land.

Several cases were recorded in which individuals sought to use both the elders' councils and the courts in settling a dispute, hoping to use the latter to maximize their interests in the former. In one case, a young man requested that a small loan from a wealthy relative be canceled when his house and coffee harvest were destroyed by fire. By custom, he should have been excused from the debt. At first it seemed that this would happen, but two years later the lender sought to recover the debt. The young man returned what he could, a small portion of the original amount, and thought the matter ended. Instead his relative continued to demand the balance.

When the lender's cattle got into the garden of the young man, he saw a chance for retaliation and went before the elders' council with an exorbitant demand for crop damages. Then, as animosity between the two men increased, the young man declared that the two were no longer relatives and opened a suit for crop damages in the subdistrict court. At this point the elders called the two men before the council, insisted that such enmity between relatives was unacceptable, and negotiated a settlement. Later the young man in conversation with the ethnographer confided that he had gone to court only to get the attention of the elders and his antagonist. His intentions all along had been to get a settlement by the council.

This example illustrates one way in which legal innovations of the state are used to further the traditional ends of magnanimity and reconciliation. In two other cases, claimants sought originally to use the sōngo to resolve their grievances, but when they began to suspect the elders' decisions might go against them, they threatened to go to court.

This should not, however, be interpreted to mean that individuals are completely rational in calculating strategies to obtain success or overcome risk. As one old generational class leader explained, people often behave like gamblers, basing their cases more on hopes than facts and ignoring the costs. It is often argued among Sadāma that to go to court is to invite ultimate disaster for both plaintiff and defendant, because of the great costs and lengthy appeals that can go on for years, ultimately using up the resources of both disputants. Not surprisingly, the opinion is widespread that the threat of going to court represents either a means of frightening an opponent or—failing in this form of bravado—a fatalistic willingness to gamble on winning no matter what the costs.

People may also use the courts as a means for demonstrating their wealth and power. A case in point was the land dispute discussed in the previous chapter, in which a wealthy old elder sought to show his superior status over a younger man. Another example in this category is a trade-off case, in which, in order to escape assault charges filed in a subdistrict court, a man and his relatives agreed to give up a land claim against the same antagonist in the neighborhood council. In another instance, a householder showed his contempt for a neighbor who planted maize across his boundary by immediately filing in a subdistrict court an action for trespassing. The trespasser quickly apologized to the neighbor and begged to be excused for his error.

Though the council remains the preferred alternative for dispute settlement, the impact of the cash economy, alcohol usage, and religious conversion have eroded some of the traditional sanctity of the elders. Indeed, many older informants were convinced that men now tend to ignore their council duties during the two-month period of coffee harvesting. Also, some young men prefer trading coffee to attending councils to learn procedures and perfect their oratorical skills. To this problem has been added the widespread practice of councils accepting the alcoholic beverage arike as payment for fines. One consequence of this practice has been drunken comportment and a threat to the customary dignity of the proceedings. And finally, religious conversion has led to sufficient community disharmony to make it more difficult to achieve consensus and compromise in council deliberations. As one distinguished elder explained, "We see halōli, the true way of life, being weakened, and we don't know whether it is due to the missionaries or to the Muslims."

In effect, religious conversion and cash cropping, as impediments to effective functioning of elders' councils, indicate the importance of linkages with the outside world. For both items show a connection with international capitalism and the formation of consequent ideological attributes.

## Impact of the Cash Economy

Producing coffee has significantly increased the amount of cash available to the Sadāma, it has led to the removal of some land from subsistence herding and food production, and it has reduced the time available for political and ritual activities. It is therefore important to explore the origins and developments of coffee production and trade, the way it has joined the people to the world economy, and what it has meant in terms of income and consumption for the peasant producer.

At the beginning of this century, members of the nobility, in cooperation with Khartoum-based Greek firms, began to commercialize the production of coffee near Harrar in eastern Ethiopia.[34] Then by 1912, after construction of the Addis Ababa to Djiboute railway, Belgium, British, and French coffee plantations were established in the same area. Among the Sadāma, however, it is difficult to determine the origins of coffee production, apart from the assertions of informants that it has always grown wild in the highlands. Indeed, there are authors who suggest that coffee may be indigenous to Ethiopia.[35] In any event, prior to Menelik's conquest the Sadāma did not use it as a food but exchanged the coffee cherries with the Arussi for butter. And as indicated at the beginning of this chapter, in the 1920s northern settlers began to appreciate the economic potential for producing and marketing coffee, considering the gabbar system a hindrance to the effective use of land and labor in the production process. But the Italian occupation and World War II intervened to prevent development of cash cropping until the 1940s. Then revival of international trade led by 1960 to the emergence of coffee as the major Ethiopian export.[36] Indeed coffee continued to account for more than 50 percent of all Ethiopian exports until the mid-1970s, when it declined to the 30 percent level, due to coffee berry disease and drought.[37]

In terms of productivity, Sidāmo Province ranked second only to Kaffa Province and by 1970 provided 20 to 25 percent of all coffee inspected by the Ethiopian Coffee Board.[38] This generated a considerable amount of wealth, as can be seen indirectly from the fact that Sidāmo Province provided the third-highest tax revenue of all the thirteen provinces in 1968–69 and the fourth highest in 1969–70.[39] Nevertheless, coffee takes up only 11 percent of all the cultivable land area in Ethiopia.[40] And since subsistence production accounts for more than 50 percent of the Ethiopian gross domestic product, the economy is less affected than most single-export economies by the notorious price fluctuation of the international market.

Marketing procedures were generally haphazard prior to 1957, when the National Coffee Board was established and given the authority to buy, decorticate, process, export, and grant credit.[41] Over the years the Board has issued a number of regulations regarding the picking, drying, and storage of coffee, but there have always been too few inspectors and extension officers to train peasant producers and to enforce these regulations. At the same time it was recognized as unreasonable to expect the peasantry to be concerned with improving the quality of their production methods without receiving higher cash incentives. Moreover, it was considered unlikely that middle-men merchants would provide higher prices unless the producers had some form of bargaining power, such as might be obtained through cooperative societies.[42]

Thus in the late 1950s there was a growing realization that a government parastatal could not do the whole job of marketing a high-quality product and ensure a fair price without cooperatives to bargain with the middlemen, monitor small holder credit, supervise local storage and drying facilities, and encourage the dissemination of new production techniques. Such a realization was to lead to a climate of opinion that would be encouraging for the type of self-help association that began to develop among the Sadāma in the early 1960s. On the other hand, there were signs in the 1960s that the government was fearful of such organizations, especially if in any way connected with religious or ethnic groups, and it sought to harass and severely regulate their activities.[43] This problem of regulation will be dealt with in detail in the following chapter.

Linkage of the Ethiopian coffee economy to world capitalism helps to explain why cash cropping has had such an impact on the Sadāma. To begin with, coffee is important in international trade, ranking second only in value to petroleum in 1978 market transactions and hence the most important of all food commodities.[44] Though there has been a decline in consumption in recent years, coffee has remained the largest single food item imported into the United States.[45] Indeed, despite increasing diversification of markets in the 1960s and 1970s, the bulk of Ethiopian coffee exports have been to the United States.[46]

The marketing process before the Second World War involved a number of small corporations in Europe and America, but following the war, declining demand and increasing competition led to mergers into large transnational corporations.[47] To lower the costs, these corporate groups found it convenient to rely less on Latin American brands than on African imports, because of less-expensive African labor. It was necessary, however, to blend the "robust" African coffee, which has a high acid content, with the milder Latin American varieties. For example, Ethiopian coffee has been found to be ideal for blending with Brazilian coffee.[48] As a consequence there has been a steady increase in the percentage of African coffee imported by Americans, from less than 2 percent in 1948 to more than 23 percent of all coffee imports in 1975.[49]

It has been argued that capital investment in isolated labor markets like the Sadāma increases the cooperation between state bureaucracies and private investors with international sources of capital.[50] This encourages the development of cooperatives as a convenient means of expanding production and increasing the returns to both the state and transnational corporations. As fluctuations in commodity prices occur, however, conflict arises between the national elites and peasant producers, the latter blaming the former for their losses, as both groups seek at least to maintain what they have already gained. The international corporations are much less affected by price downturns than Third World nations that are dependent upon one or two export commodities. Thus the growing conflict between burgeoning national bureaucracies and peasant producers to maintain their position often leads to inflation and stagnation.[51] The Sadāma began to undergo this pressure in the decade preceding the 1974 Revolution, as they experienced the consequences of fluctuating coffee prices and the resulting conflict over the increasing cost of developing a modern nation state.

The best way to understand the importance of coffee to the Sadāma is to examine the process of production, the income that farmers receive for sale of their product, and the way this has changed values and patterns of consumption. Coffee is not uniformly distributed throughout the land, but is concentrated in Āletā and Hadičō territories, primarily at an elevation of between six thousand and seven thousand feet. In starting a crop, men generally are able to avoid the purchase of seedlings by obtaining them from friends and kinsmen. For the first three or four years, few beans are produced, but after that the yield alternates between high and low from one year to the next. The mature bushes require little care other than occasional weeding, the main danger being frequent hailstorms that may destroy the crop. Once the cherries have begun to ripen, the harvest is under way, taking place in the two-month period from early December through January. Since it has become a major source of wealth, the harvesting and marketing process is confined solely to men. It is important that the beans be picked quickly and carefully in order to avoid possible damage by the elements and any injury to the bush that would reduce future yields. Furthermore, as there was no precedent for harvesting and storing a cash crop, it has been necessary to establish a new form of reciprocal labor exchange. The neighborhood work groups would have been too unwieldy because of the long delays necessitated by reciprocal labor exchange with large numbers, the problem of maintaining discipline among so many in relatively small gardens, and the great expense involved in feeding such a sizable number of workers. As a consequence, this problem of production was largely resolved by the formation of voluntary associations, as will be discussed in the next chapter.

Once the coffee is picked, the producer has several options. If he has an immediate need for cash, he may sell the cherries at a relatively low price, or, alternatively, dry the cherries and sell them in the market for slightly more. Men generally dry their coffee on a flat, cleared piece of land in front of their homes, keeping the beans out in the sun during the day and storing them in large, wide baskets at night. Though Marketing Board representatives have attempted to persuade farmers to dry the beans on racks as a means of improving the grade, sufficient incentive has not been provided to make the added effort seem worthwhile to most producers. For those who can afford to wait, there is a third alternative, namely, to dry, decorticate the cherries, and save the beans until the time of optimum price, usually in June or July.

Trading in coffee is another means of supplementing the income

Drying Coffee, Preparatory to Marketing

from one's own garden, and there are usually two or three men in a hamlet who devote much of their time to this activity during the dry season. There is, however, a certain ambivalence on the part of the average Sadānčo toward coffee trading, an activity that, with the possible exception of buying coffee futures, is considered undignified for elders. On the other hand, the production and sale of coffee by older men is considered a legitimate activity, as it is properly associated with the idealized role of the cultivator. They may also buy coffee futures by using profits from sale of their own crop to purchase a part of the next year's crop from others who have immediate cash needs. Though there is always some risk that the crop will be damaged or the price will fall, it is a reasonable probability that the individual will make a profit the following year.

Another approach involves petty cash transactions that begin in late November, when young men can be found along the trails buying small amounts such as a can or a cupful of cherries from market-bound women. It is this bargaining with women, as well as the fact that the women often have taken the cherries from their husband's gardens without permission, that discredits trade in the eyes of the elders. Though only small sums are involved, such as fifty cents for two or three cans of dried cherries or twenty-five cents for three cups of dried and decorticated beans, the bargaining is often intense. Both buyer and seller are interested in small profits of not more than five to ten cents on a single transaction. Usually traders have learned the market price from a transistor radio, when the announcer provides quotations directly from Addis Ababa.

Most farmers receive all of their income from the sale of vegetable and animal commodities, whether it be coffee as among the Āletā people; teff, barley, or ensete in the highlands; or butter and maize from the low-lying pasture lands. Moreover, as a consequence of the concentration on coffee production, which results in a food shortage in some households, men in areas where coffee does not thrive are able to derive some cash income from the sale of their produce.

In the first period of field research, income and expenditure estimates were obtained from thirty-seven household heads in three Āletā hamlets. Unfortunately, in 1973 it was possible to obtain similar information from only eleven of the original group of informants.[52] It should be remembered that, with two exceptions, these men were nonliterate and kept all of these accounts in their memories, which is certain to be responsible for a degree of error in the figures. Nevertheless, the data, minus one household head who had given up farming to become a merchant, are contained in table 3.

In interpreting the results of this survey, it is important to note that, with the exception of two men who derived some income from selling corn meal and medicines, the bulk of the income comes from the sale of coffee. As the standard deviations show, there is considerable variation in income and expenditure from one household head to another; with the exception of the 1964–65 expenditures, half of the individuals are more than one standard deviation from the mean average. Also, though the average income in the two time frames has remained essentially the same, the 1972–73 expenditures are on the average sixty-four dollars more than income. This is a large increase considering that in 1965, for thirty-three men with complete expenditure figures, only 18 percent spent more than their income, as compared with 60 percent of the 1973 group of ten.

Why should there be such an income/expenditure imbalance, and how did these household heads manage such a deficit? The explanation cannot simply be the existence of past savings, since only three of the men reported savings for either income period. The facts of the matter are that of the six men whose expenditures exceed their income, two reported savings from other years, one had borrowed sufficient money to meet his indebtedness, and a fourth man expected to balance his accounts by profits from sale of coffee futures, the acquisition of which were responsible for most of his indebtedness. The problems of a fifth man are attributable to legal fees for a land case, toward which he hoped to receive contributions from members

**Table 3.** Average Estimated Mean Income and Expenditure for Ten Household Heads, 1964–65 and 1972–73 (Ethiopian dollars)

|  | Income M | Expenditure M |
| --- | --- | --- |
| 1964–65 Estimates | 320.85 | 239.55 |
| SD | 183.21 | 159.29 |
| 1972–73 Estimates | 328.50 | 384.20 |
| SD | 170.82 | 167.31 |

Source: Author.

of his clan. And plans of a sixth man for settling an imbalance of fifteen dollars were not ascertainable.

As to the causes of indebtedness, three are in debt because they have invested half or more of their 1972–73 income in cattle, which is an investment in future food production. Indebtedness of two of the households is indirectly a capital investment, in that they have used more than their annual income for court actions to maintain control of their land. Only one man has gone into debt for an essentially luxury item, in the form of a town dwelling with a corrugated iron roof. Thus it is likely that the indebtedness of most of these men in 1973 would be offset in future years by investment gains from their land and cattle.

Table 4 shows a breakdown of the average expenses as percentages of income for all categories of expenditures in the two time periods. These figures reveal that percentage expenditures, as might have been anticipated, remain about the same in both time frames for taxes, purchase of ensete seedlings, medical expenses, fodder for animals, and hired labor.[53] On the other hand, expenditures for food and clothing, two high income-expenditure items, have actually declined. In fact, of the thirty-seven household heads surveyed in 1965, only nine were without supplementary food purchases. For the ten men

**Table 4.** Categories of Average Estimated Mean Expenditures as Percentages of Estimated Income, 1964–65 and 1972–73

|  | 1964–65 | 1972–73 |
| --- | --- | --- |
| Food | 24 | 10 |
| Taxes | 8 | 7 |
| Clothing | 53 | 24 |
| Ensete seedlings | 4 | 4 |
| Medical care | 2 | 4 |
| Domesticated animals | 4 | 29 |
| Hired labor | 4 | 6 |
| Loans | 0 | 6 |
| Fodder | 2 | 1 |
| Other[a] | 9 | 48 |

[a]Includes legal expenses, bridewealth payments,
housing, and mission contributions.
Source: Author.

interviewed in both time periods, all had food purchases in 1965, while only six had them in 1973, mostly for ensete, cornmeal, and teff.

This difference may be partially explained by the concentration on coffee in Āletā, leaving less land for food production. But by utilizing some of their income for supplementary food purchases in the markets, Āletā producers were in effect providing income for peasants from non-coffee-producing regions.[54] Moreover, coffee producers are relatively close to the all-weather road, which expedites the transmission of their commodity to the urban and international marketplace, while the cash food producers are isolated in the highlands and lowlands. Thus it is unlikely that they would be able to market their surplus food production without the demand of the Āletā coffee growers. Also, to some extent the decline in purchased foods may be due to the higher productivity from recent use of hybrid corn, to be discussed later. Another and simpler explanation is that indebtedness forced some householders to reduce the amount and quality of their food consumption in 1973. Indeed, three of the four men who made no supplementary food purchases in 1973 were heavily in debt. On the other hand, the four men whose 1973 accounts were in balance show a considerable decline in the percentage spent for food, helping to explain the overall reduction to half of the 1965 average percentage expenditures. Furthermore, percentage expenditures for clothing in 1973 had also dropped to less than half of what was spent in 1965. Only one of the two household heads who increased their 1973 expenditures has this category for his largest percentage increase.

It is significant that four of the other nine men have their largest percentage income expenditures in saving and in the purchase of domesticated animals. And five householders have devoted the largest percentage of their income to the "other" category. "Other" and "domesticated animals" constitute the two areas of greatest income expenditure in 1973, with the suggestion already having been made that these expenditures, along with court expense, are items of direct and indirect capital investment. Two men used significant amounts of their income for the infrequently occurring bridewealth expense; half of the group were Christians and reported substantial church contributions. Such expenditures helped to boost the overall total of the "other" category.

Finally, it is necessary to elaborate on the issue of saving and borrowing. Saving has not been included as an expenditure heading because some men were reluctant to confide information on the subject, even though they admitted to having such funds. Perhaps this is how some with income/expenditure imbalances were planning to resolve the problem. Two men did, however, provide actual figures on their savings, one indicating that the largest percentage expenditure of his income was devoted to saving.[55]

Since there was less reluctance to talk about borrowing, this category is included in table 4. One of the three men reporting receipt of loans indicated that he planned to use this money to resolve the problem of his income/expenditure imbalance. Another was using the money to pay off a debt he had acquired during a long illness, while in the third case it was not clear how the man planned to use his loan. Though none of these men had borrowed or loaned money in 1965, at that time five others in the survey were involved in this practice, in addition to three who had reported doing so in previous years but had stopped because of the difficulty of obtaining repayment.

There is minimal data from informants regarding expenditures on trade. Only one man in the 1973 survey reported such an expenditure, using 33 percent of his income for buying coffee futures. While in 1965 two of the ten men made money in trading, both had withdrawn from this activity in 1973. The limited involvement in trading is probably because when a young man is just starting a garden, his coffee trees are new and provide only a limited yield, so that trading is the only way to build up sufficient income to support his household. It will be recalled from chapter 5 that failure to provide a wife with clothing is a reason for marital disharmony and even dissolution of the marriage. Thus it is understandable why clothing is so important an item of expenditure and why young men with new households and gardens must trade, in order to keep the wives who are so important a labor adjunct to their future economic success. As time goes on, however, and a man's garden matures, he has less reason or time to engage in commerce, since production and harvesting of his coffee requires more of his attention and energies. This may be the reason that trading is often alleged to be undignified for older men. Indeed, out of twelve men reporting trading activities in 1965 (from a sample of thirty-seven), nine were relatively young men with new gardens. Also, one recent deterrent to trade in coffee futures has been the previously mentioned spread of coffee berry disease. As the largest saver in the 1973 survey indicated, he had originally put aside the money to buy coffee futures, but the berry disease had become so widespread that he was afraid to invest it in this activity.

To summarize, it is evident that coffee is the basis for most of the cash income in Āletā and that its production helps generate the only cash flow for peasant farmers in non-coffee-producing regions. These regions in turn produce the food that has been lost in growing coffee on Āletā land. Nevertheless, just as Ethiopian farmers in general have not become dependent for their subsistence on coffee exports, the income/expenditure figures indicate that the same is true for the Sadāma in particular. Even so, for one of the most productive coffee regions in the nation, the income figures are low and the imbalance between income and expenditures in 1973 is striking, for more than half the members of this small sample. Despite the imbalance and individual variability in income and expenditure, however, there is an overall tendency for these peasant farmers to spend their money on expanding their herds, maintaining control of their land, and providing clothing to sustain the commitment and loyalty of wives and children, whose labor is so important in the production process. There is little evidence of expenditure on luxuries, unless one considers the building of a house with a corrugated iron roof or church contributions as such.

By and large the expenditures of peasant farmers are being used to increase and protect their capacity for production. There is an implied competitiveness in this process, as indicated by the way it has encouraged development of the pursuit of self-interest to the detriment of community obligations. It will also be recalled from chapter 4 that there is a traditional regard for the encouragement of youth to respect wealth, achievement, and rivalry.

Studies in other Third World countries have indicated that competitive consumption rather than create class divisions tends to increase the productivity of farmers, at least where it involves "productive property" rather than personal luxury items.[56] For the Sadāma, before the 1970s there were few personal luxury items available to vie with utilitarian objects for the farmers' money. By 1973, however, bicycles, transistor radios, manufactured household goods, and buses for short- and long-distance travel had become part of the local scene. Many men and women had made occasional use of the new mode of transportation, one considering it a sufficiently important item of expenditure to estimate that he had spent thirty dollars for bus fare during 1972–73. Most persons, however, continued to walk or ride mules wherever they went, though there was a consensus that bus travel would make life easier in the future. And very few people had been as far as the national capital in Addis Ababa; these had made the journey only because they had land litigation on appeal to the High Court.

Does the spread of the cash economy, the signs of small-scale capital investment, and the presence of Western-style consumers' goods mean that productivity was increasing and the standard of living improving? Many elders expressed a sense of what they referred to as atote-šīma, which translates literally as "little blessing." The expression was used in a paradoxical sense to mean that things that seemed to be increasing in quantity or value were in reality doing just the opposite. These men would complain that while there was more food and money, people seemed to have less to eat; though there were more cows, there was less milk; there was also more medicine but less health. Some argued that existing taxes had increased and that the government was always threatening new taxes for developing the countryside, but there were few tangible results available to rural people in terms of more and better schools or health facilities. One distinguished old elder felt that the old ways were fast disappearing and in their place there remained only disregard for the elders by the young. There was also an expressed concern about increasing inflation, as prices for everything in 1973 were much higher than in 1965.

On the other hand, younger men, especially those active in the new self-help societies, felt that it was only the more traditionally oriented who expressed a sense of atote šīma. They felt this way because they were used to a time of smaller population, more land, and smaller herds of cattle. As one man explained it, people formerly lived shorter lives; now, however, there were less infant deaths, which meant that there were many more people using up more resources. Also, older people in their youth had little money and few things to spend it on, so they became concerned when they saw the younger generation with more money spending freely on a greater variety of goods. Nevertheless, it was admitted by all that there was much difference of opinion on whether the standard of living was improving, with some believing that life-style was declining in quality, while others were optimistic that a "modernization" process was under way, which would ultimately lead to improvements.

The optimists based their thinking on increasing opportunities for trade, a limited amount of wage labor, agricultural innovations, anticipated benefits from formal education, and self-help opportunities for making change a reality. For now attention will be focused on trade, wage labor, and agricultural inputs, as education will be discussed in the next section and self-help will be the subject of the following chapter.

The ultimate in trading activities for the ambitious youth was to become a coffee merchant and to move out of the hamlet into a nearby market town. Even if they could acquire the necessary capital, though, relatively few were actually prepared to risk the break between country and town living, something they rationalized on the basis of traditions. One might retain a household, land, and cattle in the countryside, but to live in town and become a merchant was to remove oneself from the land and the idealized role of a peasant cultivator. In fact, if one did not reside on the land and provide continuous care of the garden and cattle, there would be very little to fall back upon in the event of failure in the highly competitive role of a merchant. And in the 1970s most young people still held respect for the old ways and the elders; the elders would sanction such a move only as a means for providing an alternative to the alleged unfair practices of Amhara merchants.

One interesting example was that of Gonsamo,[57] who in 1968 turned his household and land over to his youngest son (then about eighteen) and wife, established a combination store/household in the nearest town, and in the next three years married two additional wives who were adapted to town life. His country wife, however, deeply resented Gonsamo's move to town, especially since he no longer provided her with money for clothing and expected her to contribute produce from the farm to feed his two town wives. There were also murmurings of displeasure from the hamlet elders, but they were reluctant to ostracize Gonsamo, as he did not cheat them in weighing their coffee and always gave them a fair price. Also, they found his assistance useful in dealing with the town officials. So by 1973 Gonsamo was one of four Sadāma out of a total of seventeen merchants licensed to deal in coffee. He had increased his estimated annual income from around five hundred dollars in 1965, when he was still primarily a farmer, to over four thousand dollars in 1973. Nevertheless, despite his apparent success as a merchant, he was experiencing difficulties, partly because of his lack of formal education, which made bookkeeping difficult and—at least in his view—

partly because of the machinations of his wealthy Amhara associate.

Though there was no price competition between merchants, success came only to the ones with sufficient cash reserves to withhold coffee from the market, in order to obtain the highest price from the coffee board in Addis Ababa. This maximum price in any given year was usually reached several months after farmers had sold their cherries to the middlemen merchants. Many of these merchants lacked the capital to finance their purchases or to acquire the necessary transport to haul coffee directly to the capital. Hence, of necessity, they had to enter into partnership with wealthy entrepreneurs, usually the descendants of the original northern settlers and soldiers.

Gonsamo acquired such a partner, and for a time they worked together in a spirit of mutual trust. But as he prospered and coffee prices fluctuated, the partner began to see him as a potential rival. In 1968 Gonsamo started his trade with three hundred dollars capital by loaning money to farmers to be repaid in coffee cherries. Then by withholding these cherries from the market for the maximum price offered by the board, he was gradually able to amass several thousands of dollars in profits. But before he acquired his license in 1971, it had been necessary to acquire a licensed partner, who also loaned him money to purchase coffee and provided a truck to haul it to Addis Ababa. When Gonsamo acquired the license, however, he noticed that the overhead costs began to increase, and finally the partner accused him of signing the same delivery sheet twice, claiming eight hundred dollars worth of coffee that he had not delivered. Gonsamo denied the allegation, but because of his lack of a systematic bookkeeping system, he could not provide the necessary documentation to prove his innocence. Still, he remained optimistic, having recently enlarged his store and having built a sizable new house, and he was planning next to invest in a truck.

The conflict between Gonsamo and his wealthy partner constitutes a local-level illustration of the previously mentioned problems for an alliance of transnational corporations, state bureaucracies, and private investors. In essence the latter two groups are dependent for their well-being on marketing a small number of commodities through a powerful international organization with virtually unlimited resources. When prices are high all three groups benefit, but when prices fall the dependent groups are threatened. Alternatively, high prices for single-crop-producing states provide respectable balance of payment reserves, which enable bureaucracies to expand and to implement development plans. In like manner, wealthy men at the local level increase their operations and encourage the aspirations and small-scale entrepreneurial activities of men like Gonsamo. A decline in prices, however, becomes a threat to the three dependent groups, which leads to conflicts being translated into mutual accusations of fraud, cheating, and misappropriation of funds.

Wage labor for the Sadāma was just as tenuous as entrepreneurial activities, since it was also dependent on the export of a few agricultural commodities. Two enterprises were involved, one a cannery and the other a meat-packing plant on the northern edge of the provincial boundary. The cannery work of processing green beans and tomatoes was only seasonal and employed about sixty members of the Mālga clan, at wages as low as sixty cents a day. And in the packing plant some 350 Sadāma were employed in 1973, slaughtering and processing seven hundred cattle a week for shipment to the European market. Although this was considered to be one of the most modern packing plants in East Africa, prior to 1970 it had been closed for five years because of lack of sufficient European demand for beef. Nevertheless, when in operation these facilities could provide some income for persons in a region where coffee was not cultivable.

A most important source of optimism was government encouragement for the development of new cash crops. Beginning in 1971, the French provided funds to finance five years of experimental agricultural development in nine subdistricts, embracing parts of Sidāmo and Gemu Gofa Provinces. The program, placed under the direction of the Ministry of Community Development, was to begin with a concentration on expanding the production of corn, beans, and sunflower seeds.

Maize was selected for improvement in Āletā through the use of chemical fertilizer and hybrid seeds, because the region was considered to be the most productive for this crop in all Ethiopia. It was hoped that production could be expanded sufficiently to begin export of cornmeal to West African nations. At the same time, it was anticipated that sunflower seeds would be purchased at twenty dollars a quintal (approximately 220 pounds), less the costs of inputs, and were to be prepared for export in an already-existing oil processing plant in Awassa.[58]

In addition, the ministry planners were looking ahead to the development of a glucose factory and to the use of the developing coffee cooperatives to market corn, peppers, and ensete. To implement the program in a region previously without agricultural extension services, the ministry planned to provide sufficient personnel to instruct farmers at the hamlet level in the use of the new hybrid seeds and chemical fertilizers.

In the subdistrict of most intensive field research, there were in 1973 nine young extension agents with formal education ranging from grammar school through the secondary school level. These men had received two months' training in modern farming techniques, the use of the new inputs, and the goals of the project. Interviews with four of them revealed that they were too few to organize or meet in small groups with all the farmers in the subdistrict.

They did, however, manage to have an impact in the three hamlets best known to the author. In this case individual farmers were initially visited by one of the agents, who explained the potential for higher yields if they were willing to try the seeds and chemical fertilizers. Each farmer was expected to make a small deposit for receipt of the inputs and to pay the balance when they harvested and sold their crop. As it happened, only thirteen farmers could be persuaded to try the "miracle" seeds in the first year of the project, but their yields were so remarkable that in the second year fifty-eight men actually sought out the extension agent to obtain these new inputs. The agent was so besieged by requests that he quickly depleted his supply of seeds and fertilizer. As one farmer explained, when fertilizer was applied to šana (a cabbagelike plant), the yield was twice as much as usual, and he was now getting three to four ears of hybrid corn per stalk instead of a single ear. Even the stalks from the hybrid corn made better fuel, because they burned longer than the ordinary stalks.

Still, there were farmers who were unconvinced, fearing, perhaps with more justification than they realized, that once one started to use chemical fertilizers it would be difficult to stop. Others were suspicious of the community development officials, believing that by receiving these inputs they would be giving the government a claim over their land. To men who had learned to fear that any government action might be a threat to their land tenure, it was difficult for the extension agents to provide satisfactory explanations. As to the problem of continuity constraints, it was explained that farmers could stop using the new inputs any time and still increase their production by practicing crop rotation. It was recommended that this be accomplished by growing maize one year and beans with teff the second year.

No one mentioned the dangers of an overemphasis on producing cash crops to the possible detriment of food production. So when this subject was finally broached by the author, it was explained that the area set aside by the average farmer for production of these crops was relatively small and not sufficient to disrupt subsistence production. Moreover, the extension agents argued that rather than marketing the new crops, the farmers could use them as food. This was so for teff and maize, which already formed part of the diets of many Sadāma, but not for sunflower seeds and beans, which were not consumed. The argument had another flaw, however, in that farmers were expected to pay for the hybrid seeds and fertilizers. But even if they had income from coffee, as has been shown, most men had little extra cash for such expenses. As a result, a farmer would likely be forced into selling most of his new crop. Furthermore, gardens were generally small, averaging no more than a quarter of an acre, by the estimate of the community development official in charge of the project. And considering that many men were already seeking to maximize coffee production, it was certainly not self-evident that subsistence food production would not decline, with further pressure to produce a greater variety of cash crops. Nevertheless, the scheme did interest farmers in some regions and led to some impressive results during the first two years. For example, quintals of hybrid maize increased more than fivefold, and the number of participating farmers rose from 165 to 1,034 in the space of a single year.

It is evident that "Green Revolution" inputs for the Sadāma primarily have been directed toward increasing cash cropping, rather than improving the nutrition and health of local peasant farmers, and only incidentally have been intended for use in feeding other parts of the nation. This was suggested indirectly by the director of the project when questioned about what he considered as obstacles to its success. He indicated that land holdings were too small for the application of modern technology; farmers were too easily satisfied, needing to work longer hours to increase their productivity; efficiency was further reduced by the distractions of too many country markets; there was a lack of incentive in areas where tenancy still existed; and too much time and money were wasted in taking land disputes to court. In effect, this list of impediments to the program implies that the goals were set primarily for increases in the scale of efficiency and productivity, with the welfare of the peasant farmer being taken for granted.

There are other change factors affecting the economy, such as the position of youth as producers and the impact of money in destabilizing mutuality. Young people still herd cattle, prepare gardens, and perform various other supportive chores that are crucial to subsistence and cash crop production. But the problems of land shortage, limited opportunities provided by formal education, and few alternative wage-earning activities make their future more tenuous than that of previous generations.

The problem of land shortage within the last three generations is primarily due to increasing population and to the inability to expand into new territory. The population has indeed been increasing, as the 1984 census figures indicate close to a million and a half Sadāma, compared to previous estimates of between half a million and one million persons. Furthermore, old elders were unanimous in their conviction that there has been an increase, and this left some of them in a quandary as to whether there would be enough land for their sons to pass on to their grandchildren. Many realized correctly that this could constitute a threat to the structure of authority, which rests on their allocation of land and the mediation of dispute that may arise from its occupation and use.

Nevertheless, despite this anxiety about overpopulation, opinion was divided as to what, if any, action could be taken to deal with the problem. In 1973 the government had no official policy on population control, though generally the dissemination of information on birth control was discouraged. And locally, as one of the pioneer leaders of the self-help movement suggested, it would be wrong to provide people with modern methods of birth control, since it was a matter better left to the wisdom of the creator.[59] But despite these disclaimers, some in 1973 believed that the time had come to deal with the issue. For example, at the annual meeting of the largest coffee cooperative, the subdistrict governor pointed out to the members that they were not doing enough planning for the future and that overpopulation was one of the most important problems with which they would have to deal.

There were also some men who began to talk about education as a solution. By educating one or more sons, they suggested, it would be possible to resolve the difficulty of allocating scarce land and at the same time add contributions from their children's future earnings to household income. Unfortunately, by the midseventies it had become evident that formal education would not provide a solution to the dilemma of increasing population and limited availability of land.

To understand the shortcomings of reliance on education it is necessary to consider the ambiguity and contradictions involved in goals, costs, and benefits of this form of training.

Formal education was initiated in Sidāmoland by Protestant missionaries following World War II. But by the late 1960s, primary and secondary schooling had been largely taken over by the Ethiopian government.[60] There was then, and continues into the present, considerable enthusiasm on the part of adults and youth about the potential rewards for persons with formal training, especially at the secondary and university levels.

There was, however, ambiguity as to the meaning and goals of education. When questioned on the subject, adults often expressed a vague understanding of the consequences of schooling, mentioning the importance of acquiring knowledge, a guarantee of wage labor, the ability to acquire the power of an administrative official, and a means for helping friends and relatives. As a consequence, educational goals were equally unrealistic and of a long-term nature, involving aspirations for a son or daughter to become a physician, nurse, teacher, or lawyer. Seldom, however, did an informant realize the time and costs involved in attaining these levels of professional competence.

By the 1970s, the costs relative to the benefits had become evident to both adults and young people. For example, a few young household heads who sent most or all of their children to school were finding it difficult, except on the weekends, to leave their cattle and gardens for other activities. Therefore, work such as weeding or housebuilding to raise capital for the new self-help societies to which they belonged had to be relegated to weekends. For many households, however, schooling created even more of a production dilemma, because of costly school fees and the problem of replacing the lost labor of youth. To hire labor only added to the burden of paying school fees, which some men found would not provide sufficient returns from their children's earnings to justify the costs. Only relatively well-off household heads were finding it financially feasible to support their sons through secondary school. And even they were complaining about the long period of school attendance, without any evidence that a son would soon be supporting himself and returning gratuities to the parent.

The youth themselves were upset at this lack of support and were concerned also about their possibilities of future employment. For

they were more aware than their parents of the realities and consequences of the Ethiopian educational system in the midseventies.
They knew that outside of government agencies there had always
been few employment opportunities.[61] But now it had become evident that the government was no longer able to employ even those
who made it to the top of the educational pyramid.[62]

Local wage employment as an alternative was also extremely limited. In addition to the few possibilities of work in the meat-packing
plant or the cannery, there were minor innovative ventures in the
development of wage labor. One involved contract construction of
housing, which began in 1963. This development represented a successful attempt of one entrepreneur to bypass the traditional work
group, which built houses on the basis of reciprocal labor exchange.
In the traditional process the requirements were that the recipient of
the new dwelling feed the fifty or more workers, provide a housewarming feast, and contribute his labor in building houses for others.
By contrast, the contractor would build a house with the aid of four
to eight helpers and, depending on size, for a price ranging from $45
to $145 Ethiopian. The advantages included the savings on the cost
of feeding fifty men for a week to ten days and the availability of the
contractor to build at any season. There were also entrepreneurs who
built in the countryside the popular town house of rectangular frame
construction with a corrugated iron roof. With his two or three helpers, a contractor could build such a house in less than a week and
the owner could finish the work of putting in the windows and
covering the frame with mud daub. These opportunities for wage
labor are limited, however, given the durability of traditional houses,
which last for twenty years or more before being rebuilt. Also, most
people, with their low cash incomes, must continue to rely on reciprocal labor exchange for house building.

Perhaps of greater consequence for mutuality in the future, considering their significant contribution to household production, will be
the impact of the cash economy on women. In 1973 many women
had begun to supplement their traditional trade in foodstuffs by
distilling and selling the liquor arike. Others were engaging in mis-
sion-sponsored rotating credit societies or in learning new techniques
of food preparation and clothing production under the aegis of community development extension agents. And more of their daughters
than ever before were attending the government primary schools.

Many suggested that there had been a small improvement in living
standards, resulting from the ability to acquire manufactured cotton

clothing and the advent of grist mills, which released them from the arduous task of grinding corn by hand. Women in polygynous households complained, however, that unless a husband had an unusually large income, the amount of money for purchasing clothing had to be shared among two or more wives. Nevertheless, despite the sense that they were not receiving as many benefits as men from the cash economy, there was a belief among women informants that at some time in the future their daughters would have more education and would be able to work for wages.

Despite these changes it is important to emphasize the relative stability and continuity of the basic social relations involved in subsistence production. Thus, despite murmurings among elders that they were not receiving the respect of youth that was accorded their fathers, the old men remained predominantly in control of the land. This has helped to preserve the intergenerational reciprocity between self-interest and affiliative obligations discussed earlier. The sexual division of labor in subsistence production is largely unchanged, in the sense that men still prepare the land and women harvest, prepare the food and fertilize the land with sweepings from the cattle pen. Polygyny also continues to be of economic importance to household heads with scattered garden plots. Kinship relationships in general not only have persisted, but as goods and services become increasingly obtainable only on a cash basis, the reliance on relatives is more important in small-scale labor exchanges and reciprocal assistance in providing food for ritual occasions. Clan members still collect money if it is necessary to go to court to protect one's land from expropriation by outsiders.

Indeed, as will be shown in the next chapter, the intensity of kinship bonds constitutes a problem in the formation of self-help societies. And along with the persistence of social relations in subsistence production, the traditional values pertaining to work, achievement, and wealth are merely reinforced by the advent of a cash economy. Therefore, it is now appropriate to consider how the teachings of European missionaries have provided an ideological supplement to this process.

## Proselytism and Changing Beliefs

The evangelical, Protestant form of Christianity, introduced into Sidāmoland after the Second World War, was encouraged by the

Ethiopian government as a means of providing formal education for the youth. By chance, its appearance coincided with the beginning of serious attempts to stimulate coffee production. The missionaries, in stressing certain aspects of secular, Protestant values such as work, saving, and the pursuit of wealth, were supporting values similar to those traditionally held by the Sadāma.

In other respects, however, the new religious order was quite different from the old cosmology of the people. The Christian order is based on universality, while that of the Sadāma is circumscribed by the influence of the spirits of the dead elders within the boundaries of Sidāmoland. As a consequence, the people have always owned allegiance to many deities, compared with the exclusive emphasis of Christians on the Creator and his Son. The Sadāma give priority for individual responsibility to the community, while Christians encourage commitment to God through the guidance of individual conscience. In encouraging the development of these new belief and value orientations, the missionaries were in effect encouraging an ideological incorporation of the Sadāma into the world capitalist system. For these are ideas, taken together with requiring converts to break with their old cosmology, that serve to promote the individualism and competitiveness of the Western economic style of thinking.

Prior to the end of the Second World War, few Sadāma had any direct contact with Christianity. The descendants of Menelik's soldiers and the northern colonists, as mentioned at the beginning of the chapter, had no interest in sharing their religion with those whom they considered their inferiors. After the war, in an effort at national reconciliation, the Ethiopian church began to encourage Ethiopians of all ethnic origins to be baptized and become members. Many Sadāma did in fact go through the baptismal ritual and occasionally attended church, and for a time a few even followed the stringent fasting rules. Most, however, unless they wished to be on good terms with the Amhara, quietly dropped out of the church shortly after baptism. One problem was that the priests made no effort to educate the people in the basic tenets of the faith. As one man explained, "They didn't make clear what it was about, we were only serving them . . . they prayed for themselves and didn't want us to go near the book." A second great difficulty was the fasting, since most Sadāma were unwilling to forgo milk and butter during the two months of the Lenten fast.

Some Protestant missionaries were permitted in Ethiopia before the Italian invasion, despite opposition from the established church. Though proselytizing was supposed to be limited to non-Christian areas, educational activities were both tolerated and encouraged by Haile Selassie.[63] And in the 1920s an organization sponsored by North American evangelical churches, the Sudan Interior Mission, established a hospital in Addis Ababa. In 1928 the emperor gave his permission, conditional upon acceptance of the local governor, for the group to establish a mission station in southern Ethiopia.[64] So at the urging of the governor of Walamo, who was anxious to have a modern medical facility in his district, they were given sufficient land to establish a large mission station. Thus by the time of the Italian occupation, the missionaries had managed to build a primary school and a hospital and had begun to proselytize among the Walamo people.

In the postwar era the Sudan Interior Mission began to expand into Sidāmoland. According to informants, an American missionary and his Walamo assistant appeared for the first time around 1950 in the town of Wando (see map 1).[65] They went from one household to another encouraging the people to accept Christ as their savior and to deny possession and nature spirits. On this latter issue there appears to have been some confusion, as the missionaries translated the Christian concept of Satan by the term *šatāna*, which refers to possession spirits. In reality, then, the Sadāma and the missionaries were talking about two different concepts. The results, however, were fortuitous for proselytizing, as the possibility of renouncing šatāna was a welcome prospect for those persons having difficult and expensive spirits.

For example, in the three research communities ten household heads were questioned in detail regarding their conversion experience. Eight of these men indicated that they had initially been attracted to the new faith by the possibility of controlling the excessive demands for tribute and the ill health associated with most possession spirits. One very dramatic case was that of a woman with a powerful spirit that forbade her husband to eat goat meat or to associate with others partaking of this food. As a result the poor man was in a continuous quandary about his associates, for fear that any mistaken intimacy with goat eaters would lead to serious illness. Several others in the hamlet were afraid of being burdened with spirits, so when they saw their friend and relative embrace the Christian doctrine, largely out of desperation and frustration with the goat restrictions, they waited in fearful anticipation of his demise. When he experienced no ill effects several days after eating goat meat, the others saw that Christianity was indeed a convenient means of ridding themselves of the burdens and fears of spirit possession.

A second inducement to accepting Christianity had to do with the possibility of prospective converts receiving instruction in the mysteries of the Bible. This opportunity was in contrast with the earlier experience of those who had been baptized in the Ethiopian church. Since a convert to this church often assumed that the power of the Amhara was connected with their special relationship with the Creator, it was believed that an understanding of this power was to be found in the book. When the information was not forthcoming, the Sadāma converts believed that there was a conspiracy upon the part of the priests to withhold it from them. On the other hand, the European and American missionaries, who were more powerful than their Ethiopian counterparts, were quite eager to impart their knowledge of the book, even establishing basic literacy training for adults and schools for their children.

A final attraction was the message of the resurrection and the promise of eternal life for those who accepted Christ. This inducement is understandable, given the traditional concern and ritual surrounding death. As one man explained, the customary concepts of life force and afterlife are not nearly as well defined as the Christian concepts of soul and heaven.

Though converts were attracted by new ideas, they organized their small church congregations along traditional lines. By 1965 there were twelve of these churches, each represented by four elders considered by a majority of the members to be noted for their humility, mediating ability, and generosity. These are the same attributes Sadāma have always associated with distinguished old men. These men were expected to make policy at the local level, as well as to admonish and, if necessary, expel those who broke basic rules. These proscriptions included divorce without permission of the elders, committing adultery, drinking alcoholic beverages, and eating the meat of sacrificial animals. Expulsion was the severest of sanctions, utilized when miscreants failed to heed warnings to amend their conduct and were temporarily put out of the church. In this case they were shunned by other Christians, as was the practice with traditionally imposed ostracism, until they begged forgiveness for their misdeed(s) and were readmitted.

Despite the advantages of conversion and the well-structured administration of the churches, there were definite drawbacks to becoming a Christian, which helps to explain why only a minority of the population sought membership.[66] Minority status in itself was a major barrier. In the early period of proselytism, converts were despised and ostracized by the majority, and even in the 1970s many people were of the opinion tht Christianity had brought much dissension to Sidāmoland and posed a threat to the culture. But the specific cultural aspects that all converts admitted to be hindrances to joining and maintaining membership included the rules against polygyny, social drinking, participation in burial and mourning rituals, and feeding the spirit of a dead father.

The taboo on polygyny was especially onerous. As was indicated in an earlier chapter, many household plots, especially in Āletā, are widely scattered. A man without a second wife on a distant plot thus would not only be without her labor, but would as well lack the means for reproducing additional workers to make that land productive.

Furthermore, conflict increased with the late arrival of the Seventh-Day Adventists. Norwegian Lutherans had been present from the beginning, but they were not as aggressive in the pursuit of converts as were the Sudan Interior. And now the very evangelism-oriented Adventist missionaries added to this competitiveness. The new missionaries sought to convince prospective members that they adhered to the true Sabbath. This impressed some informants who were already members of the Sudan Interior Mission, because it was also the practice of the Amhara whose power they continued to grudgingly admire. Sudan Interior missionaries argued in turn that this was merely a ritual matter and had nothing to do with the substance of Christian teachings.

Despite these remonstrances of their teachers, several Sudan Interior converts took the opportunity to establish new Adventist churches on their own land. These actions ensured that they would become leaders and that their households would constitute centers for meetings and social activities, further enhancing prestige. The end result, however, was that the competing denominations simply added another dimension to the already-existing division between traditionalists and Christians.

The new religion broadened the social and conceptual horizons of the participants. Perhaps the most important new concept was that of the universal brotherhood of man. As one of the faithful explained, it had led him to realize that since all mankind were the descendants of a man and woman created by the deity, they must be equals, so even members of the artisan groups and descendants of slaves had to be accepted by him. One man was impressed by the way converts in other ethnic groups, traditionally considered enemies, welcomed him with hospitality and love. In fact, all the new Christians remarked upon how conversion had extended their social relationships. Whereas previous social interaction had been largely limited to the neighborhood, now they associated with other Ethiopians in addition to Europeans and Americans.

In keeping with traditional pragmatism, however, it was noted that the new "spiritual brothers" had a practical as well as ethereal value. As one informant explained, he had been able to stay at the mission compound in Addis Ababa and had received assistance from the resident missionary when he was appealing a land case to the High Court. All agreed that as they became excluded from community activities by traditionalists, they were able to form small work groups with converts from other neighborhoods, which tended to enhance their productivity, especially in preparing land and harvesting coffee. In the next chapter it will be shown how these small work groups became important in the formation of self-help societies.

Throughout the previous chapters there has been an emphasis on individual choice being limited by community responsibility as sanctioned by the living and dead elders. Christianity, however, brought a new dimension of individual responsibility as a matter of conscience, not so much to the community, but to the Supreme Deity. This new concept led to a previously unknown sense of individual and group exclusiveness.

It was a paradoxical development in view of the Christian emphasis on the brotherhood of man. And indeed, some Sadāma recognized the paradox, such as the old church elder who pointed out that because people belonged to different churches, they seemed to love and cooperate less with each other than before the existence of Christian missions. Furthermore, having dedicated their allegiances to the churches, they lost some of their sense of responsibility to the elders and the community. A fundamental part of the problem was that the new morality, based on individual responsibility, was grounded in the principle that only those who believed would be saved and experience eternal life. In the past the elders had always said, in keeping with halōli (the true way of life), that killing, stealing, and lying were wrong, but one could compensate for these offenses by admitting wrongdoing and paying a fine to the elders' council. For a Christian, though, the sanctions were more severe, since the individual had sinned against the Deity and his or her soul would be punished after death. Sadāma have never before been directly responsible to the Creator.

This view of God helps to explain why, in the Christian belief system, serving possession spirits and feeding the spirit of a dead father were wrong, since these actions tended to separate the individual from the one true Deity. It also explains why learning and knowledge were so important to the Protestant missions: to be directly responsible to the Deity implied that it was essential to know in detail the dogma and history of the divine power toward which these obligations were directed. Indeed, the position of the missions on learning and responsibility contrasts with that of the Ethiopian church where, as one informant explained, only the priests had to be knowledgeable as interveners between the laity and God.

Nevertheless, the missionaries were prepared to deal with the imperfectibility of man through a more earthly sanctioning process, in the form of church elders and the confession of wrongdoing in the presence of the congregation. For both Adventists and Sudan Interior churches, public confession took the form of admitting before the assembled congregation that one had engaged in work on the Sabbath, failed to do church work, or offended another church member. And individual responsibility was extended to interpersonal relations, where it had the effect of promoting group exclusiveness. Thus, the new morality limited a convert to one wife and required avoidance of the less pure in heart who ate sacrificial foods and drank alcoholic beverages. Members could be expelled from the congregation if they were reported as having wept at a traditional mourning ritual or as having participated in social drinking with neighbors. For these were activities considered to interfere with true commitment to the Deity or to reduce individual accountability to the point where one might be led to sin by breaking a commandment.

In addition, the Protestant missions required their members to practice varying degrees of marriage endogamy; the Adventists required marriage within the denomination and the Sudan Interior, though less exclusive, restricted connubial union to Protestants. Both groups forbade marriage with members of the Ethiopian church, because the latter permitted the consumption of alcohol.

But it is possible that converts have extended exclusiveness beyond these rules. A woman church member on her way home after a church meeting was asked once if the church prayed for the soul of a member of the hamlet who had died recently. She replied that they prayed only for neighbors who were members of the church.

Ideally, increasing individual responsibility promotes greater social predictability. Thus, abstinence from alcoholic beverages and emphasis on avoidance of gossip and abuse of neighbors help Christian converts develop reputations for dependability and amiableness in their relations with others. Furthermore, Christians were widely believed to be more heavily sanctioned for violating their commandments than were traditionalists for ignoring the customary norms. One consequence was the belief that it was more advantageous to take Christians to court than traditional believers, since Christians would be more strictly enjoined to tell the truth. Also, because Christians could not engage in social activities like drinking and traditional ritual, it was assumed that they devoted more than the average amount of time and energy to productive work in their gardens. Therefore, in keeping with the tenets of their new faith, the converts gradually became stereotyped as peaceful, unusually reliable producers.

Given the emphasis on universality, responsibility, and predictability, it is perhaps not surprising that the missionaries also sought to minimize those traditional beliefs and values that they considered counterproductive to these goals. One such belief concerned the efficacy of clan deities and fathers' spirits as governing the order of the universe. In the opinion of missionaries, this tended to narrow one's interest in the world to his or her immediate social network.

Moreover, if one were self-reliant and responsible only to God, it would no longer be necessary to rely on intermediary spirits such as the dead elders and possession spirits. To cease to believe in these forces implied that it was not necessary to participate in the elaborate rituals of feeding and honoring them. In addition to increasing the spiritual purity of converts, there would also be a great saving in time and resources, which—probably unknown to the missionaries—had great appeal to the pragmatic self-interest of the newly baptized. For most Sadāma, however, the risks and costs of renouncing traditional deities and rituals were too great.

In the international economic system, a toleration for social diversity, dependability, and commitment to work when combined with an eagerness to learn are all attributes conducive to the development of an ideal labor force. Instilling these ideals is as much a matter of harnessing the emotions as the intellect, hence the importance of the religious conversion experience. But the lack of connection that the Sadāma saw between the new faith and their marginal dependence on the cash economy probably explains why only a small minority became converts. Those who did accept the new religion played a significant role in creating self-help societies. Moreover, it is important to note that the convert did not completely break with the traditional, in the sense that the churches remained structured on the authority system of elderhood, and the new individualism could be at least partly reinterpreted to fit the traditional emphasis on pragmatic self-interest.

The presence of Islam as an influence for change is of much greater historical depth than Christianity.[67] For over the last two hundred years, it is likely that trading ventures with Muslims provided many Sadāma with a knowledge of the basic tenets of their faith. It is difficult, however, to know exactly what influence these trade relations had on the economy of the people. But in an ideological sense, Islam which has developed in association with a different economic tradition, has not had the impact of Christianity in laying the foundation for links with world capitalism. Nevertheless, based on such evidence as the increasing production of *čat*,[68] more frequent appearance of Islamic clothing styles, and the building of new mosques and cemeteries, it appears that within the last quarter of a century there has been a substantial increase in Muslim converts.

Because Islam places more emphasis than Christianity on behavior and ritual and less upon dogma, it has been more accommodative of customary beliefs.[69] For example, the conversion process involves minimum stress on verbal persuasion and more involvement with indirect experience like dreaming. Analogous to the appearance of a dead father's spirit, the dream, as several informants explained, involves the appearance of the revered Shakh Husain, who demands that the dreamer embrace the faith or face death. Indeed, Sadāma themselves draw a parallel between their notable ancestors and Islamic saints. The parallel has been so developed in honoring Abo, the famous apical ancestor of the Holō clan, that the Muslims have built a small mosque near his grave site.

Also, somewhat like the "true way of life" principles that must in specific instances be interpreted by the consensual agreement of the elders' council, so must the Koran continuously be interpreted by Islamic lawyers, scholars, and saints to fit changing situations. The interpretation must always be made on the basis of an acceptance of what is understood to be community consensus.

Then there are conditional vows, like the previously discussed concept of tāno, in which Islamic saints, instead of notable apical clan ancestors, are honored with rich gifts in return for their blessings in the form of progeny or renewed health and well-being. Furthermore, Muslim healers are available to drive out those possession spirits that hosts find difficult to accommodate.

Unlike Christians, the Islamic converts have not gained access through conversion to secular education or been subjected to religious instruction by foreigners. But like Christianity, acceptance of Islam has been a popular means of ridding one's family of possession spirits. Otherwise, Sadāma have embraced the faith as a result of the previously mentioned dream visitations by Shakh Husain, often after a severe illness, or by conversion through friends or relatives.

Despite the lack of secular advantages of conversion to Islam, there are also none of the disadvantages accruing to those who join the Christian community. There is not, for example, the exclusiveness of Christianity; neither are there the elaborate ritual and ideological taboos that have made the Christian dogma so difficult for many Sadāma. Polygyny and most customary rituals are acceptable to Muslims. There are as well the advantages to conversion mentioned for Christianity, such as instruction in the sacred book, salvation and eternal life, and direct association with a powerful deity. Consequently, this helps to explain why most informants were of the opinion that both Christian and Muslim converts are increasing in number, but it is difficult to say that one religion is gaining more adherents than the other.

Finally, though Islam has not provided ideological support for international capitalism, it has indirectly contributed to the developing cash economy through the ritual use of čat. By the mid-1970s a number of farmers were beginning to realize a substantial portion of their income from the production of this plant near market towns like Yirgā Alēm; one farmer known to the author for instance, in one year realized an income of five hundred dollars from its production and trade.

## Discussion   *Sidame*

At first glance, one has the impression that the Ethiopian conquest of the 1890s simply provided the Sadāma with a form of colonialism. Certainly there are some resemblances to the European type of colonial experience undergone by many other African peoples. There was, for example, the appropriation of labor and tribute through the gabbar system, indirect rule through government-appointed balabats, appropriation of surplus value by landlords in some areas of Sidāmoland, the later imposition of land taxes, and the recent exploitation of coffee marketing by northern merchants.

Nevertheless, there were many differences from European-imposed colonialism. For instance, there was no plantation system sponsored by foreign corporations, for which the colonial authorities encouraged the development of cheap labor through the imposition of high taxes or enforced recruitment.[70] Nor were there European settlers with large estates, who sought to utilize African communities as reserves for cheap labor by preventing the people from growing their own cash crops. Furthermore, there was no encouragement of migratory labor to work in the mines, as in central Africa. Hence there were none of the consequences of an undermanned subsistence sector that also constituted a last resort for those too old or ill to continue work in the mining compounds.[71] But more important, in all these forms of colonial experience there was a direct link through the corporate structure, the administrative bureaucracy, or the settler population with the metropole and the market system of international capitalism.

Colonialism experienced by the Sadāma, with the exception of the short Italian interregnum, was imposed by other Ethiopians, until recently with no connections with international capitalism. There has been no migratory labor with a subsequent impoverishment of the household and neighborhood modes of production. With the exception of a few large absentee landlords in the Hadičō clan area, there have been no great settler estates, nor have there been any foreign plantation enterprises. Moreover, the stigmatized Amhara were by no means ethnically homogeneous, as tended to be the case of the European colonists, who exercised juridical-political control. For although 65 percent of the northern settlers and soldiers were from Shoa Province, they included large numbers of Gurage and Oromo as well as Amhara.[72] Rather than providing a homogeneous ruling class, the results were a loose patron-client system that led to the corruption of some traditional leaders. This patron-client structure that prevailed throughout prerevolutionary Ethiopia permitted so great a personal appropriation of resources that the state functioned through inefficient, decentralized, indirect rule, despite the aims of Haile Selassie to create a centralized polity. The inefficiency of the state actually favored the Sadāma in supporting the retention of their social structure and traditional belief system.

This historical analysis of change indicates that it has been largely connected with the economic base. The cash cropping of coffee has provided a new mode of production, in which Sadāma have rearranged their allocation of time, labor, and use of land. Men have begun to change their aspirations for material well-being and the futures of their sons. Women also have acquired new goals, which may ultimately lead to change in the division of labor.

The cash economy has led to a contradiction in the juridical-political sphere in the form of chiefs as personalized ritual-mediators becoming simultaneously impersonal government administrators. This is seen most directly in their desire to appropriate land and accept money for the performance of duties. Government courts have, in the view of the Sadāma, become like a marketplace in which justice can be bought and sold. Even elders' councils have been affected, as men have become concerned more with increasing their incomes than with taking time to settle disputes and establish consensual public policy.

Ideological transformations have occurred in consonance with the economic and juridical-political. Thus Christian missionaries have encouraged the development of Western standards of exclusiveness, individualism, and the work ethic. The introduction by the missions of formal education laid the groundwork for government-financed education, stressing occupational goals in the wage sector. And Islam, while more accommodative than Christianity of traditional beliefs and practices, encourages unity through universal brotherhood. Muslims have also been instrumental in expanding the cash cropping of čat for ritual activities.

Reproduction as it pertains to increasing population and a concomitant shortage of land is also an area of significant change. Census data now, in comparison with previous estimates, show a population increase, and there is no question about the reality of this problem in the minds of people. It is this developing problem of imbalance between land and population that many thought might be resolved through their sons' acquiring formal education and their subsequent entry into the wage sector. By the mid-1970s, however, after at least part of a generation had experienced education, there was no significant change. Like cash cropping, wage labor had merely been added on, articulated neither with the old domestic mode of production nor with a new system. Jobs in government or the private sector remained minimal and did not resolve the problem of population growth and land scarcity.

Nevertheless, the two traditional modes of production have remained surprisingly buoyant. The survival of the people remains contingent upon domestic subsistence production and neighborhood cooperation in maintaining community communications, water resources, housing, and rituals. Cash cropping, rather than distorting these functions, has simply been added to them.

Several reasons have been given for the durability of the traditional modes of production, including the relatively small amount of land that can be committed to coffee without curtailing subsistence production, the small percentage of expenditures devoted to food purchases, the fact that indebtedness is related mainly to protecting the land and increasing the herd, reluctance to risk leaving the land and community social network to engage in marketing coffee, and continuity of a labor system based on kinship ties. Moreover, people are even cautious about committing themselves to the "Green Revolution," for fear they will not be able to meet the costs of inputs and lose their land. Nor are they eager to increase productivity by working longer hours and giving up traditional social activities such as visiting and frequent trips to market.

Elders' councils continue to make local policy and settle disputes. This is partially for lack of government resources to control the countryside and partially because the elders are less expensive and more efficient than government courts in settling disputes. Also, while bribery and corruption eased the problems of a resource-deficient central government in compensating local officials, it reduced credibility and made customary institutions of social control seem superior by comparison.

Cash cropping in coffee has provided an indirect link to the market system of world capitalism. As such, it might be anticipated that producing and marketing this commodity could lead to differences in wealth and class divisions among the people. Class conflict is often offered as an explanation for changes in the modes of production and forms of social control.[73] Specifically, this conflict is usually associated with how capitalism transforms precapitalist systems by separating producers from the means of production, increasing dependency on capital expansion, and changing subsistence producers into wage laborers.[74]

The Sadāma have traditionally had an equalitarian social structure that enhanced the ease of movement between clans according to economic self-interest. Their mixed economy of ensete and cattle has necessitated both individualism and cooperation. In the past there were only differences in rank based on purity, prestige, and, in the case of the artisan groups, restrictions on marriage. Men of wealth have always been greatly admired and respected, but they cannot be considered as a separate class, if this categorization is taken to mean a group possessing separate organization in opposition to others and a sense of self-consciousness.[75] Moreover, there is no indication that the small number of Sadāma coffee merchants have set themselves apart or acquired the role of a broker class between peasants and the Amhara.

There is also a problem as to whether the diversity of ethnic groups constituting the descendants of Menelik's soldiers and northern colonists can be defined as a class. Furthermore, it will be recalled that there was a difference in interests between those who acquired land in return for government service and those who had come as colonialists and made their way largely through participation in mercantile ventures. Several Ethiopianist scholars suggest that persons in these ethnic groups, rather than being organized horizontally into classes, as individuals have articulated vertically in a patron-client structure.[76] Nor did this amorphous grouping of merchants, administrators, and landowners succeed in separating the Sadāma from their land and cattle, force them into dependency on cash cropping, or provide them with wage alternatives.

Even if one uses criteria for indicating the existence of social classes from other parts of Africa, such as entrepreneurship, education, and political leadership, it is not clear whether these groups constituted social classes or simply hostile ethnic groups.[77] Certainly the successful merchants and some of the landlords and government office holders managed to accumulate enough capital for investment in houses, shops, and land, which gave them a different life-style from the Sadāma. But entrepreneurial activities in the small towns were often quite competitive, so that risks were great and individuals could gain and lose fortunes in the space of a generation. Consequently, there were Amhara small holders in the countryside whose standard for living was little different from that of neighboring Sadāma. Lacking information it is difficult to know whether the children of well-to-do merchants succeeded in receiving more and better education than the children of peasants. It is reasonable to assume, however, given the conservative inclinations of their fathers, that in lieu of formal education many remained on the land or served a long apprenticeship in the family business. At least some would have received advanced education and become part of the national bourgeoisie.

As to political leadership, other than in the courts and lower echelons of the subdistrict administration, it is difficult to conceive of the Amhara as influencing, leading, or making available important information for the Sadāma.[78] The latter simply distrusted and avoided the former, except when it was necessary to defend against encroachment on their land or to use the court system to individual advantage. These outsiders as individuals often had vast economic and administrative advantage over the Sadāma, but whether they were consciously united in opposition to them remains uncertain.

It has been shown that historically many of these northerners considered the Sadāma their inferiors, refusing to intermarry or to accept them in the Ethiopian church. Nevertheless, those whose fortunes have declined have intermarried and lived in peasant communities. And since the end of World War II, there has been some willingness to encourage Sadāma to become Ethiopian Christians. The Sadāma, however, whether poor, wealthy, powerful, or powerless, continue to stigmatize the northern outsider as the Amhara enemy.

Thus it becomes difficult to distinguish between class conflict and ethnic animosity. Indeed, as one recent writer on the subject has suggested, it is often impossible to disentangle class from ethnic conflict in Ethiopia.[79] Ethnicity may come to the fore in certain situations, but at other times social class will be used to express the antagonisms leading to change. Certainly, as will be shown in the next chapter, the Amhara opposed in varying ways the establishment of self-help societies, and, by doing so, helped to promote commitment and loyalty among the members.

Finally there is the question of whether the exclusiveness of those who became mission converts justifies considering them a de facto class. But even though they became a divisive force in Sidāmoland, these converts did not purposely organize themselves in opposition to the majority. They were themselves divided denominationally, rather than working together as a single Christian group. Also, Muslim converts never sought to separate themselves from most of the rituals, activities, and beliefs of the majority. Nonetheless, the external influence of the missionaries, though it did not lead to the formation of conflicting classes, unintentionally provided the people with a new form of cooperative self-help for coping with the cash economy and the failure to develop wage labor. The emergence, form, and dynamics of these groups gave the Sadāma a new mode of production, as well as a means for participating in the change process.

9              Self-Help
Associations for Change

First Member: "Why not let the
people establish any
shop they want in
the community?"
Second Member: "If we do that, we
lose the association."

This quotation from an ongoing dialogue between two members of a new self-help society is a fitting way to begin this chapter on the organization of people to participate in the change process. It reflects the recurring theme throughout the book concerning the balancing of self-interest with community obligation. Since this issue has been so important in the past, it is perhaps not surprising that it continues to be crucial to the maintenance of social predictability in voluntary associations coping with change. The chapter begins with a discussion of the origins of the self-help movement, followed by an examination of the organization and recruitment of members, the reinterpretation of traditional authority and methods of social control, the influence of the central government, and the limits of self-help as a process.

The term "voluntary association" is widely used in the anthropological literature, but there has been considerable debate regarding its definition. At issue is the meaning of volition, which tends to be a relative matter, since so many different types of organizations are more or less voluntary. As a consequence, several anthropologists have preferred the term "common interest association."[1] Such an organization is based neither on kinship nor on "political geographical" considerations; recruitment generally is based upon achieved rather than ascribed status.[2] On the other hand, it has been argued that these organizations are really "contract associations."[3] They are volitional only to the extent of the making of the contract, but once it is made, the rights and duties entailed supersede the volition. Nevertheless, it is a form of "commonweal" contract agreed to by members as a means to achieving ends that they deem beneficial.

In regard to the Sadāma, the initial stages of formation of self-help

183

societies by groups of friends were voluntary, but as they developed, the groups became formalized and were indeed contract associations. It is important, as will be demonstrated, to recognize that status in these societies was based upon membership rather than kinship.

## Origins

To begin with, these associations have their roots in the problems connected with coffee harvesting and in the exclusiveness of religious converts. Coffee must be picked with care, for to damage the stem reduces the yield. Therefore, it is necessary to have from six to a dozen trustworthy men working together consistently for the two to four days it requires to harvest the crop of the average farmer. Consistency is important, for once the harvesting season begins, as mentioned in chapter 5, it is necessary to proceed expeditiously in order to avoid the dangers of sudden hailstorms and petty pilfering by women and children. In this situation the traditional work group of a few close agnates is too small, while the neighborhood work group is much too large for the efficient harvesting of a small garden crop.

It was the chance convergence of religious proselytizing, the emergence of coffee as a source of income, and government interest in decentralizing coffee production after the Second World War that provided the Sadāma a solution to the problem of efficient harvesting. Thus converts, having excluded themselves from many traditional community activities and arousing the antagonism of the majority, began to act on their new sense of universalism by gathering with Christian "friends" from differing neighborhoods and hamlets to perform work activities. The emphasis on friendship and love is important for understanding the efficiency of these new work groups. Traditional neighborhood work groups were not only cumbersome for small-scale work activities but notable for time-consuming bickering over work procedures. By contrast, the work procedures observed by the author of the small Christian groups were much more harmonious. Kinship-based work groups (*dī-yi*), in addition to being too small, were composed of persons obligated by agnatic or marital ties to assist one another. Since this assistance can be taken for granted, it not only created problems in forming associations, as will become evident in the next section, but it was often rendered unenthusiastically. Consequently, the small work groups of religious converts set a precedent for labor exchange based on friendship rather than kinship or community obligation. And as traditionalists began to see that nine to twenty Christians working together had developed groups for expeditiously harvesting coffee, they sought to form their own or to work with those already in operation.

But there was more to these groups. In addition to mutual exchange of labor, the members dealt with the problems of cash needs by developing a rotating credit procedure.[4] In small groups of eight or nine men, the procedure was to work together two days a week in preparing, weeding, or harvesting a garden. And in larger groups of seventeen to twenty, the usual agreement was to exchange labor reciprocally every two to three weeks. Then on designated work days they would agree to contribute fifty cents or one dollar, which would constitute a common fund to be rotated among the members. A man receiving the fund would be ineligible to participate again until other members had received their share. The cash windfall provided a member with a considerable advantage in overcoming indebtedness or in fulfilling immediate cash obligations, such as taxes or purchasing clothing for his wives and children. So it was that in time these small societies gradually acquired the designation *mahabar,* an Amharic term for groups connected with the Ethiopian church having religious and friendship functions.

It will be recalled from the previous chapter that in the 1950s coffee marketing board personnel concluded that it would be difficult to market coffee successfully without local-level organizations that could provide farmers with technical knowledge and bargaining power with local merchants. A move in this direction began in 1957 with the establishment of the Ministry of National Community Development, consisting of departments for community development, cooperatives, social welfare, and labor.

The objectives of the departments of community development and cooperatives are of especial interest. In the case of the former it was to "intensify social participation on a self-help basis in development projects, promote social reform, assist settlement and development of nomadic peoples and extend the services of many civic, social, health, educational and agricultural institutions to areas undertaken for development."[5] Clearly there are two aspects of emphasis in this statement, including participation through self-help and the role of ministry personnel as resource persons coordinating the services of various social and economic agencies. In the establishment of cooperatives, the ministry recognized that there were many traditional institutions of cooperation, but these lacked facilities to provide credit, services, and equipment needed for productive purposes.[6] Nevertheless, concrete goals for the establishment of cooperatives were not prepared until the Second Five-Year Program—1962–67. The objectives were modest, involving the creation of twenty cooperatives, training personnel to staff the cooperative department, the promulgation of cooperative legislation, and the provision of capital for providing loans to farmers. A limited program was perhaps fortuitous, however, given the failure of massive cooperative movements in other African countries during the 1960s. The government frankly admitted to a lack of trained personnel, limited investment capital, and any previous experience with the cooperative movement.

Therefore a short program for training 150 community development workers was established at Awassa, and legislation was passed in 1960 setting out principles for organizing cooperatives.[7] The guidelines included such provisions as the requirement of a minimum number of ten persons to form a primary society, the principle of one member-one vote, provision for supervision and audit by community development workers, and, most important, the settlement of disputes through arbitration without interference from the civil courts. Further, it was agreed that the new ministry would make use of the atbia, the most basic unit of government jurisdiction.[8] Previously the atbia, under the jurisdiction of a koro, had been used only as a tax-collecting unit and for dispute settlement through the rural court, but now it was to serve as the organizing base for large-scale development projects such as schools, community assembly halls, and road building. Thus the government began to move toward encouraging the self-help movement just as the Sadāma were beginning to develop small societies for efficiently harvesting their coffee.

In 1962 a group of friends under the leadership of an Adventist elder first came into contact with the new ministry. Later as an organized development society they were to become an important demonstration center for community development. Their leader Wiko saw a film made by the ministry on cooperative work groups and talked with others in his church society about the possibility of organizing a self-help society. They invited interested persons in three adjoining neighborhoods to join and soon had forty members, with mixed religious loyalties. To raise capital for supporting their enterprise they went periodically to a nearby government farm in

Awassa to weed sunflowers, eventually accumulating five hundred dollars.

In like manner all of the six government-registered societies observed by the author in 1973 began as church groups and gradually developed into self-help organizations.[9] These six societies had all become registered by 1966. Indeed, through church connections, three of these organizations first heard about the self-help principles from Wiko and his group, with his becoming a model for their own operations. Members of the other two societies first learned of the potential for formal organization in 1965 from a recently elected member of the national parliament. He told them that if they acquired some capital on their own, they could obtain loans from the government. They would then be spared the 100 percent interest rates charged by local merchants and also could obtain government recognition through registration. Further, he verified what many already suspected, namely, that they were receiving only about 25 percent of the real market value for their coffee by dealing with the local middlemen merchants. This encouraged them to think in terms of eventually acquiring their own drying sheds, decorticating mill, and a truck to transport their coffee directly to Addis Ababa.

It is important to note that the church groups as mutual aid societies, other than developing rotating credit systems, had not made any previous attempts at raising capital or obtaining loans to finance their marketing or development interests. As events transpired, however, the acquisition and allocation of funds had important implications for recruiting and maintaining members. In the beginning, the reputation that Protestant converts had acquired for fidelity and trustworthiness attracted many non-Christians. Moreover, with an increased emphasis on seeking capital funds, the religious orientation of the societies declined. In one instance this alienated a Sudan Interior missionary, who believed the capital accumulation function to be antithetical to the religious nature of the groups. The members of the society, however, felt the missionary was afraid they were becoming too independent of the mission by acquiring their own capital. In any event, members in all but one of the six societies raised their initial capital by preparing gardens, weeding, and building houses. In their neighborhoods they began to displace Gurage wage labor in gardening activities, usually charging Gurage rates to non-members and half rates for members.

Furthermore, members of the mahabar (the term of reference for these groups by the late 1960s) had varying goals in these fund-raising activities. For three of the societies the initial interest was in finding a more effective, profitable means for marketing their coffee; one group was primarily committed to rural development in the form of providing feeder roads, a grist mill, and a cooperative store; and members of two societies hoped to develop small towns that would cooperatively provide amenities to all residents. The members and leaders did not at first realize that the financing process and the goals themselves might be contradictory within the organizational framework of a single society. As will be shown later, however, there were indeed contradictions that did create organizational problems for some of the societies.

## Organization and Recruitment

As numbers increased and capital accumulated, the societies sought recognition from the government in order to become eligible for loans and for technical and political assistance. By 1973, five of the six societies registered with the government reached a level of membership averaging (mean) 45.4, as compared with 17.8 for four that were not recognized by the Ministry of Community Development.[10] To register it was necessary to elect an executive committee of nine and from them to choose a president, vice president, treasurer, and secretary.[11] The government established few rules for registration other than the requirement of the committee, accumulation of a small amount of capital, and enough members to aid in the acquisition of the capital. Hence there was variation among societies in such matters as meeting times, capital investment goals, and means of social control. For example, in 1973 only two of the six held regularly scheduled meetings for all members, and four held executive committee sessions at regular intervals.

As previously noted, only one of the mahabar did not utilize collective labor to develop an initial fund of capital. Once established, however, the five societies in the coffee-producing zone tended to rely more on the profits from marketing this commodity than on work projects. The sixth society was outside the coffee area and came to rely primarily on the profits from a successful grist mill and a retail store.[12] All required members to purchase a share, but two permitted the purchase of a cheaper, nonvoting share. These shares ranged in price from $2.50 up to $100, with two mahabar having increased the share price over the years as more persons sought to join. In only one instance was there a provision for paying shares out of capital funds for potential members without funds.

All accepted the principle of vesting decision-making and dispute-settlement authority in the executive committee, but only four societies had put the principle into practice. Furthermore, there was variation, poorly understood by most people in the countryside, in terms applied to various type societies. Though all persons had come to refer to the groups as mahabar, government agencies such as community development utilized Amharic adjectival terms to designate functional differences. These included *hibret* for cooperative ventures in retail merchandising and trade, and *gaberuč* for produce-marketing cooperatives. The term *ediguet* was used to refer to development societies. People usually interpreted development to mean the improvement of living standards in regard to housing, diet, farming techniques, education, and sanitation. So, according to the previously summarized goals, the members of some societies had opted for an emphasis on development, while in others the goals were marketing or the establishment of towns. That a mahabar could possibly engage in all three activities, but with modification of organizational articulations vis-à-vis other groups, had not been made clear to the Sadāma. This qualification was important in its implication for allocating funding and responsibilities.

Successful recruitment and maintenance of membership in a voluntary association is dependent upon the commitment of the individual. Erasmus has suggested that commitment is based on self-interest, frequency of membership interaction, sharing of common goals, and the renown of the organization.[13] Certainly in the early stages of the mahabar movement, the collective work projects for obtaining capital provided opportunities for assembling and working together at least once a week. In coffee areas all men could agree upon the goal of circumventing the middlemen merchants to get a higher price for their coffee. Moreover, all shared the basic belief that money was the equalizer that would enable them to achieve the age-old goal of wealth. Much of the awareness of wealth potential could be attributed to completion of an all-weather road for transporting coffee out of the region, for it was largely due to this road that the

Sadāma gained access to manufactured consumer goods upon which individuals could expend some of their income for the new wealth symbols.

There were also things of collective interest, such as the grist mills for easing the food preparation burden of women, communal water supplies, health clinics, feeder roads to link with the all-weather road, and schools. All of these facilities were considered desirable and accessible with the development of a cash economy. A form of organization was needed to make these shared goals possible, and because the mahabar seemed to fill that need, it was widely acclaimed.

Satisfaction of self-interest was more complex, however, since it involved varying interpretations of cost/benefit estimates. As shown in previous chapters, this is a factor of considerable historical depth, related, for example, to the pursuit of individual gain by the mythical heroes and the customary pragmatic approach of the individual Sadānčo to trade and land acquisition, as well as to spiritual beliefs and ritual. Thus it is not surprising that mahabar members provided similar responses when questioned about work projects and goals. They invariably pointed out that Sadāma were individualistic in their commitment to land and property, though willing to cooperate in community endeavors. Considering that the six societies required on the average an initial outlay of twenty-eight dollars to acquire a full share, it is evident that the original members had considerable respect for the credibility of the self-help movement.[14] Part of this enthusiasm may have been related to the anticipation of future monetary dividends from the original investment. And yet the leaders of only two of the six societies expressed hopes of being able to accumulate a sufficient surplus of funds to provide such dividends. Nevertheless, by the late 1960s there were certain tangible signs of attaining goals, such as the presence of cooperative stores, the acquisition of land for building public facilities, and the evidence in some areas that members were actually getting a better price from the mahabar for their coffee.

Furthermore, the importance of tangible rewards can be seen from the reasons given for loss of members. In general, people dropped out because of poor management of funds, excessive costs of memberships, lack of tangible benefits, and inadequate coffee prices. There were complaints in one instance that the children of nonmembers were attending a school built with labor and funds provided by members. A further problem with financial administration was a lack of understanding and mistrust of the banking system. Some persons feared that the society would not be able to regain deposited funds or that the money would be taken by the government. In one case, members quit because they claimed there was an excessive use of fines for absence from work parties, which made participation too expensive.

Committeemen admitted that failure to provide immediate rewards (like low-interest loans) and too much emphasis on long-term capital development (such as buildings and water supply systems) had discouraged some members. In fact, much of the recruiting success of one society was attributed to providing interest-free loans. But by 1973 only two of the six societies were actually providing loans.

Also, coffee marketing through the mahabar provided an uncertain advantage for some members. An advantage existed for those with small amounts of coffee who were in need of immediate cash, for they could sell soon after harvest to the mahabar and have this income supplemented from profits, minus service charges, when the society sold later at higher seasonal prices. But farmers with large coffee harvests, hence less in need of immediate cash, could be at a disadvantage in marketing through the mahabar. These men could hold their coffee for the seasonal price high, avoid the cooperative service charge, and make a greater profit by selling to the Amhara merchants. Those that gave up their membership for this reason, however, ignored the competitive advantage provided by the society in forcing the merchants to pay a higher price.

Under the circumstances, it is perhaps not surprising that altruism and personal dedication were of little relevance in the recruiting process. And, in fact, only one society attempted to obtain members with professed beliefs in self-help ideals and willingness to work.

Still, in the late sixties and early seventies there was an almost contagious enthusiasm and belief that the self-help movement would change the quality of life. Much of this euphoria must be attributed to the dedicated visionaries who became leaders of the six registered societies. All of these men were mission converts who brought to the self-help movement the same evangelistic spirit they had found in Christianity. By taking on the new beliefs and breaking with tradition, they had shown themselves to be innovative and willing to take risks.

Their persistence in the faith, despite persecution and a degree of exclusion from the community, provided them with reputations for integrity.

Four of the six leaders were unusual for men of their age in having attained two or more years of primary schooling. Though starting as leaders of small Christian societies, they gradually encouraged non-Christians to join, realizing the limitations of exclusiveness in labor-intensive projects and in efforts at capital accumulation. Their church ties were useful in establishing social and communication networks between distant societies, which provided opportunities for keeping up with organizational changes, obtaining assistance in resolving problems, and establishing goals. The dedication of these men helped instill enthusiasm in members to remain loyal in the early stages of organization, when the societies were threatened by merchants and lower-echelon government officials fearful of the potential power of the movement. Their initial integrity was important in holding together a membership that joined the mahabar largely for reasons of self-interest.[15]

For all but one of the societies, opposition from outside interest groups provided a means for creating membership unity as formal organization proceeded. This external resistance came from merchants, residents of an administrative town and, in at least one instance, a Protestant mission.

The leaders of three of the mahabar were confronted by middlemen coffee merchants with accusations ranging from unauthorized building of feeder roads to treason. For example, the executive committee of one society was accused before the district governor by representatives of the Wando Share Capital Association of building an unauthorized feeder road to supply their cooperative store.[16] The store constituted a threat to the merchants' retail activities as well as presaged the possible development of a coffee-marketing facility independent of their control. Even the provincial governor was eventually brought into the dispute and ordered the arrest of the executive committee members. At this point, others from the society went to the community development officials in Awassa, who returned with them, looked over their work, and went immediately to the provincial governor. They informed him that the project was well within the limited goals established by the ministry. In the end, the minister of community development came from Addis Ababa to negotiate a settlement. Nevertheless, the merchants continued to harass the society long after the store was well established, in 1972 going so far as to accuse the members of collecting money to purchase arms for a rebellion.

When another mahabar began to build a store, the same merchants took its executive committee to court, claiming the establishment of a rural retail outlet was tantamount to a boycott of the Wando stores. These charges were in turn dismissed for lack of evidence by the subdistrict court.

Another tactic was to attack the leadership of the five registered societies in the district by spreading rumors and maligning their integrity. In the case of one of the leading and most successful society presidents, the approach was to persuade a European missionary to denounce the man as attempting to collect money to promote his own fortunes, rather than working for the people. When the disparaged leader brought suit for defamation of character, the court found in his favor and issued a general edict ordering the missionary to stop vilifying Ethiopian people and their customs. After this failure, the Amhara shopkeepers accused the man before the subdistrict governor of attempting to arouse the people of the countryside against the government. Then, following several years of claims and counter-claims by the merchants and the mahabar president, and as the popularity and support for the self-help movement increased, the governor sided with the president.

So bitter was the opposition of the merchants that the Minister of Community Development decided on the ploy of trying to bring these urban and rural protagonists together in one society, believing that working together toward a common goal would overcome their differences. Toward that end he encouraged the members of the merchants' association to form a mahabar and to join the five rural societies in the Wando Gaberuč Mahabar for the cooperative marketing of coffee. To provide working capital the merchants contributed eleven thousand dollars and the four rural societies ten thousand dollars.

Nevertheless, the majority of rural members elected as president of this cooperative union the very leader the merchants had sought to discredit, and they chose one of the leading merchants treasurer. It was a clever but naive compromise, for the townsmen then sought to undermine the cooperative by spreading rumors among the peasant farmers that the organization was useless and that they could get a better price for their coffee by selling to individual coffee dealers.

Even more damaging was the failure of many members of the old share capital association to sell their coffee through the cooperative. This reduced profits and increased overhead costs for members supporting the new marketing society. The strategy of the Amhara to destroy the rural cooperatives, however, had an effect opposite from what was anticipated. A few of the members dropped out, but many indicated that these actions only strengthened their resolve to support their president and the union.

Another form of opposition was provided by the merchants and bureaucrats of an administrative town well removed from the north-south highway bisecting Sidāmoland. They were fearful of replacement by a mahabar that had begun establishing a new town along the highway and that by 1973 had acquired a population of three hundred persons. As in the case of the Wando merchants, their efforts to stop the development by disparaging the leadership and threatening the members with various legal maneuverings were frustrated by agencies of the central government. When it started, for example, the new mahabar received money from UNICEF and assistance for building houses and stores from the building college, a branch of the national university. Even Emperor Haile Selassie visited the site and so approved of the efforts of the leadership and the members that he personally named the town. As the society president explained, however, it would not have been possible to hold the members together without opposition from the bureaucracy and the mercantile interests in the established administrative center.

If external opposition was a means for encouraging unity, it was evident that attempts to form societies with closely related kin had the opposite effect.[17] It has been suggested that modern forms of cooperation require "institutionalized suspicion" in order to control the potential for corruption and to ensure equitable decision making by those in authority.[18] Where personal bonds of trust take the place of impersonal rules, members find it difficult to accept procedures such as auditing, since the connotation of suspicion threatens the mutual trust that is the hallmark of kinship bonds. If equality and efficiency are to be maintained, members should show a certain amount of skepticism about the performances of one another and especially of the executive committee personnel.

In the case of the Sadāma, an informant pondering the cause of mahabar failures pointed out to the author the problem of trying to organize closely related kin. He quoted an old proverb: *Fā-tōnu gūsso ad jis hōw-lo* ("a relative is like a small cloak"). A broader interpretation is "relatives always make a person seem less important than do nonrelatives." This has to do with mutuality between close relatives being a form of "generalized reciprocity," in which individuals are not specific about the nature or timing of the exchange but are always obligated.[19]

This is the form of reciprocity described in previous chapters regarding cooperation between agnatic kin and between in-laws, in production and ritual activities such as mourning and elderhood promotion. By comparison, mutuality based on self-interest is more in keeping with short-term reciprocities, involving skepticism about the motives and actions of others, in addition to greater interpersonal respect. The traditional precedent for this form of exchange has been the role of the stranger in acquiring land in a new clan area through formal agreement and various arrangements for obtaining and maintaining personal control of property.

Though people do become suspicious of relatives and engage in disputes with them over property, such quarrels are in violation of the norms of altruism that should govern mutuality between kin. Altercations occur because the generational and birth-order differences provide for a certain amount of structural inequality, leading to a competition and rivalry among siblings that is used to support the authority system. To overcome this built-in rivalry and inequality, the prescribed respect and amity among close relatives make it possible to take for granted their minimum assistance when called upon. Such inequality, ambivalence, and delayed response, however, is inimical to the establishment of voluntary associations, whose members are seeking to maximize the equality and efficiency of mutuality.

Informants in all the mahabar in the study agreed that it was difficult, if not impossible, to organize societies with close relatives, and some could point out specific failures where the principle of membership heterogeneity had been ignored. For example, in one neighborhood there were five small societies that had not been registered because the closely related relatives were said to have spent too much time arguing over, rather than completing, work assignments to raise capital. By contrast, one of the best-organized societies was composed of members from two different clans who were always competing to outdo each other in raising money, providing more laborers, and doing more work.

Furthermore, closely related kin were usually most effective in small group situations, while established associations had to rely upon larger numbers for the labor-intensive projects that provided the initial source of capital. The obligation to perform in such work groups could not be postponed without sanction, which contrasted with the situation among close relatives, where obligations tended to be long term and prescribed amity made it difficult to evoke punitive sanctions.

Thus the early stages of the organization of the self-help movement have shown the importance for effective organization of kinship diversity, unity through opposition, and dynamic leadership. These principles have parallels to development activities in other parts of Africa.[20] For example, Teso cooperatives in Uganda have sought to avoid conflict between fathers and sons by not recruiting closely related kinsmen.[21] Leaders of a small Bukusu clan in western Kenya endeavored to establish a transport system as a financial benefit to all of their relatives.[22] When arguments developed over the distribution of profits, however, the whole scheme collapsed amid the animosity and ill feelings created among close relatives. In Niger members of self-help societies organized on the basis of age similarity were found to work together more effectively than those established on the basis of kinship.[23] In the Cameroons the failure of a cooperative credit association consisting of closely related kin was attributed largely to the inability of members to participate on an equalitarian basis and to compete for leadership positions, because of the norms requiring deference and respect for age.[24]

The importance of external opposition in generating membership solidarity has been demonstrated in Kenya. Here the establishment of a high rate of participation in rural self-help societies has been attributed to resentment of the failure of national political leaders to meet expectations for a higher material standard of living.[25] In western Kenya it has been noted that the caliber of leadership and participation in Bukusu cooperatives began to decline as people felt less threatened by Asian traders.[26] Moreover, such opposition to Asian commercial dominance was an important factor in the formation of Ugandan cooperatives.[27] And in Tanzania the founders of a small cooperative community were able to promote enthusiasm for joining by stressing their "modern" antitribalism and nationalistic loyalties. This contrasted with the emphasis of surrounding communities on ethnic homogeneity and provincialism.[28]

A plethora of material is also available on the organizational significance of leadership. In Tanzania a Sukuma cotton cooperative was established by men who were intercultural in experience and outlook.[29] Success of their leadership contrasted with the failure, in the same area, of cattle and fishing cooperatives formed by men lacking the ability to reinterpret external ideas and technology to fit the local situation. Also, leadership in the formation of cooperative societies in Uganda was provided by men with considerable intercultural experience, such as Protestant evangelists, sons of chiefs, or men of wealth.[30] Liberian associations have chosen their leaders on the basis of exceptional mediatory abilities, oratorical skills, and the holding of high status in other groups.[31] In like manner, Malian cooperative founders have been noted for their ability as intermediaries between villagers and the government, and they have possessed relatively high degrees of literacy.[32]

## Authority and Controls

Social predictability in small groups is generally contingent upon acquaintance with other persons, procedures for cooperation, ability to influence the performance of others, and third-person control when exchange relations break down.[33] In effect a major problem for small voluntary associations is control of the so-called free rider. As mahabar increased in size, being composed of persons who joined primarily in hopes of improving personal living standards, then personal acquaintance became less effective than third-person control.

The ideal approach was for the members of executive committees to reinterpret the old values and expectations of elderhood authority in mediating conflicts and establishing precedents for new norms of mutuality. And in essence the executive committee became an elders' council, often being referred to by this term, since the members followed similar procedures and utilized the sanctions of fines and exclusion. Nevertheless, there were differences, such as committee authority not being based on halōli ("the true way of life") or connections with the deities. Also nonelders as well as elders served as full-fledged decision makers.

In the survey area, three of the six registered societies held regularly scheduled meetings for resolving disputes and making policy. A fourth had been following a similar procedure until koros and judges, fearful of a loss of fees, managed to convince the local subdistrict governor to ban their meetings. This opposition was justified on the grounds that the committeemen were attempting to function as a court of law. But at the time of field research the committee was seeking to have this order nullified by obtaining a permit from the Ministry of Community Development.

So important was this form of third-person control that a prerequisite for membership in three of the societies was an agreement to bring all disputes before the committee. Only if the committee was unable to effect a resolution was it permissible to take the case to court. As there was near unanimity about the validity of this approach, members of a fifth society were planning to institute this requirement, and the sixth mahabar, which had started primarily as a coffee-marketing cooperative, was expecting to follow suit as soon as the members shifted their organizational emphasis to community development.

Over a period of several months in 1973, it was possible to observe executive committees of two of the societies settling disputes and making policy. In the process rules were being evolved for balancing the goals of individual aim with group responsibility. Just as in an elders' council, members of the society other than those on the executive committee could, if they preferred, join in the proceedings. Indeed, of fourteen cases brought before the two committees, eleven pertained to the establishment of community norms resulting from disputes between individual members. Three disputes involving slander, household boundaries, and access to land were of the type brought before an ordinary council.[34] Delicts pertaining to the establishment of new norms could be grouped into four categories: issues of planning and management, health and safety matters, problems of taxation, and trade. The following examples will show some of the issues and consequences following from the resolution of these cases.

One dispute pertaining to zoning rules and two regarding the building of feeder roads had to do with community planning done by executive committees and approved by the general membership. There was a situation, for example, in which surveyors' stakes had been removed from a proposed feeder road. This involved an old man Kadella (a pseudonym), who had been requested to appear before the committee. Kadella admitted that he had in fact pulled the stakes in protest, because he felt that the committee was taking too much of his land. He indicated a willingness to apologize for his actions, but he insisted that the layout of the road was not as originally approved by the society members.

For his actions some wanted to impose a heavy fine. But others argued that it was his first offense and that he was an old man who had always supported the society. It was finally agreed to impose only a small fine. To this decision Kadella assented, though he continued to insist they were taking too much of his land and none from his neighbors. Consequently, the committeemen agreed to send three members to look once again at the boundaries and see if they had been unfair in establishing the dimensions of the road.

Kadella had pulled up the stakes to draw the attention of the committee to what he considered to be a personal injustice. In effect, he was arguing that such unfairness could not be part of any plan approved by the mahabar. The committeemen in return were indicating that individual members could not interpret plans for their own benefit. Nevertheless, they were always prepared to reexamine initial decisions in order to avoid any injustice to the individual. The proceedings in the case were orchestrated in the manner of a traditional elders' council, in terms of a seemingly acrimonious debate followed by a consensual agreement and a concern for lightening the sanction of a person who admitted his wrongdoing.

A second planning case involved a zoning issue in which one man complained to the committee that another had extended his house into an area intended as a public road. This created uncertainty about the complainant's property rights. Once again the solution of the committee was to adhere to the outline of the plan in maintaining the dimensions of the proposed roadway, but they provided the complainant the option of building on a lot reduced in size or selecting another building site.

A third case involved the responsibility of the individual member to keep abreast of association plans and activities. The defendant had plowed under road survey stakes, claiming he had not understood the purpose of the markers. When he admitted his error, the committee reduced his fine to a token, with the admonishment that ignorance of association plans and rules was no excuse.

The most interesting of four cases involving health and safety issues concerned a dispute regarding neglect of duty. As background it is necessary to know that the association in question contained members from three different hamlets, the boundaries of which overlapped in a newly established mahabar community. Each of these hamlets had numerous members of the society, so a man designated by the traditional title of morīča (work leader) had been assigned by the committee to administer security functions in each area. It was his responsibility to assign members to protect the households, community shops, and other facilities from theft during the hours of darkness. For example, in hamlet A when all the members had taken a turn at guard duty, the morīča was to inform his counterpart in hamlet B who was in charge of making assignments, and so on, until all in C had taken a turn and responsibility reverted once again to A.

The case itself resulted from the theft of a small amount of the cash crop čat from a field that was ready for harvest. In the course of the committee's discussion of the deed, it was established that the guard had been absent from his post on the evening of the theft. It was indicated that the guards whose turn it was for duty would be responsible for locating the stolen čat. And the one missing from his post should be punished for negligence if in fact the field was within his jurisdiction.

In defense, the absent guard Bogalli maintained that he had not been formally notified that it was his turn for duty. Furthermore, he explained that he had quarreled with several persons in the hamlet to which he was assigned and was afraid he might be attacked while on duty.

Some committeemen argued that fear of assault was a sufficient excuse for neglecting the duty; others thought that the only issue was irresponsibility in protecting members' property; and a third group thought the committee should more specifically delimit the area and require Bogalli to assume his duties. After much heated debate, a consensus was reached that the reluctant guard should be fined and required to assume his duties. So Bogalli was fined and told that unless he went to his guard post he would lose his financial share and his membership in the society. Nevertheless, he maintained that he was still afraid and asked for time to consider the alternatives.

The committeemen also considered the responsibility of the work leader for assignments and for making sure that guards attended to their duties. It surfaced that the work leaders had quarreled among themselves as to whose turn it was to provide security. Then, following a lengthy discussion, it was agreed that a leader had the responsibility to take on security duty when requested, even though he did not believe it was the turn of his group. It was inexcusable to leave the property unguarded. And if he believed that his men had been unjustly treated, the work leader should have brought the matter to the attention of the committee.

In the end both men paid their fines and were excused by the committee. The case provided an interesting example of agreement on the general principles of security but uncertainty about the specifics of jurisdictional limits and what was to happen when the sequence of responsibility broke down. Limits of responsibility were clarified by the committeemen in the dialogue with the reluctant guard and his work leader. Also, the case established the precedent that, regardless of personal conflicts and animosities, guard duty could not be neglected if it was to retain membership in the association. Furthermore, responsibility for continuity of security was to take precedence over any personal belief in the inequity of the sequence.

There were three other cases involving the balancing of self-interest with community obligation: one concerning the butchering of animals, another involving the closing time of bars, and another dealing with a case of physical assault. In one of the communities the committee had initially set aside a butchering place somewhat removed from the marketing area. This was done to minimize the stench and the dangers from potential disease carried by swarms of flies. As the area was inconvenient to the butchers, they began to slaughter behind their shops in the midst of the marketplace. People complained, and the butchers were summoned before the mahabar committee. One butcher admitted that he had found it expedient to slaughter behind his shop, but he apologized and, as usual, asked to be excused from paying a fine. The committeemen, however, were angry with the man for this blatant violation of the rules and fined him ten dollars. A second butcher claimed he was unaware of the violation, which he attributed to his employees. The committeemen pointed out that employers were responsible for the actions of their employees and fined him also ten dollars.

In regard to the drinking establishment, the committee had established a rule for closing at sundown on market days so as to limit excessive drinking, which often led to violence. Over a period of time it had become evident that the proprietors, eager to maximize their profits, continued to dispense drinks long after sundown on market days. When the matter was brought to the attention of the committee, some wanted to fine all of the owners, though after much discussion it was agreed to temper this suggestion with an initial warning to obey the rules.

The physical assault dispute was considered to be a more serious matter. It involved the woman owner of a bar who accused a young man of attacking her with a knife during an argument over an unpaid bill. In the discussion of the case, it developed that the defendant had previously made a written agreement to stay out of the plaintiff's establishment. Now she wished the committeemen to see that the agreement was enforced, as well as to require the young man to compensate her for a hand injury. Several witnesses indicated that they had observed the defendant use a knife to cut the woman's hand during the altercation over the bill. Nevertheless the young man, who had been in trouble many times before, protested that the woman and the witnesses were lying and that she had cut her hand accidentally. In private, the committeemen complained that this young defendant was always in trouble and some thought he should be excluded from the community. Others argued that at nineteen or so he was too young for such drastic action and that the committee instead should seek to discover the reasons for his continual mischievousness. Consequently, three members were appointed to look into the matter and report back to the committee.

The three cases thus provide further illustration of the ability of the executive committee to perform as a council of elders in establishing precedent-setting rules of behavior. It was decided that responsibility for community health and well-being took precedence over individual convenience and profit. Also, violence should be minimized to protect the community, even when leading to a reduction of profits and to intolerance of youthful exuberance.

Two tax cases involved disputes between individuals rather than between members and the committee. One of these might best be called the case of the responsible taxpayer. This dispute involved a man who had transferred title to land occupied by a tenant. Neither the new owner nor the tenant had paid the money for the land tax. Indeed, the new owner argued that since he had not yet taken possession of the land, he should not be liable for the tax.

As in most disputes the committeemen were divided in their opinions as to who was responsible; some insisted the original owner should pay, others suggested that this was unfair because the tenant was using the land, and a third group even felt the matter was outside the jurisdiction of the society. But after much argument it was agreed that the committee did have jurisdiction and that the new owner was responsible for the tax. He was told, however, that there was nothing to prevent his getting the tax from the tenant.

The other tax case involved an old man who complained he was being forced to pay land tax to two different balačika. When these two were called before the committee to answer the accusation, they each claimed that the old man was living in their respective collection areas. Under questioning it became apparent that they were both seeking to maximize their tax collecting, because of difficulties with people resisting payment. The complainant, having little understanding of the tax system, had fallen prey to the demands of both collectors. Four committeemen were assigned to establish a dividing line that would ensure that the old man paid only one tax.

In both tax cases there was an attempt to resolve some of the ambiguities of an old tax system that had never been legally or administratively well defined, hence the necessity of defining jurisdiction over a household that had not been clearly allocated to one area or another. There was also the problem of uncertainty about the tax responsibility of buyers and sellers for land occupied by a third party. These were matters that the government might have been expected to resolve. In effect, the committee was ruling that the power of official status could not be used at the expense of those who lacked such status. The latter were as much members of the community as tax collectors, and they could not be exploited just because of their ignorance or certain ambiguities of residence. Nor, as in the land transfer case, could an individual ignore his responsibilities to another member of the community and to the state in receiving transfer of land, simply because he was not using the land.

Finally, there were two cases dealing with trading rules. One involved a problem of fair price, based on seasonal differences in the price of corn, and the inability to resolve amicably an altercation between two close relatives. It began when Sukari accused Banda of reneging on a promise to repay a debt consisting of a sack of corn. Banda admitted his failure to meet the obligation but claimed that he had been the victim of a very poor harvest. Moreover, he thought it was unfair of Sukari, a paternal cousin, to accuse a close relative.

Banda rejected the initial admonition of the committeemen to repay his obligation immediately. So Sukari became angry and accused him of hoarding corn in anticipation of a higher market price. Nevertheless, the committeemen were reluctant to continue the case, believing it should be mediated by Banda's father. But the father indicated that he had tried and failed to settle the matter. Furthermore, he suggested that if they delayed a settlement much longer, the harvest would soon take place, and the bag of corn would be worth only half of what it had been when the loan was made. The committeemen, however, ignored this issue of price fluctuation and suggested that since Banda was without corn, he should repay his debt with a single sack after the coming harvest. It was a solution that Sukari could not accept.

There was also controversy with regard to a second case in which a complainant purchased land from another man, only to find later that part of his land was to be used as a road. The buyer argued that he should have received additional land to compensate for this loss. After much discussion the committee was unable to reach a consensus and asked the community development worker to break the deadlock. This he did by indicating that the seller should be required to provide the buyer with the amount of land originally agreed upon. Though this was not agreeable to the seller, both parties finally accepted a compromise put by the committee to change the dimensions of the roadway.

Perhaps the difficulty in resolving these cases was related to the fact that, unlike problems of community organization and taxation, these were matters affecting individual control over cash or land. In the case of the unpaid obligation, the sentiments of the committee were divided between the traditional values of generosity and the individualistic utilitarianism of the marketplace. In the end they took the position that customary generosity between relatives should apply to association members and should take precedence over individual profit taking. The unacceptability of the decision may be indicative of the impact of cash economy values upon the kinship amity principle.

There was also the problem of defining the rights of a buyer in regard to the intrusions of the community in reducing the amount of a land purchase. Even though it was necessary to bring in an outside arbiter when the members failed to reach a consensus, the solution involved a return to the traditional form of compromise, favorable to both parties, by changing the dimensions of the road. Finally, it is important to note that, when needed, the committee had no hesitation in calling upon the government worker to resolve a contentious issue.

In summary, a consideration of the planning disputes shows the disputants accepting the recommendation of the committee to sacrifice individual preferences for maximizing convenience and control of property, so that others may with greater ease come together to work and trade. Much the same was true of the health and safety cases, where the protection of the community was given precedence over accessibility of work facilities, the profitable trade in liquor, personal reluctance to participate in society affairs, and the waywardness of youth. Also, one of the tax cases shows the responsibility of the individual for his obligations to the government. More important, in the other case there is indication of a concern to provide justice at the local level in rectifying the negligence and inefficiency of government representatives. Finally, the old contradiction between the pursuit of wealth and the requirements for generosity was a factor in the trade disputes. Moreover, compromise was shown to be of continuing importance when two men cannot agree over rights in amount or access to property.

The executive committees thus provide the juridical-political controls for insuring cooperation in the self-help societies. The operations of these committees show a continuity for the respect of authority associated with the ideology of elderhood and the functioning of elders' councils. In the process of decision making and dispute settlement, there are many indications of an ongoing concern for the attributes of halōli, such as mutuality, fairness, generosity, and consensual compromise. It is as if there has been a reinterpretation of the authority and labor of the elders and youth in maintaining cooperation within and between communities. The meaning is similar, but the form has changed from the elders' councils and the generational class system to the executive committee and society members.

As was done for the association attributes of kinship, leadership, and solidarity, it is now possible to assess the role of juridical-political controls in the wider African context. Unfortunately, much less information is available on this subject, inasmuch as there has been little opportunity in most areas to develop it at the local level. In Kenya, for example, a government-imposed arbitration system for cooperatives was found to involve procedures that were too lengthy and cumbersome, and it discouraged dispute settlement within the societies.[35] Among successful coffee and cotton cooperatives in Tanzania, however, there has been some use of community elders in settling disputes and imposing sanctions.[36] And leaders of the Banyang clan societies in the Cameroons have also used their positions to conciliate disputes and have counseled members to avoid the courts.[37]

## Government Influence

I now consider in detail the role of the Ministry of Community Development, mentioned at the beginning of the chapter, as the principal government agency contributing to the emergence of the self-help movement. This will be done by examining how the role of the community development worker articulates with the society, the atbia (lowest government unit of 130 gaša), and the subdistrict levels of administration.

Given the relatively small number of workers, it was not possible to assign more than one or two to a subdistrict. Ideally he or she was assigned to a district with ten atbia and a population of at least twenty thousand.[38] The worker served as executive secretary of a subdistrict development committee chaired by the governor, which was responsible for coordinating all development activities within this administrative area. The Āletā Wando subdistrict provides a good example of the composition of such a committee around 1973. Committee members consisted of the following:

two school principals,
subdistrict health worker,
regional coffee board inspector,
community development worker as secretary,
top-ranking police officer,
subdistrict corn project worker,
two representatives from each atbia development committee,
the koro of each atbia,
the subdistrict governor as chairman.

As was pointed out by the executive secretary of the committee, not all of these members were favorably disposed toward development projects. The most enthusiastic were generally the professional development workers and many of the representatives from atbia committees. Despite opposition, however, there had been a number of successful projects over a period of four or five years. Among them he listed the construction of three elementary schools, three assembly halls, literacy training for one thousand adults, clubs established for juveniles, road construction, initiation of a women's welfare department, and construction of water systems in several communities.

At an intervening administrative level between the subdistrict and the mahabar, the 130-gaša unit known as the atbia (approximately 1,100 acres) was most important, since all adults eighteen and older residing in the area were supposed to provide labor and funds for major development projects. This was also the territorial unit most involved in coordinating the activities of the various societies. In fact, it was the members of the societies, rather than the general adult population, who spearheaded most development activities. For instance, one of the most highly organized atbia in the research area had ten registered societies with three hundred listed members. These members had contributed over one thousand dollars from various work activities on atbia projects and in 1972, in an effort to improve sanitation, constructed more than two hundred toilet and garbage pits.

In terms of organization, atbia committees were usually composed of representatives from each society, a small group of elected members, as well as the koro, who acted as head of the committee. The organization and productivity of these groups was uneven, however, considering that in some subdistricts there were as many as thirteen atbia (1,690 gaša) for one worker to organize, in addition to administrative duties with the societies and the subdistrict committee. There were also district and provincial development committees for coordinating activities at the subdistrict level, so as to conform with regional and national planning. Fortunately, the overtaxed community development workers were not involved in these activities.

As one young worker explained, his role was primarily to establish rapport with the local people. It was essential to demonstrate that as government representatives they were present to help people plan and realize goals that had been established locally, rather than to impose government-made plans and development targets. The people were to help themselves in planning and bringing about desirable changes, with community development officials providing expertise in making available whatever resources the government could provide. This was more than mere rhetoric, as indicated by the fact that society members were not personally threatened by the presence of these government-paid development workers.

The following example of an altercation between executive committee members and a worker is illustrative of the point. It took place within the context of the weekly meeting of the committee, when several members expressed dissatisfaction with the cooperative store accounts, which had just been presented by Kebede,[39] the community development worker. Their concern was based on a belief that he had not given a reliable report of the inventory and sales income to the newly elected treasurer.

Though Kebede insisted he had given full information to the new treasurer, several members expressed skepticism, claiming that all of this material should have been presented to the committee by the newly elected official, not by him. Kebede then tried to change the subject by indicating he had just forwarded the new annual plan for society projects to the subdistrict governor. But this ploy only served to outrage several committeemen, for they insisted that he had exceeded his authority by not obtaining prior approval of the committee. To this admonition he could only apologize and point out, justifiably, that he was responsible for such a large area that he could not always be available to consult with them. Nevertheless, the vicepresident reminded him that the first matter for future consideration would not be the plan, but a presentation before the committee by himself and the new treasurer of all the society accounts.

The case indicates the negligence of the worker in following society rules for transferring funds and records after a change in treasurers. He also failed to keep the committee fully informed about the operation of society enterprises. This may be due to the previously mentioned problem of being responsible for too many societies in too large an area. But regardless of whether his failures were due to intentional neglect or inability to cope with the work load, it is evident that the committeemen were dissatisfied with his performance and would not hesitate, if matters did not improve, to petition the Ministry of Community Development for his removal. In the meantime they were likely to observe his work with caution and skepticism.

Despite widespread community acceptance, there were clearly certain shortcomings to the role of the development worker as a change agent. They were expected to act as catalysts in the development process, providing technical assistance to people who were organizing themselves at their own pace and according to their willingness to accept change. Ideally, the worker was to have been available as a resource person when the membership of the society had exhausted their knowledge and skills in trying to resolve a problem. As indicated, however, development workers were often too widely scattered and the demands upon their time too great for them to perform this function effectively.

**Table 5.** Location and Dispersal of Community Development
Workers in Five Subdistricts

| Location | Number of Atbia | Subdistrict Workers | |
|---|---|---|---|
| | | Male | Female |
| Dalli | 12 | 2 | 1 |
| Wando (Āletā) | 13 | 1 | 1 |
| Agherasalam | 9 | 1 | 0 |
| Bensa | 10 | 1 | 0 |
| Hārbigōnā | 3 | 1 | 0 |

*Note:* Subdistricts are composed of atbia,
units of approximately 1,100 acres.
*Source:* Author

Table 5 shows the distribution of workers in five subdistricts. Though in several instances the ratio specified by the Ministry of Community Development (one worker to ten atbia) is close to being achieved, the population density was often much higher than twenty thousand per worker. For example, forty thousand persons were in the Āletā Wando subdistrict. And even though there were a man and a woman worker assigned to the district, the work burden of the former was much greater than that of the latter, given the limited organization and involvement of women. Indeed, informants often complained that they had not seen the development worker in their atbia for several months. The problem of contact frequency was often further complicated by the isolation and limited access to many atbia, especially during the rainy season.

Another difficulty was that the supportive role of a development worker, rather than encouraging self-help, could occasionally lead to dependency. One ministry administrator expressed concern that too often projects worked well as long as the worker was present, but that in his or her absence the people did nothing. Perhaps this was not so much reflection of dependency as an indication of overassertiveness on the part of individual workers in developing projects that were not of interest to the people. Nevertheless, the opinion of informants was nearly unanimous that most workers managed a balance between providing assistance upon request and encouraging, rather than imposing, the general development goals of the government.

Still, by 1973 there were indications of certain ambiguities in the government intervention process, which will be discussed in the following section.

## Limitations

Though dynamic leadership, kinship heterogeneity, cohesion promoted by hostile external groups, and social control through reinterpretation of the traditional authority structure have all helped in the establishment of these societies, there have also been limiting factors. These impediments to organization concern techno-ecological problems, individual as opposed to cooperative ideals, and the contradictions of certain forms of government intervention.

There was a lack of knowledge about appropriate technology for various types of work and about the operational limits of machines. For example, in two societies the grist mills were continually subject to prolonged breakdowns. In one instance the problem was traceable to the attachment of an oversized motor to an inappropriately small mill. Both mills were being inadequately maintained, in addition to being rapidly worn out from continuous running at high speed. This problem was due to the demand of women who had come long distances with grain and who were anxious to get home, as well as to the concern to increase profits by grinding a maximum amount of grain in as short a time as possible. Another techno-ecological problem was coffee berry disease, which destroyed the berry but not the plant. Since the estimated spraying cost of four hundred dollars an acre was prohibitive, government plant scientists were attempting to breed rust-resistant plants, a long-term process that left many farmers wondering if there would be any future in growing coffee.

A limiting factor has been the individualistic commitment to tangible short-term gain as opposed to the cooperative endeavor of prolonged labor and investment in projects that may benefit the individual only indirectly. Some of this could be attributed to a lack of understanding, such as the widespread fear that money deposited in the bank by a treasurer could be taken for personal use or could be confiscated by the government. This difficulty was overcome in one society by having three men in charge of finances: one who collected the money, another who was in charge of petty cash disbursement, and a third who kept the records.

Long-term capital accumulation for future investment in the building of public facilities, pulping and drying mills, and motor trucks was for some members too distant and intangible. Many preferred tangible, quick returns associated with such personal items as a house with a galvanized metal roof or high yields resulting from hybrid seeds and chemical fertilizers. And, in a sense, the establishment of cooperative or independent retail shops in the countryside, meant to provide people with more time for productive labor by eliminating long treks to distant towns and markets, actually encouraged spending for immediate gratification. In fact, the prospect for quick and high returns from retail shops became so attractive in one society that the competition from member entrepreneurs led to the bankruptcy of the cooperative store. In other societies, however, the executive committees strictly limited the number and type of shops permitted to compete with the cooperative store. A further handicap in coffee-producing areas was the difficulty of convincing members of the necessity for paying out of their coffee receipts the various overhead costs for maintenance, accounting, and the servicing of loans. This was no minor problem, considering that independent coffee merchants either had lower overhead costs or were willing to cut profits to compete with the associations.

Repayment of loans was another troublesome problem. After two years, the one coffee cooperative providing a sizable number of low-interest loans was refused continuance of the loan program by the bank because a large percentage of borrowers had failed to make any effort at repayment. Though this delinquency was partially attributable to crop failure and a misunderstanding of repayment procedures, funds were used inappropriately, and some borrowers believed it would be possible to avoid repayment. To overcome this latter difficulty, a subcommittee of the executive committee was proposed to evaluate the ability of all prospective borrowers to repay their loans and to impress upon them that failure in the repayment process could result in the forfeiture of their land to the banks.

Finally, though the government had been generally supportive, certain traditional administrative practices and contradictions of organization worked to the detriment of the self-help movement. As noted in the previous chapter, the central government, dominated by Haile Selassie, was committed to the practice of balancing one administrative branch against the other to prevent any potential threat to the power of the emperor. Thus, while the government ostensibly

supported the Ministry of Community Development efforts to promote and maintain the self-help movement, it also continued to
bolster those elements of local administration who were opposed to
the policies of the ministry, namely, posts often held by descendants
of the northern colonists and Menelik's soldiers.

As an example, money was often collected within the various
subdistricts for specific development projects such as roads, schools,
or dispensaries. According to law, the money should all have been
spent for these projects, within the subdistrict in which it was collected, but the district governor in Yirgā Alēm often ignored the law
by refusing to authorize expenditure of such funds. It was estimated
that as much as $200,000 in subdistrict development assessments
had accumulated in the district treasury. A widespread belief developed among the farmers that, with the exception of a few inexpensive
show projects (for example, a road to nowhere in Yirgā Alēm and a
bandstand for official ceremonies), most of the money had been appropriated by high-ranking members of the district administration.
Though a willingness of the central government to tolerate this violation of the law was contradictory to their expressed commitment
to rural development, it limited the enhancement of power and popularity of community development officials by preventing them from
distributing large sums of money for desirable projects in the
countryside.

The organization of atbia as development units also tended to
conflict with support for the self-help societies. As an indication of
this problem, several informants suggested that self-help societies
had not gotten started in their area because many people thought it
unnecessary to go through the wearisome task of organization. They
believed that the government, through the atbia, would do it for them.
While this particular opinion may indicate lassitude as much as
discouragement, members of one of the most highly organized societies complained that atbia and subdistrict assessments of money and
labor weakened the self-help movement. Furthermore, it was objected
that directions for subdistrict projects were often formulated in Addis
Ababa, without consultation at the local level.

## Appraisal and Comparison

The importance of leadership, social solidarity, and kinship heterogeneity in the organization of rural populations for change has

been recognized throughout Africa. Why then have these organizations generally been failures?[40]

It is true that techno-ecological problems, self-aggrandizement, and corruption have everywhere been problems.[41] Nevertheless, technological obstacles can often be overcome by applying machinery and tools appropriate to the available skills, environment, and financial resources of the people. Self-aggrandizement and corruption, as has been demonstrated by the Sadāma, can be controlled at the local level. This has been amply illustrated by the role of the executive committees, reinterpreted from the traditional elders' councils, as consensual decision-making and dispute-settlement bodies. There is very little evidence for use of this principle of decentralized decision making from other parts of Africa; instead, there has been reliance on control from the top down. This may help to explain why so many development projects have ended in failure.

A number of analysts have demonstrated that in many new African nations small-scale associations, ostensibly created for bringing about rural social and economic change, have in reality been imposed by governments to extract a surplus from the peasantry.[42] Government-imposed schemes for cooperative development in rural Niger provide a notable example.[43] Publicly the government espoused an "animation" program, in which rural development of Hausa communities was to come from the local rather than national level, through a dialogue between peasants and administrators. From the beginning, however, there was a contradiction in the assumption that Hausa attitudes had to be changed from "traditional" and "fatalistic" to "modern," while simultaneously assuming that the old social system had all the elements of cooperation necessary to bring about change. But by the 1970s this dialogue had become minimal, and the strategy, according to the field worker, had become one of increasing the influence of the state in rural areas by inducing peasants to finance their own development, ensuring repayment of government loans, providing a marketing monopoly for the cash crop of peasants, improving the system for collecting taxes, and employing a burgeoning bureaucracy of development agents.

In many of the attempts at changing rural African societies, it has been assumed that this can be accomplished only through agents of the state and expatriate professionals, with peasants being treated as obstacles to "transformation" and "improvement."[44] Following independence, much the same thing happened in Senegal, with the imposition of cooperatives by a national bureaucracy bent on establishing political hegemony in rural areas through control of marketing procedures.[45] Other than administrators, the only people to benefit from this system were wealthy peasants and local notables.

Elsewhere, the famous ujamaa villages of Tanzania were established on the model of a successful voluntary self-help endeavor of the 1960s.[46] These villages were meant to transform rural Tanzania into a nation of productive, self-reliant communities. The scheme failed, largely as a result of government-imposed policies. The initial 1973 guidelines for organization stressed local control; people were to participate in the development and implementing of plans for change. Instead, when matters did not proceed according to schedule, the government resorted to bureaucratic rules and controls. When peasants did not resist this scheme of imposed village living, it was largely because they hoped to gain access to better land, favorable credit terms, machinery, schools, and other services. Indeed, farmers often found the new communities too far removed from the land they had hoped to obtain. Among the Nyamwize, for example, people resented the extra burden of walking the long way to their fields, feared that it would be difficult to control insect pests at a distance, disliked having to carry harvests great distances to storage centers, and dreaded the health hazards of living in compact settlements.[47]

Almost everywhere in Africa those who have achieved the most from these imposed systems of change have been the more powerful members of communities, who, because of their wealth and influence, are often sought out by government officials as "successful" farmers.[48] As a consequence, they have gained favored access to loans and agricultural inputs from external agencies.

These examples from other parts of Africa contrast with the experience of the Sadāma. Grass roots social control has been based on a reinterpretation of the consensual authority of the elders' councils to fit the deliberative process of the associations. The people themselves are quite aware that old forms of communal cooperation were seldom based upon altruism but required the authority of the elders to ensure that all persons contributed their labor.

In this connection it is interesting to note that during the period of field research, only one instance of self-enrichment at the expense of the organization came to the attention of the author. The president and founder of a successful society attempted to make an agreement to share the profits of the small health clinic with the pharmacist. The latter also agreed, apparently unwillingly, to employ the president's son. When other members of the executive committee heard rumors of the affair, they called both men and asked for an explanation. The president refused to answer questions and subsequently withdrew from society affairs. Consequently, the vice-president assumed all leadership functions and it was confidently anticipated the president would lose his position in the next election.

In the development of the self-help movement among the Sadāma, it is evident that the people were the beneficiaries of historical accident. They experienced the elaboration of a sequence of unforeseen events giving rise to a new direction in the change process.[49] This is not to imply, however, that a sequence of causation cannot be traced to explain what happened after the occurrence of the events.

The convergence of the international coffee market with a feudal central government and religious proselytization were historically unpredictable, seemingly unrelated events that in retrospect can be shown as analytically related to one another and that had an effect on the emergence of the associations. As I noted in the previous chapter, Protestant missionaries were initially permitted to proselytize by an impoverished government, as a means of providing educational and health benefits for the rural population. Religious conversion of a small minority ultimately led to the inculcation of new ideals about universality, responsibility, and work consistency, all part of the ethic of Western capitalism. The rejection of many traditional beliefs and rituals by these converts alienated them from the majority, forcing them to develop their own work societies.

Meanwhile, in the 1950s National Coffee Board administrators began to see a need for cooperatives to improve maketing efficiency. This came at a time when farmers had begun to supplement subsistence farming by cultivating coffee. As farmers in areas conducive to coffee production began to utilize more of their land for this purpose, they began to purchase small amounts of food from areas where coffee could not be grown. In this way they generated cash income for farmers outside the coffee-growing zone. And finally, in the late 1950s, the government decided to embark upon a program to encourage rural development through self-help, by creating the Ministry of Community Development.

In sequence it is difficult to see any planned connection between these five factors. Retrospectively, however, there is a surprising interdependence in the formation of a capitalistic labor ethic for an alienated minority who had to organize their own work groups, ultimately establishing marketing cooperatives deemed necessary by the coffee board, and supported by a government agency seeking to further modernization.

It is not intended to infer that, as in other parts of Africa, the central government would not have preferred to use the self-help societies to extend political controls and appropriate more of production in support of a nascent national bureaucracy. Nevertheless, there had been no experience with colonial capitalism that could have led to development of a hierarchy of exploitative classes. Instead there was a semifeudal, patron-client system that resulted in the fragmentary nature of the Ethiopian polity described in the previous chapter. In return for the opportunity to exploit the local peoples economically, the government had initially relied on the original invaders and their descendants for protection against European colonial encroachment. Only after the Second World War was a national constitution and an administrative facade provided by the state. But the lower echelons of this administration were often staffed by the very northerners the Sadāma had come to stigmatize as the Amhara conquerors.

Despite these trappings of modern government, authority remained personalized on a patron-client basis. The emperor at the top of the pyramid was able to maintain a precarious balance of power by favoring first high-ranking patrons on one side, then their counterparts on the other, in a triangular arrangement of fragmentary opposing forces. These latter forces consisted of loose coalitions of clans or self-help societies, administrative leaders and their factions, as well as merchant-landowners and their clients. With the exception of a few corrupt koro and mote/balabats, there was no emergence of an indigenous bourgeoisie to act as intermediaries between the mass of the peasants and the administrators, or merchant/landholding Amhara. Indeed, these corrupt officials tended to be despised by most Sadāma and identified with the government.

Consequently, people continued to rely on the traditional authority system, using government institutions only in situations likely to promote individual advantage. By the late 1960s the national ministries for community development and agriculture were staffed with young technocrats who were strongly committed to rural development. This provided another option for the Sadāma in protecting their interests vis-à-vis local government officials and merchants. As has been shown, the society leaders sought assistance from community development officials in overcoming resistance of local government administrators to the dispute-settlement and policy-making functions of the executive committees.

The Sadāma did not have a truly colonial experience. Indeed, historical accident, in terms of the sequence of events and structural changes linking the peasantry to the state and international capitalism, has been more favorable to them than peasantries subjected to colonialism in other African nations. The people have had the opportunity to develop, rather than have imposed upon them, their own societies for bringing about change. What of the future for the self-help movement and the implications of these people's experience for other African and Third World nations in general? This issue of participation and decentralized controls will be discussed in the next chapter.

10          Theories of
Development and the
Future of the
Self-Help Movement

In chapter 8 we examined the historical process of contact between
the Sadāma, the state, and the international cash economy. Then in
the previous chapter the response of the people in forming self-help
societies was shown to have resulted in a new form of cooperation
that has been added to the ensete-herding mode of production. It is
now appropriate to examine the basis for articulation of these new
and old modes of production in regard to theories of development. It
will then be possible to give some consideration to future prospects
for self-help societies in the aftermath of the 1974 Revolution.

## Theoretical Formulations

The past for the Sadāma has been fraught with change, and there
is no evidence that the people have ever been passive subjects in a
so-called traditional cohesive community. On the contrary, as individuals they have always been active participants in the change
process. The last half-century has differed from the past only in the
increased momentum of change and the impact of technology. Or-
ganizationally these aspects of change have been expressed through
the imposition of the state and world capitalism, euphemistically
referred to as "development" or "modernization." Much effort,
largely unsuccessful, has been expended by social scientists to explain resistance to or acceptance of these changes. These efforts have
resulted essentially in techniques for analyzing change in particular
societies, rather than an overall theory of social change.[1] There have
been, however, at least three major attempts at elaborating overall

theories of socioeconomic change that are pertinent to the situation of the Sadāma: the classical theory of economic growth, dependency theory, and the Marxian modes of production approach.

Growth theory has two aspects, one pertaining to "development" and the other to "modernization." The development aspect has been associated with a post-World War II conception that a Keynesian form of economics, emphasizing planning and financial aid, could be applied to the Third World to encourage an "ordered growth."[2] This expectation is based on an analogy drawn between the experience of the industrial nations in the depression of the 1930s and the conditions of the post-war, underdeveloped Third World. Thus it was widely believed that the so-called problem of underdevelopment could be overcome by putting idle resources to work in the creation of capital, which in turn would increase employment. It was soon recognized, however, that the economic problems of the Third World were different from those of industrial nations. The Third World relied more heavily upon imports, which tended to create inflationary pressures, which in turn made it difficult to expand employment and meet the increasing demands of consumers.

"Modernization" is a concept that appeared with the advent of the cold war in the 1950s, when the USSR and the United States emerged as the two major world powers.[3] Both powers began to vie with one another to gain the allegiance of old and emerging Third World states, by holding out the possibilities for modernizing their economies through financial and technological aid. It was a competition in which the USSR offered the possibility of creating socialism, while the United States proposed membership in the capitalist free market system.

Regardless of whether it was development or modernization by growth through capital investment and technological change, there was an implied analogy in these concepts with the nineteenth-century distinction between the "civilized" and the "noncivilized."[4] Now, however, modernization became a measure of the progress of Third World societies in approximating the institutions and values of industrial states. Conceptualization of this form of dualism led to a tendency to treat the former as if they were societies without history, free of conflict, and lacking in power struggles. They were negativ ¹v defined as "traditional" as compared with the positively de′ "modern" societies. But there was no attempt, other than apr to the addition of capital investment and increments of in technology through a sequence of stages, to explain the process involved in change.[5]

Dependency theory seeks to explain the process of underdevelopment. It is a theory that emerged largely out of the problems of exchange relations between Latin American countries and metropolitan centers, as a result of the failure of these countries to establish economic independence.[6] Historically, a situation arises in which the lesser-developed economy always operates far below capacity, and the only way to overcome this problem is to achieve national autonomy. Generally, dependency theorists ignore class conflict, stressing instead nationalism and removal of parasitic elites that are thought to be responsible for continuing dependency.[7] Consequently, a fundamental premise of those convinced of this view is that national development must take place through industrialization, independent of foreign aid and investment. In the past it has been assumed that this can be accomplished by import substitution.

Though there is considerable variation in theoretical positions among dependency theorists, fundamental agreement exists on at least four major premises.[8] One is that the condition of underdevelopment is a result of the expansion of industrial, capitalist states and that the growth of these states is predicated upon the dependence of the nonindustrial states. Second, and as a consequence of the first premise, development and underdevelopment are perceived as opposite sides of the same coin, so that development of one country is based upon the underdevelopment of another. Third, underdevelopment is a permanent rather than a temporary condition; development models from industrial countries are not relevant to the needs and problems of Third World peoples and lead to inappropriate policies or to none at all. And finally, the subordinate, dependent relationship between countries is also conceived as becoming part of the internal social structure and culture of the Third World country.

In regard to specific Latin American problems, it is claimed that prices of raw materials exports have never advanced significantly, so that the real development that was supposed to occur, according to classical theories of international trade, has not happened.[9] Such gains as have been made in the production and export of raw materials have not accrued to domestic benefit, but have been exported in terms of lower prices for the industrial states. At the same time, exports of manufactured goods have continued to increase in price. Consequently, the only remedies lie in the encouragement of import substitution, integration of the economies of the dependent countries, control of raw commodity prices so as to limit price fluctuations, and a transfer of resources from industrial countries as compensation for low raw material prices.

A more extreme view is that the interests of dependent Latin American countries and industrial states, especially the United States, stand in opposition and can never be considered as complementary.[10] The conflict is due strictly to linkages with capitalism. Thus local economies, cultures, and social structures not merely are shaped, but are being determined by the industrial, capitalist states and their agents within Latin America that benefit from dependence. Under these conditions, foreign aid and investment lead only to further dependence.

A somewhat broader variant of dependency theory is the so-called world theory, enunciated principally by Wallerstein.[11] This approach assumes a capitalist accumulation of resources, a world-wide core-periphery division of labor, and the presence of the nation-state.[12] Movement is predicted to occur in the form of economic growth and stagnation cycles, shifts in the distribution of power among core states, and modifications from colonialism to indirect control by the core over the periphery. This last movement usually means a shift toward political independence. Supporters of this theory also postulate certain long-term trends characterized by continued expansion in the size of the world economy and trends towards the predominance of wage labor, consumerism, capital concentration and automation of the productive process.

Wallerstein has been concerned to elaborate this thesis historically. He takes the position that the capitalist system emerged in the sixteenth century with some areas of Europe becoming modernized and others becoming traditional. Thus sixteenth-century Europe became the center of capitalism, eventually expanding from this base to the whole world. And the relationships between core and peripheral areas at this time period are considered analogous to the contemporary situation prevailing between developed and underdeveloped countries.

The core areas are such because they evolved a greater variety of economic activities, as well as control over international commerce by a bourgeoisie merchant class. On the other hand, the peasants in peripheral areas (for example, Poland), linked to the land by a property-owning aristocracy, became producers of agricultural commodities. The land-owning class in turn became dependent on the core areas of international capitalism for disposal of their crops. In sum, these various core, periphery, and semiperiphery areas each had specialized functions that made them interdependent parts of a world system. It is a situation in many ways similar to contemporary industrial–Third World relationships.

Wallerstein has also proposed a sequence of changing core-periphery relations for Africa.[13] He considers a first period, extending from 1750 to 1900, as involving the gradual shift from the slave trade and its consequences to the development of colonial interests in cash cropping of commodities. These interests were for the expanding industrial core of nineteenth-century Europe and America. Then in a second phase, from 1900 to 1975, the African periphery became important in providing minerals and the cheap labor to exploit these resources. By the 1970s, however, a power shift occurred in the core, so that the former dominance of the United States was replaced by increasing competition from Western Europe, Japan, and the USSR. But the postwar industrialization of these countries created an oil crisis that threatened the developing productivity of the new African states.

Finally, in the conclusion of his essay he predicts a third period, from 1975 into the future, in which there will be problems of famine and weak markets for the peripheral African countries. Furthermore, there will be great shifts in population from rural to urban areas. In turn this will lead to a large-scale mechanization of agriculture, not to produce food for the masses so much as to increase cash crop production for export. As a result, most Africans will become wage laborers, with the possibility of a developing class consciousness leading to revolution.

"Mode of production" theorists, in true Marxist style, utilize class conflict as the key element in their theory. This is quite different from dependency theorists, despite Wallerstein's prediction of the proletarianization of the African peasantry. Though there is considerable debate and disagreement about the nuances of the concept "mode of production," there is a consensus about its basic meaning. The term includes the two aspects referred to as forces and relations of production.[14] The former designates material factors such as technology, ecology, demography, and the tasks performed by labor; the latter involve the appropriation of the results of labor in utilizing the forces of production. Appropriation is based upon the extraction of surplus value by nonproducers from the labor of producers. A convenient way of understanding appropriation in a cash economy is to conceive of it as that part of the value received for sale of a commodity in excess of the capital (wages and other inputs) advanced for its production.[15]

Many orthodox Marxists insist that forces and relations interact in a dialectical fashion and, though conceptually different, are inseparable.[16] On the other hand, some French anthropologists support the position that the relations of production determine the mode of production. Thus Meillassoux has presented the thesis that in African societies elders control the labor of youth through manipulation of marriage rights, in what he refers to as the "lineage mode of production."[17] And, as was indicated at the end of chapter 7 in the discussion of authority and ideology, Terray postulates that there are as many modes of production in a society as there are differing forms of cooperation.[18] In his view, these forms of cooperation help to account for a diversity of juridical-political and ideological superstructures in noncapitalist societies.

There has also been much debate about the historical sequence of modes of production, but in general there seems to be no adequate theory regarding transition from one to another. Indeed, each mode of production is considered to be historically unique. Nevertheless, the recent work by Hindess and Hirst provides an analysis of six widely discussed modes including "primitive communism," "slave," "Asiatic," "ancient,""feudal," and "capitalist."[19] Their representation of primitive communism comes closest to the situation of the Sadāma, in that they consider appropriation under this mode to be based upon redistribution of the product of labor, rather than of labor itself, as in a class-structured system. Relationships of production are based upon kinship and household control of the means of production.

In Third World societies the emergence of cash crop farming introduces the influence of the capitalist mode to whatever may be the existing indigenous mode(s) of production. When this happens, Amin has suggested there are two alternative possibilities for articulation: either the noncapitalist mode is completely absorbed in the capitalist or an unequal exchange is established.[20] Anthropologists have been especially interested in investigating the process involved in this articulation of production modes.[21] There are various forms the process may take, the most drastic involving separating producers from their means of production, such as their land and/or animals, and forcing them into wage labor. Another approach involves advancing credit and utilization of the so-called putting-out system.[22] These are procedures in which middlemen merchants encourage cultivators and their families to engage in household industries, by advancing them credit and the materials for producing pottery, garments, rugs, baskets, and the like. The developing relations appear to be more in the nature of exchange. In fact, however, these arrangements enable the merchant to utilize the labor of the peasant, usually at a considerable gain in surplus value for the merchant, while the peasant becomes increasingly dependent on the cash economy sector.

It is through the appropriation of the labor of producers by nonproducers that a class system and conflict evolve. Orthodox Marxists view this procedure as a necessity, leading ultimately to fully developed capitalist and proletarian classes. Indeed, for the orthodox it is the dialectic between opposing classes that leads to change, first to the capitalist, but ultimately to the socialist mode of production. Recent theoretical approaches, however, do not involve the assumption of linearity, but recognize the possibility of variable origins for capitalism, with the chance for continuing ties to precapitalist forms of production.[23] Nevertheless, the dynamics of change continue to be considered dialectical, always based on conflict and contradiction. Unlike the classical evolutionary thinking of the Marxists, only the overall direction need be economic. Political, ideological, and technological variables, independent of classes and class struggle, may create significant movement in a new direction, through dialectical interplay with the economy.

## Application of Theories to the Sadāma

Growth theory does not seem to be significant in explaining the recent change process in Sidāmoland. Recent foreign investment in coffee, other than support for the north-south, all-weather road, has been negligible. As to individual capital investment, farmers simply obtained coffee plants from friends or relatives. And the few pulping mills in existence have been financed by Ethiopian capital. Nor have Ethiopians, unlike citizens of many Third World nations, relied heavily on international trade. Even so, Ethiopia had an adverse balance of trade every year from 1958 to 1971,[24] and fluctuations in international coffee prices have had a severe effect on foreign currency reserves.[25] But it has been primarily market plantation owners, transport companies, and the government who have been adversely affected and not the masses of small, peasant farmers. Nevertheless, it is evident that Ethiopia has not been able to provide for development, agricultural or industrial, out of these earnings, even though growth in coffee production for export increased from sixteen thousand tons in 1945 to approximately eighty-eight thousand tons by 1965.[26] By 1971, production fell to a little over eighty thousand tons and the value from 188 million to 175 million Ethiopian dollars.[27]

It is apparent, however, that formal education, first by the missions and later by the government, was oriented toward encouraging Western work values and wage labor. Furthermore, the United States and other European powers invested in and encouraged the development of the one major Ethiopian university. Nevertheless, prior to the 1974 Revolution there were less than a dozen Sadāma who had ever seen the inside of a university. And finally, the wage labor opportunities, which so many families desired for their children, did not materialize.

There is also minimal evidence for any attempt through use of foreign aid to make so-called idle resources productive, so as to increase capital investment and employment. The only exception is the investment in the green revolution provided by French aid. But it is not clear as to whether this will be supplemented by other government efforts to promote cash cropping in oil seeds and maize. Nor is it certain that if such investment were forthcoming, adequate incentives would be provided to gain widespread farmer participation. Moreover, the realistic concerns of Sadāma about the high costs of the new inputs, their fear of losing control of their land, and a preference for activities other than long hours of labor has caused them to be labeled traditional and backward by the technicians administering the programs.

Nevertheless, while there is practically no support for a thesis of growth through capital investment and great increases in wage labor, there is some indication for the applicability of dependency theory. In Ethiopia as a whole, there has been practically no industrial development.[28] One indication of this fact is that the value of manufactured goods as exports in 1971 amounted to less than 3 million as compared with commodity exports of slightly over 300 million Ethiopian dollars.[29] Though Ethiopia is a relatively small participant in international trade, the emphasis upon the production of food and raw materials tends to place the country in a peripheral position vis-à-vis the states of the industrial core. There is also, in keeping with Wallerstein's prediction, some indication that the dominance of the United States as a trading partner had begun to wane by 1975, with the new industrial nations of West Germany and Japan substantially increasing their share of Ethiopian exports.[30]

Though pulses and oil seeds have in recent years increased as percentages of the total volume of exports, coffee remains predominant. This is because relatively cheap labor costs make it advantageous for the large international corporations to blend African coffees with the more expensively produced Latin American varieties. But the effect of fluctuating coffee prices, while having a minimal impact on the core industrial institutions, has had a more substantial local influence on the few Sadāma who have become dependent on coffee sales by assuming the status of middlemen merchants. Furthermore, the 1965 and 1973 comparative sample of income and expenditure by household heads shows that coffee production has not led to an increase in material well-being. Income has stagnated, with little change during the eight-year interval. And expenditures and indebtedness, along with inflation, have actually increased.

One way in which the Ethiopian authorities sought to develop productivity in agriculture was with the so-called package projects. Though there were only three or four of these programs in all of Ethiopia and none in Sidāmoland, they help to illustrate how a model designed by European experts to encourage rural development may actually further the dependency process. The goal of a package project was to coordinate agricultural inputs, services, and infrastructural improvement with increases in peasant productivity and income in select areas. In fact, the results were actually the reverse in the most notable program, the Chilalo Agricultural Project.[31] In this instance, the results after seven years of development were advantageous for large-scale capitalist farming ventures. Small holders gained little, and tenants were actually evicted from landholdings of large operators, in favor of capital-intensive, agribusiness enterprise.

Wheat yields on many landholdings in the Chilalo area were actually trebled and services such as credit were expanded dramatically. In the case of credit services, however, it was landowners and large cultivators who accounted for the greatest percentage of borrowers with the largest loans.[32] In general, the project failed to reduce the original income differences between large and small cultivators. It is suggested that this was due to the fact that the loans were never administered by associations, such as cooperatives, in which all the members were able to participate.[33]

Finally, the assistance anticipated by the Swedish planners of the program from local notables and government officials never materialized. This was simply because their interests and goals were inimical to the income enhancement of small-scale cultivators.[34] Thus the benefits of much of the productivity increases that occurred accrued to the benefit of large landholding producers and not to the small peasant farmers. The effect was simply to increase the peripheral position of Ethiopians as slightly more efficient commodity producers, dependent on world commodity prices.

There was no landholding class dominating coffee production among the Sadāma. For the small holder producers, coffee constituted only an adjunct to the household subsistence production of most peasants. The only rural wage labor was that provided for some itinerant Gurage workers, to dig up the land for spring planting. Certainly there was no movement of the people from rural to urban areas. Also, given the high cost of oil, the ecology, and the small holdings of Sidāmoland, it is unlikely that large-scale, mechanized agriculture would be practicable. Moreover, the prediction from Wallerstein's thesis for the development of class consciousness as a prelude to revolution has not occurred. Instead a revolution has been implemented in Sidāmoland without the emergence of an indigenous capitalist system and the subsequent class conflict.

Two aspects of mode of production theory have shaped our study of the Sadāma. These include the emphasis on historical development and differing ways of organizing cooperation for production of material means and reproduction of the social system. Earlier chapters have dealt with the household and community forms of cooperation in production, as well as changes in the distribution of the people, social structure, and values. This has been followed by historical consideration of the emergence of cash cropping and the consequences of its links to international markets. As a result, a new mode of production developed based on the mutuality of members and the marketing procedures of self-help societies. These societies, though usually considered to be a part of the distribution process, in the case of the Sadāma are more appropriately associated with production; before the advent of self-help societies, peasants were dissatisfied about producing coffee for prices they considered to be exploitative, since the market was nearly monopolized by Amhara merchants.

This study does not support the hypotheses associated with Meillassoux's "lineage mode" of production, that elders appropriate the surplus value of youth labor.[35] Rather it is our contention, more in keeping with what Hindess and Hirst have referred to as "primitive communism,"[36] that there is a circular reciprocity and redistribution between generations. Indeed, exploitation has existed primarily in connection with the tributary policies following Menelik's conquest. When tribute gave way to government taxation, land control in some areas of Sidāmoland continued until the 1974 Revolution in the hands of the descendants of northern colonists and soldiers. In these areas, Sadāma were exploited to the extent of having to give annually one-third or more of their crop production in rent. Aside from tribute and rent the Sadāma have suffered in recent times from the aforementioned appropriative marketing techniques of the Amhara merchants. But there has been no internal exploitation of one group of Sadāma by another. This has made it possible to reinterpret the meaning of the authority of elders' councils to fit the new form of self-help executive committees, a juridical-political development in keeping with their cash cropping mode of production.

For the most part, the impact of capitalism has remained negligible and has not led to the absorption of the community and household modes of production. And the unequal exchange with the northern middlemen merchants has been overcome by the emergence of the self-help societies. Nor have the Sadāma, as has been emphasized so often in previous pages, been separated from their means of production and been forced into wage labor. In fact, people have sought, without widespread success, to provide opportunities for some of their children to enter into wage labor, as a solution to the increasingly unfavorable population-land ratio. Furthermore, they have never become engaged in household industries that could have led to nascent class formation. And as to credit, it has not been obtained on a class-exploitative basis, but only by traditional methods or, more recently, through society loans.

Certainly there has been conflict between the Sadāma and the so-called Amhara, but it remains questionable as to whether it has been dialectical, in the sense of leading to significant changes in the lifestyle of either group. On the other hand, political fragmentation has been as important as the economic variable in supporting the emergence of the self-help societies. There is as well the element of contradiction, both purposive and unintended, in government policy. The unintended contradiction of supporting regional development projects to the detriment of the self-help societies has seemingly lessened the availability of resources and in some instances discouraged membership in these societies. But purposive contradiction, in which the government has sought to maintain a balance of power by playing one administrative branch off against another, has actually enabled the Sadāma to do the same thing in protecting the associations from hostile local interests.

Thus mode of production theory contributes more to understanding the experience of the Sadāma than the dependency or growth theories. All three approaches tend, however, to minimize the participation of individuals in the dynamics of change. And yet it has been the individuals—from the heroes depicted in clan mythology to the butchers, reluctant watchmen, and unhappy farmers who argue before the executive committees about new rules and changes in access to land—who have chosen and continue to choose among the alternatives shaping the direction of change. They have, of course, not been able to determine the chance course of internal and external events that have provided them with these alternatives. Indeed, the people have been especially fortunate that the sequence of historical events has been sufficiently ambiguous, of lengthy duration, and cumulative, so as to permit reinterpretation of old forms of council participation to fit the new arrangement of committee structure. This has provided continuity for ensuring that individual choice can be reconciled with community obligation.

Dependency and mode of production theories help us to abstract the problems of alternative selection, as well as to conceptualize the successes and failures of the Sadāma in the choice process. Thus the education solution to the adverse population-land ratio failed because of the lack of wage labor positions. The people learned about the potential for self-help in coping with economic change by observing the experience of the socially isolated Christian converts. Paradoxically, they have been aided in this approach by the opposition of more powerful but politically fragmented outsiders. At the same time the Sadāma have also used the ingenuity of their own leadership, a realistic knowledge of the limits of kinship organization, and customary concepts of authority to ensure a relative balance between self-aggrandizement and community responsibility. The question is whether they can continue to participate in modifying the impact of the state and world capitalism, choosing among the alternatives provided by historical accident. As it happens, the 1974 Revolution provides some interesting possibilities as to the direction of future change.

## The 1974 Revolution

In early 1974 a revolution began in Ethiopia, the consequences of which are as yet unclear. At least two events of the Revolution have been of momentous significance: one was the establishment of a nationwide network of peasant associations, the other was the redistribution of rural land, limiting the amount per household to a maximum of ten hectares, prohibiting the use of hired labor,[37] making land nontransferable, and abolishing all landlord-tenant relations.[38] One peasant association was to be established for every eight hundred hectares of land to administer the reform and to establish marketing cooperatives, mutual aid societies, schools, clinics, and village communities. Initially there were to be five levels of administrative linkages ranging from the association through the district and administrative region to the national All-Ethiopia Peasant Association.[39] Judicial and administrative functions were confined to the subdistrict and district levels, but by late 1975 these activities had been delegated to the newly formed associations.[40]

To implement both programs, urban high school and university students were mobilized and sent into the countryside in all parts of Ethiopia. Ostensibly this was due to a shortage of government personnel, but it was also a means of diffusing anticipated unrest among the most energetic and outspoken part of the population by enlisting them in the idealistic *zemača* campaign.[41] The campaign continued, with varying results, in most administrative regions until the end of 1975.[42] The students organized thousands of associations in a relatively short time and assisted in land redistribution to individuals, as well as establishing collective agricultural plots for each association. They met resistance in those areas from large landowners and landlords, as well as from peasants antagonized by the occasional use of authoritarian attitudes and interference with the local decision-making process.[43] These actions caused the government to fear the possibility of losing control in the rural areas, so that the military quickly intervened wherever disorders occurred.[44] In this way, government officials made it clear that they intended to keep control of the associations from the top of the organizational pyramid.

In the beginning there was much ambiguity about the activities and structure assigned to the new peasant societies. A proclamation of late 1975, however, provided for a progression from minimal to total collectivization of the means of production.[45] This change was to be accomplished by first transforming associations into service cooperatives to establish storage facilities and to provide low-cost agricultural inputs, marketing services, consumers' shops, and encouragement of modern agricultural practices. Two or more associations, with three delegates from each elected to an executive committee, would form a service cooperative. In addition to judicial and administrative functions, the committees were delegated a policy function and authorized to form armed defense squads. Other than enforcing the decisions of the executive committee in settling disputes and ensuring labor on the collective, it seems that the defense squads were to ensure tax collection, which had become the responsibility of the associations.[46] The government planners envisioned these service cooperatives evolving into producer cooperatives in which most of the members' private plots would be transferred to collective production, with remuneration being based on individual labor contribution.

It is evident that the organization and endeavors of service cooperatives are very similar to the prerevolutionary self-help societies of the Sadāma. Possibly this is due to previous knowledge and experience with these associations, as well as the importance of coffee in generating interest in cooperatives. Unfortunately, there has been no research as to how, or if, the transformation of self-help societies to service cooperatives occurred.

One survey, however, of Shashemene subdistrict, which contains part of the Mālga clan, indicates some of the developments in broad outline.[47] Abate and Teklu show that in 1977 all peasant associations in the subdistrict had defense squads and judicial subcommittees that were settling disputes involving land, criminal offenses, and violations of association rules.[48] Just as in the case of the self-help societies, organizational divisions and functions were largely ignored and interested members participated equally with executive committeemen in decision making and the dispute-settlement process.

And, similar to prerevolutionary conditions, there was minimal participation by association delegates in subdistrict decision making. It seems that consensual agreement was still important in making policy and settling disputes, although provision existed for decision by majority vote in both the executive committee and the general assembly of all members.

Land redistribution in this subdistrict had minimal impact on the small farming communities, since most peasant holdings were well below the ten hectare maximum.[49] Nevertheless, in the early stages of association organization, zemača workers had sought to hold individual land allotments to one hectare a household, with the rest of association land being devoted to collective farming. But after 1975, as more of the young attained their majority (age eighteen), the shortage of land became so acute that much of what had been set aside for collective farming had to be divided among the new members.

Indeed it seems that, as elsewhere in Africa, the peasant farmers of Shashemene subdistrict rejected the concept of collective farming.[50] Under this system, household heads were expected to devote a portion of their labor to collective production. By 1979, however, despite executive committee efforts ranging from warnings to imprisonment, the duration of time contributed per member had declined and absenteeism had risen to 40 percent of household heads. Such income as was derived from the collective plots was not reinvested according to government plan but was being divided among the members. Again there is a similarity to the short-term incentives that were so important for recruiting members to self-help societies.

Though the study of Shashemene subdistrict population includes some members of the Mālga clan, there is no information on the Sadāma in general. It was possible in 1984, however, for the author to return to Ethiopia for a short visit. During that time discussion was held with several old informants, regarding events since the Revolution. These men indicated that after the Revolution, the old self-help societies became models for the new peasant associations. For two years, from 1975 to 1977, government agencies were run largely by Sadāma, local affairs were controlled by the peasant associations, and, as a consequence, the former power of the middlemen merchants was broken. In one instance a former mahabar, which had become a service cooperative, took over a large coffee-pulping mill. Then for a two-year period the members of the cooperative made several millions of dollars in profits, which the committee invested in trucks to carry their coffee directly to Addis Ababa, in clinics and primary schools in the countryside, and in a modern secondary school in the town of Wando (see map 1).

In 1977 military representatives of the central government took more direct control of affairs in Sidāmoland. Centralization resulted in tax increases, coffee marketing quotas, and a tendency toward surveillance rather than resource support from government officials. Then peasants began to complain of high taxes, which now include a flat income tax for all household heads, as well as numerous ad hoc assessments for development projects planned by government officials. Also, Sadāma were required to sell their coffee through the cooperative, ending the alternative of selling on the open market where prices were sometimes higher.[51] Finally, as in the Shashemene situation, attempts were made to establish producer cooperatives, but resistance by the people ultimately led to abandonment of the project.

## The Future

There is indication that the establishment of rural cooperatives in postrevolutionary Ethiopia has involved a mixture of voluntary participation and government imposition. The unsuccessful attempt to create a situation of wage labor through collectivization has been essentially a way of separating peasants from control of the means of production. Thus the rulers of Ethiopia appear to be confronted with the choice of imposing centralized agricultural production and minimizing local decision making, or decentralizing and encouraging voluntary participation through self-help. Despite some movement toward imposed organization, the government has also espoused ethnic decentralization and participation.[52] So far, however, guarantees of ethnic self-determination have involved more rhetoric than action.

The failure of centralized government control of agriculture elsewhere in Africa has already been noted. There is also precedent for this failure in the application of similar policies in other parts of the world economic system. When the Russians faced this choice in the 1920s, they chose centralization. The cost in lives and misery was great, and there are those who argue that Soviet agriculture, as a consequence, has never been able to support effectively the urban industrial sector.[53] There had, however, been arguments for a decentralization approach. Nikolai Bukharin, a high-ranking party official and theoretician, recognized that peasants wished to control their own land and that collectivization would be dependent upon force, state funds, and increasing bureaucratization.[54] On the other hand, he was convinced that collectivization could be established voluntarily through the initial use of marketing cooperatives that would provide small farmers with immediate benefits. State control of credit would furnish the incentive for joining, and through experience peasants would come to realize the superiority of collective activities over private enterprise. Instead of the orthodox class warfare there would be a competitive class struggle in which the socialist cooperatives would outproduce, undersell, and provide better products than private entrepreneurs. Actually, the importance of Bukharin's position was not so much the near-utopian role that he assigned to cooperatives, but the emphasis he placed on providing peasant farmers with a choice. In his view, this choice should not have been subordinated to industrialization and urban bureaucracy, but industrial growth should have been dependent on agricultural development and the consumer demand of the rural majority.

Unlike the Russians, the Chinese after their revolution developed a system of household mutual-aid teams and producer cooperatives organized into brigades.[55] Decentralization was decided upon after it was discovered that large, centralized communes produced less than did small agricultural units. Mutual-aid teams were deliberately organized on the principle of kinship heterogeneity, so as to prevent kinship ties from inhibiting criticism and competitive production within groups. These teams presently farm both collective and private soil plots, with private plots being more productive and being preferred by the peasant cultivators.

Examples from capitalist economies also show that farmers are more effective producers if they control their means of production and avoid centralized bureaucracy. Thus, French farmers have created informal networks of cooperation to combat government agencies seeking to change their methods to fit bureaucratic ideals.[56] They voluntarily exchange labor and farm machinery so as to avoid government-sponsored cooperatives, with their formal bookkeeping procedures and expensive administrative overhead.

In a somewhat different approach, Spanish government authorities have encouraged consolidation of small farms to form producers' cooperatives.[57] These are said to have worked well because administrators have functioned as resource persons, serving and encouraging the cooperative members. The government has avoided such centralized controls as investigations of labor contributions and rigid rules about the division of profits. Instead, officials have preferred to see administrative policies evolve at the local level, as the responsibility of the members of the various societies.

Established capitalist and socialist economies thus both provide a precedent for organizing agricultural production by encouraging development of decentralized, small producers units with local participatory control. Furthermore, there is contrary evidence to the assumption that small peasant holdings are less efficient and productive than large farms with hired labor and machinery.[58] Comparative research on both large and small farm units in Latin America and South Asia has shown that small farms produce more output per unit of land under cultivation than large ones. The reasons for the small holders' success is their reliance on household labor, the simplicity of self-management, the quality of care and attention provided by people whose survival is dependent on their produce, and the willingness to work whenever necessary to maintain production. And, as has been shown in the case of the Sadāma, these farmers reinvest a substantial part of their incomes in their farms.[59]

There are other reasons for the higher level of production and efficiency of small peasant farms.[60] Because smallness of scale gives them greater control over the production process, they can adapt quickly to new opportunities. Some coffee farmers in Sidāmoland, for example, were able to switch part of their land devoted to coffee to oil seeds within a year of discovering the favorable price of the seeds. Another advantage is the possession of a thorough knowledge of local environmental conditions. This enabled Sadāma in a short time to establish a relatively favorable balance between cash cropping and subsistence production. Such an ability to integrate innovative with old patterns of subsistence farming makes it possible to take limited risks. In the process, farmers are able to avoid the great monetary and ecological costs of large and expensive inputs of chemical fertilizers and insecticides. An example is the case of those Sadāma who were instructed how they could avoid these high input costs by practicing crop rotation.[61]

Finally, the costs of small holdings are low compared with those for large government-controlled state farms and settlement schemes with high capital costs for infrastructure, salaries for administrators, and wage labor costs. This is of course not to minimize the potential problems, previously discussed for the Sadāma, of the imbalance that comes from overgrazing too many cattle or from having farms that are too small for practicing crop rotation. Nevertheless, these are problems of which the Sadāma and other peasant farmers are aware and which can often be resolved at the local level with appropriate government extension support.

Given the failings of centralized controls, combined with the dismal decline during the 1970s in African agricultural production, the findings regarding decentralization and local participatory control are worthy of serious consideration by any African government. [62] Moreover, the international outlook for commodity prices, export opportunities, commercial borrowing, and foreign aid appears to be unfavorable for low-income countries in the foreseeable future.[63] Voluntary self-help activities of peoples like the Sadāma are thus especially significant. Within the framework of the self-help societies, farmers have responded enthusiastically to participation in modifying their system of production.

If there continues to be a government policy of assistance, rather than imposition, it is possible that the Sadāma could use the new service cooperative to alleviate the unfavorable population-land ratio. There is a worldwide estimate that 25 percent of the rural labor force could be employed in nonagricultural occupations such as food processing, handicrafts, leather, textiles, metal working, construction, commerce, and marketing.[64] These activities are most useful in meeting local demand, while at the same time they use simple technology and labor-intensive techniques, and they require a minimum of capital investment. The members of such service cooperatives could plan and establish small-scale irrigation projects, rural electrification, and road maintenance programs that would employ many of their sons who may inherit insufficient land to provide family subsistence. These projects would, of course, require a minimum of government support in the form of small loans, as well as engineering and management assistance.

11 Conclusion

> It has become fashionable to question the "absolute desirability" of economic development, to deride as unscientific its identification with progress, to accuse its protagonists in the West of "ethnocentrism," of hypostatization of their own culture, and of insufficient respect for the mores and values of more primitive peoples.—Paul Baran, *The Political Economy of Growth*

The above quotation by a prominent political economist contains a frequently expressed plaint against anthropologists. They are alleged to seek to preserve Third World peoples as museum curiosities or "noble savages" who must be protected from the onslaught of industrial peoples. Indeed, it is a criticism sometimes advanced by anthropologists against others in their own profession. For example, Western anthropologists are sometimes accused of ignoring the theories and views of the people they are studying, when these views contradict the theoretical orthodoxy of the discipline.[1] Furthermore, as mentioned in chapter 1, some social scientists claim that peasant cultivators are only interested in avoiding risks that might jeopardize a minimum standard of living. They suggest that Third World peoples are afraid to risk innovations that might bring financial gain.

Throughout the book I have sought to show that the Sadāma are a people quite adaptable to change on their own terms. According to their own narrative history and from what is known from documents in recent times, individuals have often taken risks that have sometimes favored and at other times gone against the enhancement of their life-style. Therefore, it is possible to agree that some social scientists have been unrealistically overprotective of "their people" and occasionally professionally ethnocentric.

On the other hand, I would quarrel with the view of growth theorists, as explained in the previous chapter, that progress in development is associated with the difference between traditional and modern societies. It is unrealistic and ethnocentric to assume that Third World peoples equate development with becoming like Western industrial peoples. A theme of this book has been that the Sadāma do have a history and that, through their self-help societies, they have in the past and continue in the present to make many of their own choices among alternatives for change. Thus the origins and history of the Sadāma indicate a continuing effort to gain and maintain control over more and better resources. To establish an ideal balance between herding and horticulture, the people have been prepared to undergo and adapt to drastic changes, such as learning a new language, switching from grain to ensete production, incorporating people from other ethnic groups, and fighting to the death those who would prevent them from obtaining these optimum conditions. Residence for several centuries in their mountainous homeland has enabled them to develop a harmonious subsistence economy based on a relatively small population cultivating the durable ensete, symbiotically linked to herding, and a hoe/digging-stick technology.

The Sadāma have utilized these resources through relations of production dependent upon bonds of birth, marriage, and friendship, which have provided them with sufficient sustenance, a small surplus for trade, and support of the ritual so necessary for perpetuating the social system. In the course of time they developed both community and household modes of production. The former is based on cooperation structured through the generational class system and the latter upon the bonds of agnatic and affinal kinship.

Interclan exchange and relative ease of movement between clan areas have been essential because of the need to acquire ensete seedlings, found only at certain elevations, and to maintain distant herds or to move cattle between different ecological zones on a seasonal basis. Such movement has helped the people to maintain an equalitarian way of life, though historically the descendants of Bushē sought to impose their authority over the descendants of Maldea. But the acquisition of additional land by Maldeans made them equal in wealth, if not in symbolic purity, with Bushēans. Only the artisan clans, originally lacking the land and cattle factors of production, have been stigmatized as to purity and restricted by marriage endogamy. Nevertheless, these restrictions have helped to ensure the production of hides, pottery, and iron tools, so important to the activities of all cultivators.

Throughout the book I have described an interplay, often conflictive, between individual variation and community cohesion. The origin myths are replete with individuals who violate the principles of the true way of life, halōli, only to become famous by acquiring more land and cattle for themselves or by leading their deviant followers to greater prosperity. Nevertheless, the ideology based on the original edicts of the creator, on a cult of dead elders, and on the principle of the true way of life, all articulated with appropriate rituals, support the predominance of community obligations. This ideological-ritual complex provides the charter for the juridical-political system of elderhood authority. This authority, based on consensual compromise and exercised through the various levels of elders' councils, holds together the household and community modes of production.

Within the past century the Sadāma have experienced conquest, followed by a period when their labor was appropriated by the conquerors. At the same time, they were forced to provide tribute, and some household heads became tenant cultivators. But though high crop rents remained until the 1974 Revolution as a heavy burden on a few, tribute and forced labor were replaced by taxation as Ethiopia took on the facade of a modern bureaucratic state.

This development coincided with the emergence of cash cropping in coffee, and the Sadāma became peasant farmers. Also coincidental with the emergence of a cash economy and the bureaucratic state were the arrival of new religious beliefs from Western industrial countries. These beliefs provided ideological support for the cash economy. More importantly, they created a rift among the Sadāma between the minority of converts and the vast majority of adherents to traditional beliefs and rituals. This had the unforeseen consequence of encouraging the advent of the self-help movement. The movement in turn led to a new mode of production based on mutual assistance in harvesting and marketing coffee in appropriate regions, as well as on community development.

Cash cropping in coffee as a new mode of production has not replaced or dominated domestic and community modes of production, for the Sadāma have never become fully articulated with world capitalism, having retained control of their land and cattle and not being incorporated into a wage labor system. Moreover, they have been able to use the factionalism of a personalized, loosely structured state to oppose the remnants of the conquerors' descendants. One outcome has been their ability to reinterpret old concepts of authority to fit that of the new self-help societies. Thus they have experienced a sense of continuity in making rules to deal with the new economy that control the age-old conflict between self-interest and community obligation.

The results in terms of growth in incomes and changes in standards of living have been modest. Only a few household heads have sufficient income to invest in expanding their herds, buying coffee futures, and/or protecting their land. Nonetheless, growing coffee has not forced them into dependency on the cash sector or led to class differences and conflict. It is true that their choices among alternatives have been limited, but the process has remained largely under the control of the people. Consequently, they have a sense of enthusiasm, pride, and identity with their accomplishments. Moreover, unlike the situation when change is imposed from the top down, the Sadāma realize their own responsibility for the rules and policies they have created.

This situation in Sidāmoland has developed from a combination of historical accident, grass roots decision making, effective leadership, and the aid of government officials as facilitators of local planning and goals. People have been attracted to the self-help movement in hopes of gaining personal advantages, such as in marketing coffee and in gaining convenient access to consumers' goods and in community improvements that will benefit individual households. These individual goals are not necessarily of the kind to favor the purposes of the societies or the community as a whole. Hence the importance of dedicated leadership and the reinterpretation of elders' authority principles to fit the executive committees. The outcome has made it possible to ensure cooperation by utilizing the old process of consensual compromise in subordinating self-interest in favor of community endeavors, but never permitting the latter to dominate the former. This process of policy making and dispute settlement by the Sadāma has been effectively supplemented by community development officials as resource persons, who advise them on planning, use of technology, and business procedures, and who serve as intermediaries with other government and business organizations.

As indicated in chapter 1, there are many specialists in Third World development who are skeptical and even hostile to grass roots participation in the change process. Others suggest that force is the only means by which to extract a surplus of production from the peasantry to feed a developing urban, industrial population. It has been emphasized by some of these analysts that if African governments rely on decentralized participation, there will be no modernization or significant change in the existing societies, because polygyny, gerontocracy, and ritual, supported by the peasant mode of production, is incompatible with socialist or capitalist modes of production.[2] Furthermore, African farmers are independent of governments in their subsistence and can withhold their surplus production as they choose. Though supporters of this position admit that forced acquiescence will not benefit rural peoples, it is generally seen as a historical inevitability in line with the Western experience of industrialization.

In essence this is the old ethnocentrism of the dualistic concept of traditional versus modern. But without the opportunity to participate in the decisions of affecting change in their style of living, there is likely to be considerable resistance from farmers. In Senegal, for example, government attempts to centralize control of the principal cash crop of peanuts led to smuggling, abandonment of cultivation, indifference, and resignation to the whole process of agricultural development.[3] Since the Senegalese government was dependent upon the revenue from this one crop, the survival of the administration was threatened. By the late 1970s, many Bukusu farmers in western Kenya had become so disillusioned with government-imposed coffee cooperatives that they cut back or discontinued production of this vital export crop.[4] Elsewhere a government-imposed centralized village scheme in Tanzania is often blamed for the drastic decline in food production during the mid-1970s.[5] Even though this argument ignores the importance of external influences, at the very least villagization did lead to resistance and dislocation of the production process, by forcing farmers to develop new techniques rapidly in adapting to unfamiliar environmental conditions.[6] And finally there is the more recent example of the failure of government-sponsored state farms in Mozambique.[7] The state had hoped to feed the urban population and the peasantry by relying on community-organized, highly mechanized, large acreage farms. But by 1981 it was admitted that not a single state farm had been profitable. Peasants had become wage laborers on these huge holdings with no real commitment to the task. They preferred instead to attend to their family plots. So the state farm program has been discontinued and the emphasis has shifted to encouraging increased productivity on small household farms, organized into producers' cooperatives.

These problems are often attributed to Western thinkers having proposed, and many African elites having accepted, that the key to modern development is continuous and unwavering economic growth. Yet many of the aspects of politico-economic change confronting African peoples are the results of historical accidents that provide for numerous alternatives. The important question is whether people will be given an opportunity to choose among these various options. Certainly people can, as the experience of the Sadāma shows, effectively participate in change at the local level. They bring a vast experience to the challenge of choosing, and also a knowledge of the relationship between their environment, tools, and organization that has enabled them to survive through the millennia. When people are permitted to draw upon their heritage in making choices, they approach the changing situation with confidence. Moreover, the opportunity to choose among alternatives, rather than being subjected to an externally made choice, maximizes the possibility for innovation.

# Notes

## 1. Introduction

1. *Sadāma* is the term the people use to refer to themselves as a group; *sadānčo* refers to an individual of this group.

2. Igor Kopytoff, "Socialism and Traditional African Societies," in W. H. Friedland and Carl G. Rosberg, eds., *African Socialism* (Stanford: Stanford University Press, 1964), pp. 53–62.

3. See especially the summaries in the issue on "African Socialism" in *Africa Report 1963*. This was certainly the assumption of Kenneth Kaunda in his attempts to develop "microsocialism" in Zambia (Stephen A. Quick, "Bureaucracy and Rural Socialism in Zambia," *Journal of Modern African Studies* 15 [1977]: 395). Also, Nyrere expressed similar views in attempting to develop ujamaa villages in Tanzania (Zaki Ergas, "Why Did the Ujamaa Village Policy Fail?—Towards a Global Analysis," *Journal of Modern African Studies* 18, no. 3 [September 1980]: 391–92).

4. See, for example, Shem E. Migot-Adholla's summary on this problem, "Traditional Society and Cooperatives," in Carl G. Widstrand, ed., *Cooperatives and Rural Development in East Africa* (Uppsala: Almquist & Wiksell, 1970), pp. 19–36.

5. Quick, "Bureaucracy and Rural Socialism," p. 395.

6. Ergas, "Why Did the Ujamaa Village Policy Fail?" pp. 387–92.

7. See, for example, the interesting summary by Joel Samoff, "Underdevelopment and Its Grass Roots in Africa," *Canadian Journal of African Studies* 14, no. 1 (1980): 5–36.

8. For a detailed discussion of the attributes of peasantries see Eric R. Wolf, *Peasants* (Englewood Cliffs: Prentice-Hall, 1966), p. 204; Claude E. Welch, "Peasants as a Focus in African Studies," in Alan K. Smith and Claude E. Welch, eds., *Peasants in Africa* (Waltham: Crossroads Press, 1978), pp. 1–5; Robert Redfield, *The Little Community and Peasant Society and Culture* (Chicago: University of Chicago Press, 1960), pp. 5–79; Frederick

Gamst, *Peasants in Complex Society* (New York: Holt, Rinehart & Winston, 1974), pp. 10–19.

9. Gamst, *Peasants in Complex Society*, p. 11.

10. See, for example, Nelson Kasfir, "Departicipation and Political Development in Black Africa," *Political Studies in Comparative International Development* 9 (1974): 3–25, and Samoff, "Underdevelopment and Its Grass Roots," pp. 34–35.

11. L. Scaff and E. Williams, "Participation and the Primacy of Politics in Development Theory," in J. Booth and M. Seligson, eds., *Political Participation in Latin America*, vol. 1 (New York: Holmes & Meier Publishers, 1978), pp. 44–49.

12. Peter Worsley, *The Third World* (Chicago: University of Chicago Press, 1970), pp. 164–74.

13. See, for example, James C. Scott, *The Moral Economy of the Peasant* (New Haven: Yale University Press, 1976), pp. 4–12; J. Migdal, *Peasants, Politics, and Revolution* (Princeton: Princeton University Press, 1974), pp. 71–72. Others have argued that individual peasants are so concerned with survival that they are unwilling to take a chance on innovations that will bring financial gains. See the recent work of Goran Hyden, *Beyond Ujamaa in Tanzania: Underdevelopment and an Uncaptured Peasantry* (Berkeley: University of California Press, 1980), p. 13.

14. Samuel L. Popkin, *The Rational Peasant: The Political Economy of Rural Society in Vietnam* (Berkeley: University of California Press, 1979).

# 2. The People and Their Environment

1. In this grouping he includes the Bako, Gibe, Gimira, Jarjero, Kafa, Maji, and the Omēto (see map 2), George Murdock, *Africa: Its Peoples and Their Culture History* (New York: McGraw-Hill, 1959), pp. 187–88.

2. Ibid., p. 200.

3. Ernesta Cerulli, *Peoples of South-West Ethiopia and Its Borderland* (London: International African Institute, 1956), p. 85.

4. Ibid., pp. 86–87.

5. Ulrich Braukamper, "The Ethnogenesis of the Sidāma," in Jean Chavaillon, ed., *Abbay: Documents pour servir à l'histoire de la civilisation Éthiopienne*, Report no. 9 (Paris: Centre Régional de Publications de Meudon-Bellevue, 1978), p. 123.

6. Teff is a species of grass grown in Ethiopia as a cereal grain. It is the major food staple in the northern highland plateau of the nation.

7. Helmet Smeds, "The Ensete Planting Culture of Eastern Sidāmo, Ethiopia," *Acta Geographica* 13, no. 4 (1955): 24.

8. A second crop of maize is sown in early August and harvested in November.

9. William A. Shack, *The Gurage: A People of the Ensete Culture* (New York: Oxford University Press, 1966), p. 62.

10. See, for example, Shack's similar findings among the Gurage, ibid., p. 50.

11. Office of the Population and Housing Census Commission, *Ethiopia 1984: Population and Housing Census Preliminary Report* (Addis Ababa-Government Printer, 1984), p. 28.

12. Central Statistical Office, "Estimates of Rural Households and Populations in Thirteen Provinces" (Addis Ababa, 1972, mimeo), p. 11.

13. Smeds, "Ensete Planting Culture of Eastern Sidāmo," p. 34.

14. Shack, *The Gurage*, p. 44.

# 3. Origins and History

1. For greater detail on this subject see John Hamer, "The Origins of the Sadāma: A Cushitic-Speaking People of South-Western Ethiopia," in Jean Chavaillon, ed., *Abbay: Documents pour servir à l'histoire de la civilisation Éthiopienne*, Report no. 9 (Paris: Centre Régional de Publications de Meudon-Bellevue, 1978), pp. 131–39.

2. Ahmad Gran led a famous jihad (holy war) in the early sixteenth century to destroy the Christians in highland Ethiopia. His immense armies and their sweeps through central and northern Ethiopia are said to have unsettled many of the peoples in these regions and to have contributed to massive migrations by the Oromo. See Richard Greenfield, *Ethiopia: A New Political History* (New York: Praeger, 1965), pp. 52–54.

3. Braukamper, "Ethnogenesis of the Sidāma," pp. 125–26, in material taken from the neighboring Hadiya, also suggests that Maldea rather than Bushē is connected with semitic-speaking people to the north in eastern Bali.

4. Braukamper, however, suggests in "Ethnogenesis of the Sidāma" that the two ancestral groups entered present-day Sidāmoland at different times and places.

5. The descendants of the Gugi are the ethnic group to the south of Sidāmoland (see map 1) who at one time occupied much of the land between the Gidabo and Billate rivers and land extending eastward through the Āletā and Gārbičo territories.

6. This group includes as well the Hadiyya, Kambata, Darasa, and Burji. See Grover Hudson, "Highland East Cushitic," in M. Lionel Bender, ed., *The Non-Semitic Languages of Ethiopia* (East Lansing: Michigan State University, 1976), pp. 232–77.

7. Ibid., p. 244.

8. Braukamper indicates the possibility that the Hoaffa were originally part of the Hadiyya people situated to the north of the Sadāma. See Braukamper, "Ethnogenesis of the Sidāma," pp. 125–26.

9. The Maldeans did not remain permanently south of the Gidabo River until the Āletā group of clans defeated the Bushēans. Since shortly thereafter the Maldeans reconstituted the generational class system, it is possible to estimate the time span by counting the number of its leaders. As the five generational classes change every seven years, with a new leader for each class, it is possible to estimate a time span of 150–160 years for the victory of the Āletā clans.

10. The blessing was tantamount to granting permission to return.

11. These groups constituted the nuclei of the present-day Wiāno, Dāma, Alēwāno, Hoyē, and Hitāla clans (see figure 1).

12. After their defeat, the Bushēan elders sent their relatives, the Hadičō, to harass the Āletā on their southern flank. These people were potterers and as such were stigmatized as inferior to ordinary farmers and herders. It is unclear as to whether they were ever a military problem for the Āletā, but their presence was considered by the Bushēans as a means for demeaning the military prowess of their enemies.

13. At present there are twelve Āletā clans, as compared with the five in existence when Locke crossed the Gidabo. This number, in conjunction with the contemporary high density, is indicative of population expansion.


## 4. Kinship, Hierarchy, and Resource Distribution

1. For definitions see John Middleton and David Tait, eds., *Tribes without Rulers* (London: Routledge & Kegan Paul, 1958), pp. 3–4, and A. R. Radcliffe-Brown and Daryll Forde, eds., *African Systems of Kinship and Marriage* (New York, Oxford University Press, 1950), pp. 39–40.

2. The Holō and Gārbičō clans have an elaborate ritual, in which every seventh year household heads and their sons visit the graves of their dead ancestors and honor them with offerings of honey. But grave locations disintegrate and become lost over generations, and names associated with particular graves become jumbled, so that in time the sequence becomes largely a myth.

3. Radcliffe-Brown and Forde, *African Systems of Kinship and Marriage*, p. 4, provides a discussion of these basic attributes of a corporate descent group.

4. In the highlands, the thatch-covered framework is made of bamboo, which produces a shape like an overturned wicker basket coming to a point at the top.

5. If leviratic marriage is practiced, the father's brother will maintain his deceased brother's wife on the land during his lifetime. Such a marriage is dependent upon the choice of the widow. From my observation, the eldest son usually permits his mother's co-wife to remain, often with the agreement

that she permit him to retain most of the proceeds from sale of any cash crops planted on the land.

6. For a succinct account of this period, see Greenfield, *Ethiopia*, pp. 72–113.

7. Charles W. McClellan, "The Ethiopian Occupation of Northern Sidāmo—Recruitment and Motivation," in Robert L. Hess, ed., *Proceedings of the Fifth International Conference on Ethiopian Studies* (Chicago: University of Illinois at Chicago Circle, 1979), p. 519.

8. John M. Cohen and Dove Weintraub, *Land and Peasants in Imperial Ethiopia* (Assem: Van Gorcum, 1975), pp. 36–37.

9. Alula Abate and Tesfaye Teklu, "Land Reform and Peasant Associations in Ethiopia—Case Studies of Two Widely Differing Regions," *Northeast African Studies* 2, no. 2 (Fall 1980): 49. A length of rope was used to measure the land into gaša, a unit of area varying in size from thirty to seventy hectares (1 hectare = 2.47 acres). Presently a gaša is supposed to measure forty hectares.

10. Allen Hoben, *Land Tenure among the Amhara of Ethiopia* (Chicago: University of Chicago Press, 1973), pp. 145–46.

11. Claude Meillassoux, "From Reproduction to Production," *Economy and Society* 1, no. 1 (February 1972): 98–100.

12. Catherine Coquery-Vidrovitch, "The Political Economy of the African Peasantry and Modes of Production," in Peter C. W. Gutkind and Immanuel Wallerstein, eds., *The Political Economy of Contemporary Africa* (Beverly Hills: Sage Publications, 1976), p. 95.

13. For more details of this practice see John Hamer, "Goals, Status, and the Stability of n-Achievement: A Small Sample from Southern Ethiopia," *Ethos* 6, no. 1 (1978): 48–49.

14. See, for example, Meyer Fortes's discussion of this problem in his *Kinship and the Social Order* (Chicago: Aldine, 1969), p. 238, n. 15.

15. On the subject of differing forms of reciprocity see Marshall Sahlins, "On the Sociology of Primitive Exchange," in Michael Banton, ed., *The Relevance of Models for Social Anthropology* (London: Tavistock Publications, 1965), p. 147, and Maurice Block, "The Long Term and the Short Term: The Economic and Political Significance of the Morality of Kinship," in Jack Goody, ed., *The Character of Kinship* (London: Cambridge University Press, 1973), pp. 83–84.

16. This fee consists of a cash payment of three dollars Ethiopian and a large bowl of ensete smothered in butter.

17. For details on the rituals and the food avoidances, see John Hamer, "Myth, Ritual, and the Authority of Elders in an Ethiopian Society," *Africa* 46, no. 4 (1976): 327–39.

18. See, for example, Donald N. Levine, *Greater Ethiopia: The Evolution of a Multiethnic Society* (Chicago: University of Chicago Press, 1974), p. 39; Cerulli, *Peoples of South-West Ethiopia and Its Borderland*, pp. 125–26; Eike

Haberland, "Special Castes in Ethiopia," in Robert L. Hess, ed., *Proceedings of the Fifth International Conference on Ethiopian Studies* (Chicago: University of Illinois at Chicago Circle, 1979), pp. 129–32.

19. David M. Todd, "Caste in Africa?" *Africa* 47, no. 4 (1977): 399–404.

20. Ibid., pp. 404–5, 409.

21. Ibid., p. 410.

22. Hamer, "Myth, Ritual, and the Authority of Elders," p. 332.

## 5. Marriage and the Sexual Division of Labor

1. Roger Keesing, *Kin Groups and Social Structure* (New York: Holt, Rinehart & Winston, 1975), pp. 89–90.

2. A succinct description of the distinction between elementary and complex marriage systems is provided by Robin Fox, *Kinship and Marriage* (Middlesex: Penguin Books, 1967), pp. 222–28.

3. Ibid., pp. 232–33.

4. In the mid-1960s, $1.00 U.S. was equal to $2.50 Ethiopian; by the mid-1970s, the exchange rate was $1.00 U.S. to $2.00 Ethiopian.

5. This excerpt is from the field notes of proceedings in which the anthropologist participated.

6. Evidence exists of a period of "adolescent sterility" extending approximately from the ages thirteen to sixteen. During this period, the female is less likely to conceive than when she reaches the period of nubility (from seventeen to twenty-two, give or take two years), and when she does there is a high level of infant and maternal mortality, as well as high miscarriage rates. M. F. Ashley Montagu, *The Reproductive Development of the Female* (New York: Julian Press, 1957), pp. 190–91. See also M. Nag, *Factors Affecting Fertility in Non-Industrial Societies, A Cross-Cultural Study* (New Haven: Human Relations Area File Press, 1968); N. Howell, "Toward a Uniformitarian Theory of Human Paleo-demography," *Journal of Human Evolution* 5 (1976): 25–40; R. E. Frisch, "Population, Food Intake, and Fertility," *Science* 199 (1977): 22–30.

7. Even a stranger may be the hero. It must be remembered that such persons are treated in most situations as if they are members of the clan in which they reside.

8. Arike is a beverage distilled from barley and maize by women in the countryside.

9. This is based on the mean estimate of income for thirty-seven household heads from a sampling made during 1964–65.

10. Shack, *Gurage*, p. 67, also notes that for the Gurage, north of the Sadāma, a shortage of land is making it increasingly difficult for men to become polygynous.

11. In the early 1970s a Sadāma revitalization movement known as Wando Magāno required its adherents to return one-half the bridewealth in the event of a marriage termination, the other half being retained by the wife's family as compensation for loss of her virginity. John Hamer, "Crisis, Moral Consensus, and the Wando Magāno Movement among the Sadāma of Southwest Ethiopia," *Ethnology* 16, no. 4 (October 1977): 410.

12. Because of recent abolition during the Italian occupation, slavery is a sensitive topic on which my information is limited. It seems that descendants of slaves could after several generations purchase their freedom by paying the original purchase price to descendants of the original owner. Such a person would then be a member of the owner's clan and would be given land by the elders.

13. M. Abir, "Salt, Trade, and Politics in Ethiopia in the Zāmōnā Māsafent," *Journal of Ethiopian Studies* 4, no. 2 (1966): 1–10.

14. Richard Pankhurst, "The Maria Theresa Dollar," *Journal of Ethiopian Studies* 1, no. 1 (January 1963): 8–26.

# 6. Beliefs, Ritual, and Authority

1. Such tales, called *mamāša*, are metaphorical and are used frequently in the course of council meetings to persuade others to take a certain course of action.

2. It is believed that paying a fine is the means of releasing a wrongdoer from the consequences of his actions and of making him once more an acceptable member of the community.

3. Karl Eric Knutsson, *Authority and Change: A Study of the Kallu Institution among the Macha Galla of Ethiopia* (Göteborg: Ethnografika Museet, 1967), pp. 53–54.

4. Hamer, "Crisis, Moral Consensus, and the Wando Magāno Movement," pp. 399–413.

5. John Hamer and Irene Hamer, "Spirit Possession and Its Socio-Psychological Implications among the Sidāmo of Southwest Ethiopia," *Ethnology* 5, no. 4 (October 1966): 392–408.

6. Ibid., p. 394.

7. Ibid.

8. Indeed, a female host is referred to as a *gaēno* ("mule") and a male as a *ferājo* ("horse").

9. A person with a spirit of unusual power may become noted for predictions about the future and suggested cures for illness. The spirit, taking the form of the host, may appear in a dream to others and request that they come to the host with gifts and provide services such as cooking, preparing a garden, gathering firewood, and other similar tasks.

10. To have a pleasant disposition is referred to as having a good stomach, while to be quarrelsome and dissatisfied is to have a bad stomach.

11. Hamer, "Myth, Ritual, and the Authority of Elders," pp. 332–34.

12. The right and left are differentially equated with "good" and "evil," depending on the situation. For example, if a person is departing on a journey and he hears the call of the kukīsa bird on his left, he recognizes this as a good omen, but if the cry comes from the right, then the journey should not be made. On the return journey the omens and directions are reversed.

13. Goida is the campsite for the Āletā (see map 1).

14. Max Gluckman, *Politics, Law, and Ritual in Tribal Society* (Chicago: Aldine, 1965), pp. 257–58.

# 7. Authority and Social Control

1. I have described the lua in detail elsewhere and will in this context present only a summary of that work. For more details see John Hamer, "Sidāmo Generational Class Cycles: A Political Gerontocracy," *Africa* 40, no. 1 (1970): 50–70.

2. Lucy Mair, *Primitive Government* (Baltimore: Penguin Books, 1962), p. 80.

3. Asmarom Legesse, "Class Systems Based on Time," *Journal of Ethiopian Studies* 1, no. 2 (1963): 2.

4. If men in attendance at mourning ceremonies are of the same clan, relative chronological age will determine the order in which they approach the bereaved kinsmen, but when they are of different clans, as is often the case, then the principle of generational class seniority is followed.

5. Hamer, "Myth, Ritual, and the Authority of Elders," pp. 331–32.

6. Marshall Sahlins, *Tribesmen* (Englewood Cliffs: Prentice-Hall, 1968), p. 21.

7. Elman R. Service, *Origins of the State and Civilization: The Process of Cultural Evolution* (New York: Norton, 1975), pp. 150–52.

8. An abāya is a miniature of a womāša and seems to be a symbolic continuation of the tradition of giving what was formerly a highly valued form of currency.

9. Service, *Origins of the State and Civilization*, p. 94. Wolf makes much the same distinction between chiefs and their followers who are "embedded" in the kinship system and those who are able to use their own descent group to control tribute. The latter ultimately become a socioeconomic class apart, controlling public works and managing redistribution and warfare. Eric R. Wolf, *Europe and the People without History* (Berkeley: University of California Press, 1982), pp. 96–97.

10. Robert L. Carneiro, "Political Expansion as an Expression of the Prin-

ciple of Competitive Exclusion," in Ronald Cohen and Elman R. Service, eds., *Origins of the State: The Anthropology of Political Evolution* (Philadelphia: Institute for the Study of Human Issues, 1978), p. 207.

11. E. E. Evans-Pritchard, *The Nuer* (Oxford: Clarendon Press, 1940), pp. 184–89.

12. This is different in non-Āletā areas, especially among the Shabādino and Yānāssi, where the functions of the lineage sōngo are similar to those of a clan sōngo in Āletā.

13. Old men smoke the water pipe together as a sign of peace and acceptance of each other's presence. When water from the pipe is used in rituals for restoring harmony, it is always the oldest man present who officiates.

14. I use pseudonyms for the persons involved.

15. It will be recalled from the previous section that harmony must prevail between persons and groups before a new class is initiated, in the hope that the beginning of each new class will portend a time of peace among the people.

16. Today the deceased's relatives could accuse the husband in an Ethiopian court of law; the procedure would involve the previously discussed process of negotiation.

17. All of the elders originally accompanied Hami to view the property, when correct procedure required only one to carry out this task.

18. Barren ground is used for the ceremony because the people wish the sorcerer to wither and die as has the grass on the ritual ground. Salt is used in the ordeal for suspected sorcerers as a token that it will hasten their demise, just as salt can hasten the drying up of grass.

19. Emmanuel Terray, *Marxism and Primitive Societies* (New York: Monthly Review Press, 1972), pp. 177–78.

## 8. The Process of Change

1. In this regard see Levine, *Greater Ethiopia*, pp. 40–64.

2. Concerning these issues of Ethiopian history, see John Markakis, *Ethiopia: Anatomy of a Traditional Polity* (Oxford: Clarendon Press, 1974), pp. 23–25; D. L. Donham, "From Ritual Kings to Ethiopian Landlords: Malle, Southwestern Ethiopia, c. 1894–1974," in D. L. Donham and Wendy Jones, eds., *Working Papers on Society and History in Imperial Ethiopia: The Southern Periphery from the 1880s to 1974* (Cambridge: African Studies Center, 1980), p. 163; Greenfield, *Ethiopia*, p. 96.

3. Greenfield, *Ethiopia*, p. 105.

4. R. A. Caulk, "Firearms and Princely Power in Ethiopia in the Nineteenth Century," *Journal of African History* 13, no. 4 (1972): 620.

5. R. A. Caulk, "The Army and Society in Ethiopia," *Ethiopianist Notes*

1, no. 3 (1978): 19; Cohen and Weintraub, *Land and Peasants*, p. 37 and n. 44.

6. Charles W. McClellan, "Ethiopian Occupation of Northern Sidāmo," pp. 515, 519.

7. Ibid., p. 519; Donham, "From Ritual Kings to Ethiopian Landlords," p. 163.

8. Caulk, "The Army and Society in Ethiopia," pp. 21–22.

9. Donham, "From Ritual Kings to Ethiopian Landlords," p. 162; Cohen and Weintraub, *Land and Peasants*, pp. 35–36.

10. McClellan, "Ethiopian Occupation of Northern Sidāmo," p. 515.

11. Wolf, *Europe and the People*, pp. 80–81.

12. See, for example, A. J. Barker, *The Civilizing Mission: A History of the Italo-Ethiopian War of 1935–1936* (New York: Dial Press, 1968), pp. 307–9; James Dugan and Lawrence Lafore, *Days of Emperor and Clown: The Italo-Ethiopian War, 1935–1936* (Garden City: Doubleday, 1973), pp. 327–29.

13. Greenfield, *Ethiopia*, pp. 306–12.

14. Charles B. Rosen, "The Dynamics of Provincial Administration in Haile Selassie's Ethiopia: 1930–1974," in Gerald M. Britan and Ronald Cohen, eds., *Hierarchy and Society: Anthropological Perspectives on Bureaucracy* (Philadelphia: Institute for the Study of Human Issues, 1980), pp. 89–122.

15. During 1964–65, cows were selling in Ethiopian currency at prices ranging from $50 to $60, sheep and goats from $12 to $15, and donkeys at $60 to $75. Based on an estimate for minimum price and number of animals equally divided among the two leaders, each would receive the equivalent in cash value of approximately $556. As will be shown later, this is more than twice the estimated average income of a Sadānčo.

16. The husband was the son of a northern colonist and therefore categorized as an Amhara.

17. Jack Goody, "Introduction," in Jack Goody, ed., *Succession to High Office* (Cambridge University Press, 1966), p. 27.

18. Robbins Burling, *The Passage of Power: Studies in Political Succession* (New York: Academic Press, 1974), pp. 50–52; Goody, "Introduction," pp. 27–28.

19. See, for example, the material on Tigray Province in Rosen, "Dynamics of Provincial Administration," pp. 89–122.

20. Cohen and Weintraub, *Land and Peasants*, pp. 35–36.

21. Though *kannazmač* is traditionally an Amhara military title meaning "general" of the right wing, these titles have frequently been given to court or civil officials. See Donald N. Levine, *Wax and Gold: Tradition and Innovation in Ethiopia Culture* (Chicago: University of Chicago Press, 1965), pp. 158–60.

22. Norman Singer, "The Ethiopian Civil Code and the Recognition of Customary Law," *Huston Law Review* 9, no. 3 (January 1972): 466–67.

23. Ibid., pp. 464–65.

24. Ibid., p. 458.

25. Ibid., pp. 484–93.

26. Norman Singer, "A Traditional Legal Institution in a Modern Legal Setting: The Atbia Dagnia of Ethiopia," *U.C.L.A. Law Review* 18, no. 2 (December 1970): 312–15.

27. Markakis, *Ethiopia*, p. 296.

28. Singer, "Traditional Legal Institution," p. 317, n. 34.

29. Markakis, *Ethiopia*, p. 297.

30. Singer, "Traditional Legal Institution," pp. 321–25.

31. Ibid., pp. 326–34.

32. Markakis, *Ethiopia*, p. 298.

33. The exception was a young man from a well-to-do peasant family who after receiving some legal training was posted to a court in a distant province.

34. Lars Bondestan, "Notes on Foreign Investments in Ethiopia," in Carl Widstrand, ed., *Multinational Firms in Africa* (Uppsala: Scandinavian Institute of African Studies, 1975), pp. 125–26.

35. See, for example, Greenfield, *Ethiopia*, p. 324, and Mesfin Wolde-Mariam, *An Introductory Geography of Ethiopia* (Addis Ababa: Berhanena Selam H.S.I. Printing Press, 1972), p. 118.

36. Richard Reimer, "Ethiopian Agricultural Exports: A Brief Survey," *Rural Africana*, no. 28 (Fall 1975): 134.

37. Ibid., p. 121.

38. Wolde-Mariam, *Introductory Geography of Ethiopia*, p. 118.

39. Central Statistical Office, *Statistical Abstracts 1971* (Addis Ababa: Government Printer, 1971), p. 143.

40. Taye Gulilat, "Coffee in the Ethiopian Economy, II," *Journal of Ethiopian Studies* 1, no. 1 (January 1963): 53; Robert Liebenthal, "Certain Development Issues in Ethiopia and Their Relationship to Rural/Urban Balance: A Perspective Based on World Bank Experience," *Ethiopian Notes*, no. 3 (Spring 1978): 52.

41. Gulilat, "Coffee in the Ethiopian Economy," p. 47.

42. Ibid., pp. 48–49.

43. Markakis, *Ethiopia*, pp. 180–81; see also Associations Registration Regulations Legal Notice no. 321 (Addis Ababa-Government Printer, 1966).

44. United Nations, *1980 Trade Yearbook* (Rome: Food and Agriculture Organization, 1980), p. 180.

45. Theodore E. Downing, "The Internationalization of Capital in Agriculture," *Human Organization* 41, no. 3 (Fall 1982): 272.

46. Gulilat, "Coffee in Ethiopian Economy," pp. 53–54; Central Statistical Office, *Statistical Abstracts 1971*, p. 110.

47. By 1978, Nestlé and General Foods controlled 75 percent of the instant-coffee market. Downing, "Internationalization of Capital," p. 272.

48. Gulilat, "Coffee in the Ethiopian Economy," p. 54.

49. Downing, "Internationalization of Capital," p. 273.

50. Ibid., p. 275.

51. See, for example, Bjorn Beckman's analysis of the cash economy in Ghana in his "Ghana, 1951–78: The Agrarian Basis of the Post-Colonial State," in Judith Heyer, Pepe Roberts, and Gavin Williams, eds., Rural Development in Tropical Africa (New York: St. Martin's Press, 1981), pp. 143–65.

52. Income and expenditures are items that most men are reluctant to reveal, partly because of fear that such information can be used to increase taxation, partly for fear of causing jealousy that could lead to sorcery, and partly, in recent times, because of the desire of some to avoid redistributing their wealth. In 1973 several of the previous informants were unavailable; some had become reluctant to discuss these matters, and there was insufficient time to contact others.

53. Some men annually absorb hired labor expenses in hiring itinerant Gurage labor to dig up their land for spring planting. Some farmers consider this a time-saving investment when they are busy picking and preparing coffee for market.

54. Though we lack income data from these regions, the opinion of informants is that the figures probably would be considerably lower than in the coffee regions.

55. For the thirty-seven householders interviewed in 1965, six reported actual dollar amounts of savings.

56. Charles J. Erasmus, In Search of the Common Good (New York: Free Press, 1977), pp. 106–10.

57. The name is, of course, fictitious.

58. Awassa, located on the northern border adjoining Arussi Province, has recently replaced Yirgā Alēm as the capital of Sidāmo Province.

59. At the time he told me this, his wife was pregnant with their eleventh child.

60. Markakis, Ethiopia, pp. 148–49. See also Patrick Gilkes, The Dying Lion: Feudalism and Modernization in Ethiopia (New York: St. Martin's Press, 1975), p. 92, who indicates the ratio of enrollment in Sidāmo Province of public (28,082) to mission and private schools (8,848) was not quite so high, at a little more than three to one.

61. Markakis, Ethiopia, p. 156; Levine, Wax and Gold, p. 146.

62. Markakis, Ethiopia, p. 156. Also see Desta Asyeghn, "Schooling and Inequality in Prerevolutionary Ethiopia," Ethiopianist Notes 2, no. 2 (1978): 10–11. The author indicates that by 1974, 25 percent of the nation's secondary school graduates were unemployed and only 23 percent of those taking the school exams qualified for university entrance.

63. Markakis, Ethiopia, p. 147.

64. Raymond Davis, Fire on the Mountains (Grand Rapids: Zondervan, 1966), pp. 27–31.

65. The missionaries soon began to proselytize in the three communities where the author conducted the most intensive part of the field research.

66. In this connection it should be noted that when a household head becomes a church member, his wife and children are, as a rule, baptized with him.

67. For more details on Islamic proselytizing see John Hamer, "Islam and the Sadāma," in Richard V. Weekes, ed., *Muslim Peoples: A World Ethnographic Survey* (Westport: Greenwood Press, 1984), pp. 1320–31.

68. The plant čat *(Catha edulis)* is widely cultivated in the Middle East and the Horn of Africa. The leaves produce a mild narcotic effect and are chewed by Muslims at prayer. See J. Spencer Trimingham, *Islam in Ethiopia* (New York: Barnes & Noble, 1965), p. 228.

69. G. E. Von Grunebaum, *Islam: Essays in the Nature and Growth of a Cultural Tradition*, American Anthropological Association, vol. 57, no. 2, part 2, memoir no. 81 (Menasha, Wis.: Banta, 1955), pp. 4–5.

70. Theodore Brett, "Colonialism, Underdevelopment, and Class Formation in East Africa," in Chris Allen and Gavin Williams, eds., *Subsaharan Africa* (New York: Monthly Review Press, 1982), pp. 3–10.

71. Werner Bierman, "The Development of Underdevelopment: The Historical Perspective," in Ben Turok, ed., *Development in Zambia: A Reader* (London: Zed Press, 1979), pp. 133–34.

72. McClellan, "Ethiopian Occupation of Northern Sidāmo," p. 516.

73. See, for example, Dale L. Johnson, "Class Analysis and Dependency," in Ronald H. Chilcote and Dale L. Johnson, eds., *Theories of Development: Mode of Production or Dependency* (Beverly Hills: Sage Publications, 1983), p. 234, and the general Marxian view that all major historical changes are based on class struggle in Karl Marx and Friedrich Engels, *Basic Writings on Politics and Philosophy*, ed. Lewis S. Feuer (Garden City: Doubleday, 1959), p. 7.

74. Henry Veltmeyer, "Surplus Labor and Class Formation on the Latin American Periphery," in Ronald H. Chilcote and Dale L. Johnson, eds., *Theories of Development: Mode of Production or Dependency* (Beverly Hills: Sage Publications, 1983), p. 201.

75. See footnote 20 in Paul Brietzke, "Review: Class and Revolution in Ethiopia by John Markakis and Nega Ayele," *Northeast African Studies* 1, no. 3 (Winter 1979–80): p. 104, which is a quotation from Marx's "Eighteenth Brumaire of Louis Bonaparte." In this quotation Marx suggests that persons whose way of life, because of prevailing economic conditions, separates them and places them in hostile opposition to others constitute a class.

76. For example, the approach of John Markakis and Nega Ayele, *Class and Revolution in Ethiopia* (Nottingham: Spokesman, 1978), in explaining the 1974 Revolution on the basis of class conflict, has been criticized on the grounds that prerevolutionary Ethiopia was essentially feudal in structure,

with a hierarchy based on patron-client relations. In this connection see Brietzke, "Review," pp. 99–105; David Wilson, "Review Essay: Class and Revolution in Ethiopia," *Horn of Africa* 4, no. 4 (1981–82): 15–22; and Donald Crummey, "State and Society: Nineteenth-Century Ethiopia," in Donald Crummey and C. C. Stewart, eds., *Modes of Production in Africa* (Beverly Hills: Sage Publications, 1981), pp. 229–30.

77. Rayah Feldman, "Rural Social Differentiation and Political Goals in Tanzania," in Ivar Oxal, Tony Barnett, and David Booth, eds., *Beyond the Sociology of Development: Economy and Society in Latin America and Africa* (London: Routledge & Kegan Paul, 1975), pp. 164–80.

78. Periodic parliamentary elections were the only times that these outsiders sought to influence the peasantry by buying their votes with money, food, and drink. In the last election in 1973 most of the seats were won by candidates who were Sadāma.

79. Edmond J. Keller, "Revolution, Class, and the National Question: The Case of Ethiopia," *Northeast African Studies* 3, no. 1 (1981): 43–67.

## 9. Self-Help Associations for Change

1. See, for example, Edward Norbeck, "Associations and Democracy in Japan," in R. P. Dore, ed., *Aspects of Social Change in Modern Japan* (Princeton: Princeton University Press, 1967), pp. 185–200; John Anderson, "Voluntary Associations in Hyderabad," *Anthropological Quarterly* 37 (1964): 175–76; James Kerri, "Studying Voluntary Associations as Adaptive Mechanisms: A Review of Anthropological Perspectives," *Current Anthropology* 17, no. 1 (1976): 24.

2. Kerri, "Studying Voluntary Associations," p. 24.

3. Paul Bohanon, *Social Anthropology* (New York: Holt, Rinehart & Winston, 1963), pp. 155–58.

4. John Hamer, "Voluntary Associations as Structures of Change among the Sidāmo of Southwest Ethiopia," *Anthropological Quarterly* 40, no. 2 (1967): 80–81.

5. Ministry of National Community Development, *Labour, Cooperatives, Social Welfare, and Community Development* (Addis Ababa: Commercial Printing Press, 1964), p. 37.

6. Ibid., p. 23.

7. Ibid., p. 24.

8. It will be recalled that a subdistrict is composed of a number of atbia, each containing 130 gaša. For example, the Wando subdistrict, the area of most concentrated field research, is divided into thirteen atbia.

9. Ten societies were actually studied, but only six had achieved a level of organization sufficient to warrant registration by the Ministry of Community Development.

10. Enrollment figures were not obtained for one of the six registered societies.

11. English terms were retained for president and vice-president, but Amharic designations were used for treasurer (wate-amado) and for secretary (safi).

12. In 1965, income from the mill varied from ten dollars to as much as forty-five dollars a day during the maize-producing season. Unfortunately, I failed to obtain figures on the 1973 mill income, though the mill appeared to be even busier than in 1965.

13. Erasmus, In Search of the Common Good, p. 118.

14. This sum is significant, as can be seen by relating it to the average (mean) income in the small sample in chapter 8 (see table 3), of which it would constitute nearly 10 percent.

15. One of these men, as will be discussed later, succumbed to the temptations of self-aggrandizement by misusing society resources.

16. This association is analogous to a Western-style chamber of commerce, protecting the interests of the merchants of the town of Wando and raising money for local activities of value to the members.

17. A more detailed account of this problem is to be found in John Hamer, "Rivalry and Taking Kinsmen for Granted: Limiting Factors in the Development of Voluntary Associations," Journal of Anthropological Research 38, no. 3 (Fall 1982): 303–14.

18. Ronald F. Dore, "Modern Cooperatives in Traditional Communities," in Peter Worsley, ed., Two Blades of Grass (London: Manchester University Press, 1971), pp. 54–55.

19. Sahlins, "On the Sociology of Primitive Exchange," p. 147.

20. For a detailed analysis see John Hamer, "Preconditions and Limits in the Formation of Associations: The Self-Help and Cooperative Movement in Subsaharan Africa," African Studies Review 24, no. 1 (March 1981): 113–32.

21. Joan Vincent, "Rural Competition and the Cooperative Monopoly: A Ugandan Case Study," in June Nash, Jorge Dandler, and Nicholas Hopkins, eds., Popular Participation in Social Change (The Hague: Mouton, 1976), pp. 82–85.

22. Jan J. De Wolf, Differentiation and Integration in Western Kenya (The Hague: Mouton, 1977), p. 61.

23. Henri Raulin, "Organized Cooperation and Spontaneous Cooperation in Africa (Niger Republic)," in June Nash, Jorge Dandler, and Nicholas Hopkins, eds., Popular Participation in Social Change (The Hague: Mouton, 1976), pp. 37–38.

24. Hans F. Illy, "How to Build in the Germs of Failure: Credit Cooperatives in French Cameroon," Rural Africana, no. 2 (Fall 1978): 64–65.

25. Edgar V. Winans and Angelique Hangerud, "Rural Self-Help in Kenya: The Harambee Movement," Human Organization 36 (1977): p. 336.

26. De Wolf, Differentiation and Integration, p. 103.

27. Vincent, "Rural Competition and the Cooperative Monopoly," pp. 75, 79, 92–93.

28. W. Arens, *On The Frontier of Change: Mto wa Mbu, Tanzania* (Ann Arbor: University Microfilms Press, 1979), p. 142.

29. Warren Roth, "Traditional Social Structure and the Development of a Marketing Cooperative in Tanzania," in June Nash, Jorge Dandler, and Nicholas Hopkins, eds., *Popular Participation in Social Change* (The Hague: Mouton, 1976), p. 52; Warren Roth "Three Cooperatives and a Credit Union as Examples of Culture Change" (Ph.D. diss., Catholic University of America, 1966), pp. 338–41.

30. S. G. Bunker, "Forms and Functions of Government Intervention in a Uganda Cooperative Union" (Paper presented at the Fourteenth Annual Meeting of the African Studies Association, 1971), pp. 16–17.

31. Hans Dieter Seibel and Andreas Massing, *Traditional Organizations and Economic Development: Studies of Indigenous Cooperatives in Liberia* (New York: Praeger, 1974), pp. 225–26.

32. Nicholas S. Hopkins, "Leadership and Consensus in Two Malian Cooperatives," in David Brokensha and Marion Pearsall, eds., *The Anthropology of Development in Sub-Saharan Africa*, Monograph 10 (Lexington, Ky.: Society for Applied Anthropology, 1969), p. 67.

33. See, for example, Erasmus, *In Search of the Common Good*, pp. 50, 320.

34. For a detailed discussion of case types see John Hamer, "Preference, Principle, and Precedent: Dispute Settlement and Changing Norms in Sidāmo Associations," *Ethnology* 19, no. 1 (January 1980): 94–108.

35. Pheroze Nowrojee, "The Settlement of Disputes in Cooperative Societies," in Carl G. Widstrand, ed., *African Cooperatives and Efficiency* (Uppsala: Almquist & Wiksell, 1972), pp. 78–79; Hamer, "Preconditions and Limits," pp. 119–20.

36. Gottfried O. Lang, Warren J. Roth, and Martha B. Lang, "Sukumaland Cooperatives as Mechanisms of Change," in David Brokensha and Marion Pearsall, eds., *The Anthropology of Development in Sub-Saharan Africa*, Monograph 10 (Lexington, Ky.: Society for Applied Anthropology, 1969), p. 57; Roth, "Three Cooperatives and a Credit Union," pp. 306, 329.

37. M. Ruel, "The Modern Adaptation of Associations among the Banyang of the West Cameroon," *Southwestern Journal of Anthropology* 20, no. 1 (1964): p. 9.

38. Ministry of National Community Development, *Labour, Cooperatives, Social Welfare, and Community Development*, p. 41.

39. This again is a pseudonym, as in all cases where personal names have been used.

40. See especially Orlando Fals Borda, Raymond Apthorpe, and Inayatullah, "The Crisis of Rural Cooperatives: Problems in Africa, Asia, and Latin America," in June Nash, Jorge Dandler, and Nicholas Hopkins, eds., *Popular*

*Participation in Social Change* (The Hague: Mouton, 1976), pp. 446–55; Lionell Cliffe, "Rural Political Economy of Africa," in Peter C. W. Gutkind and Immanuel Wallerstein, eds., *The Political Economy of Contemporary Africa* (Beverly Hills: Sage Publications, 1976), p. 124.

41. Hamer, "Preconditions and Limits," pp. 120–23.

42. See, for example, Cliffe, "Rural Political Economy of Africa," p. 123; Gavin Williams, "Taking the Part of Peasants: Rural Development in Nigeria and Tanzania," in Peter C. W. Gutkind and Immanuel Wallerstein, eds., *The Political Economy of Contemporary Africa* (Beverly Hills: Sage Publications, 1976), pp. 134–35; Hamer, "Preconditions and Limits," pp. 123–26; Donal B. Cruise O'Brien, "Cooperators and Bureaucrats: Class Formation in a Senegalese Society," *Africa* 41, no. 4 (1971): pp. 263–77; Roger King, "Cooperative Policy and Village Development in Northern Nigeria," in Judith Heyer, Pepe Roberts, and Gavin Williams, eds., *Rural Development in Tropical Africa* (New York: St. Martin's Press, 1981), pp. 278–79.

43. Pepe Roberts, "Rural Development and Economy in Niger, 1900–75," in Judith Heyer, Pepe Roberts, and Gavin Williams, eds., *Rural Development in Tropical Africa* (New York: St. Martin's Press, 1981), pp. 208–18.

44. Williams, "Taking the Part of Peasants," p. 136.

45. Cruise O'Brien, "Cooperators and Bureaucrats," pp. 264–65.

46. See the works of Williams, "Taking the Part of Peasants," pp. 138–41, and Hyden, *Beyond Ujamaa in Tanzania*, p. 75, both of whom indicate that a major reason for the success of the Ruvuma Development Association was the lack of government interference and the reliance on local controls.

47. R. G. Abrahams, *The Nyamwezi Today* (London: Cambridge University Press, 1981), p. 79.

48. Williams, "Taking the Part of Peasants," p. 147.

49. Melville J. Herskovits, *Man and His Works* (New York: Random House, 1948), pp. 588–93.

## 10. Theories of Development and the Future of the Self-Help Movement

1. Caroline Hutton and Robin Cohen, "African Peasants and Resistance to Change: A Reconsideration of Sociological Approaches," in Ivar Oxal, Tony Barnett, and David Booth, eds., *Beyond the Sociology of Development: Economy and Society in Latin America and Africa* (London: Routledge & Kegan Paul, 1975), p. 122.

2. P. W. Preston, *Theories of Development* (London: Routledge & Kegan Paul, 1982), pp. 62–65.

3. Ibid., pp. 72–74.

4. Ibid., pp. 83, 89–91.

5. See especially W. W. Rostow, The Stages of Economic Growth (Cambridge: Cambridge University Press, 1960).

6. Preston, Theories of Development, pp. 152–53; C. Richard Bath and Dilmas James, "Dependency Analysis of Latin America: Some Criticisms and Suggestions," Latin American Research Review 11, no. 3 (1976): 3–4.

7. Preston, Theories of Development, pp. 158–59.

8. Bath and James, "Dependency Analysis of Latin America," pp. 3–54.

9. Ibid., p. 6.

10. Ibid., pp. 10–11.

11. Immanuel Wallerstein, The Modern World System, vol. 1, Capitalist Agriculture and the Origins of the European World Economy in the Sixteenth Century (New York: Academic Press, 1974), and vol. 2, Mercantilism and the Consolidation of the European World Economy (New York: Academic Press, 1980).

12. Richard Rubinson, "Introduction," in Richard Rubinson, ed., Dynamics of World Development (Beverly Hills: Sage Publications, 1981), pp. 12–15.

13. Immanuel Wallerstein, "The Three Stages of African Involvement in the World Economy," in Peter C. W. Gutkind and Immanuel Wallerstein, eds., The Political Economy of Contemporary Africa (Beverly Hills: Sage Publications, 1976), pp. 30–50.

14. See especially Barry Hindess and Paul Hirst, Pre-Capitalist Modes of Production (London: Routledge & Kegan Paul, 1975), p. 9; Bridget O'Laughlin, "Marxist Approaches in Anthropology," in B. J. Segal, A. R. Beals, and S. A. Tyler, eds., Annual Review of Anthropology (Palo Alto: Annual Reviews, 1975), pp. 346–69.

15. Alice Littlefield, "Exploitation and the Expansion of Capitalism: The Case of the Hammock Industry of Yucatan," American Ethnologist, 5, no. 3 (1978): 497.

16. O'Laughlin, "Marxist Approaches in Anthropology."

17. Meillassoux, "From Reproduction to Production," pp. 93–105.

18. Terray, Marxism and Primitive Societies, pp. 177–78.

19. Hindess and Hirst, Pre-Capitalist Modes of Production.

20. Samir Amin, Le development inégal (Paris: Editions de Minuit, 1973).

21. The special issue of the American Ethnologist entitled "Political Economy," vol. 5, no. 5, 1978, has several excellent articles illustrative of this endeavor.

22. Nicholas S. Hopkins, "The Articulation of the Modes of Production: Tailoring in Tunisia," American Ethnologist 5, no. 5 (1978): 468–83; Littlefield, "Exploitation and the Expansion of Capitalism," pp. 495–508.

23. Norma S. Chinchilla, "Crisis and Transformation of Dependency in the World System," in Ronald H. Chilcote and Dale L. Johnson, eds., Theories of Development: Mode of Production or Dependency (Beverly Hills: Sage Publications, 1983), pp. 159–64.

24. Central Statistical Office, *Statistical Abstracts 1971*, p. 89.

25. Wolde-Mariam, *Introductory Geography of Ethiopia*, p. 166.

26. Ibid., p. 165.

27. Central Statistical Office, *Statistical Abstracts 1971*, p. 98.

28. Reimer, "Ethiopian Agricultural Exports," pp. 119–20.

29. Central Statistical Office, *Statistical Abstracts 1971*, pp. 98–101.

30. Reimer, "Ethiopian Agricultural Exports," p. 135.

31. John Cohen, "Effects of Green Revolution Strategies on Tenants and Small-Scale Landowners in the Chilalo Region of Ethiopia," *Journal of Developing Areas* 9 (1975): 335–58.

32. Tesfai Tekle, "An Approach to Rural Development: A Case Study of the Ethiopian Package Projects," in John W. Harbeson and Paul Brietzke, eds., *Rural Development in Ethiopia* (East Lansing: Michigan State University, African Studies Center, 1975), pp. 93, 100.

33. Ibid., p. 101.

34. Ibid., p. 102.

35. Meillassoux, "From Reproduction to Production," pp. 98–101.

36. Hindess and Hirst, *Pre-Capitalist Modes of Production*, p. 9.

37. Exceptions were made for widows, the incapacitated, and children under eighteen who inherited land.

38. Proclamation to Provide for the Public Ownership of Rural Lands, no. 31 (Addis Ababa: Government Printer, 1975).

39. Since the revolution, the term *kifle-hager* ("administrative region") has been used instead of *tekla-gezat* ("province").

40. Allen Hoben, "Perspectives on Land Reform in Ethiopia: The Political Role of the Peasantry," *Rural Africana*, no. 28 (Fall 1975): 68.

41. *Zemača* is usually translated as "development through cooperation."

42. Marina Ottaway, "Land Reform and Peasant Associations: A Preliminary Analysis," *Rural Africana*, no. 28 (Fall 1975): 43–48; Abate and Teklu, "Land Reform and Peasant Associations," pp. 11, 20.

43. Abate and Teklu, "Land Reform and Peasant Associations," p. 14; Paulos Milkias, "Zemecha—An Assessment of the Political and Social Foundations of Mass Education in Ethiopia," *Northeast African Studies* 2, no. 1 (Spring 1980): 22–23.

44. Ottaway, "Land Reform and Peasant Associations," pp. 40–48.

45. Abate and Teklu, "Land Reform and Peasant Associations," pp. 20–21.

46. Ibid., p. 28.

47. Ibid., pp. 12–19, 23–36.

48. Ibid., pp. 17–19.

49. Ibid., p. 31.

50. Ibid., pp. 34–36. The rejection has been general throughout Ethiopia. See, for example, Hoben, "Perspectives on Land Reform," p. 68, and Ottaway, "Land Reform and Peasant Associations," p. 49.

51. Lirenso shows that for Ethiopia in general, the objectives of the Agricultural Marketing Corporation changed in 1978 from competing with private traders for commodity procurement to quota schemes and fixed prices. This change has apparently created dissatisfaction everywhere among the peasantry because of confusion about the role of private traders and because of quotas that do not fit cropping patterns. Marketing corporation prices are often falling below those offered by private traders. Alemayehu Lirenso, "Grain Marketing in Post-1974 Ethiopia: Problems and Prospects" (Paper presented at the Eighth International Conference of Ethiopian Studies, Addis Ababa University, November 26–30, 1984), pp. 6–7, 18–21.

52. Marina Ottaway and David Ottaway, *Ethiopia: Empire in Revolution* (New York: African Publishing Company, 1978), p. 158.

53. See, for example, M. Lewin, *Russian Peasants and Soviet Power* (New York: Norton, 1975), pp. 515–16; A. E. Adams and J. S. Adams, *Men versus Systems* (New York: Free Press, 1971), pp. 5–8, 250; R. D. Laird and B. A. Laird, *Soviet Communism and Agrarian Revolution* (Middlesex: Penguin Books, 1970).

54. S. F. Cohen, *Bukharin and the Bolshevik Revolution* (New York: Oxford University Press, 1980), pp. 78–79, 195–96, 170–75, 140–45.

55. Erasmus, *In Search of the Common Good*, pp. 252, 256–61.

56. B. Lisa Groger, "Of Men and Machines: Cooperation among French Family Farmers," *Ethnology* 20, no. 3 (July 1981): 163–76.

57. Erasmus, *In Search of the Common Good*, pp. 321–26.

58. The World Bank, *World Development Report 1982* (New York: Oxford University Press, 1982), pp. 81–82.

59. Ibid., p. 6.

60. Williams, "Taking the Part of Peasants," pp. 146–47.

61. See the section on "Impact of the Cash Economy" in chapter 8.

62. The World Bank, *World Development Report 1982*, p. 42, indicates that during this time period, per capita agricultural output increased in Latin American countries and Southeast Asia but actually declined in Africa from 2.7 percent in the 1960s to 1.3 percent in the 1970s. At the same time, there was a rapid acceleration of population growth in African countries.

63. Ibid., p. 2.

64. Ibid., p. 79.


## 11. Conclusion

1. See in this instance the views of Maxwell Owusu, "Ethnography of Africa: The Usefulness of the Useless," *American Anthropologist* 80, no. 2 (1978): 310–34.

2. See especially Williams, "Taking the Part of Peasants," pp. 148–49, and Hyden, *Beyond Ujamaa in Tanzania*, pp. 209–60.

3. Cruise O'Brien, "Cooperators and Bureaucrats," pp. 275–76.

4. Hamer, n.d., unpublished field notes.

5. See especially M. F. Lofchie, "Agrarian Crisis and Economic Liberalization in Tanzania," *Journal of Modern African Studies* 16, no. 3 (1978): 451–74; Philip Raikes, "Agrarian Crisis and Economic Liberalisation in Tanzania: A Comment," *Journal of Modern African Studies* 17, no. 2 (1979): 309–16; Rodger Yeager and Norman N. Miller, "Food Policy in Tanzania: Issues of Production, Distribution, and Sufficiency," *Universities Field Staff International Reports*, no. 17 (1982): 10–13; Ergas, "Why Did the Ujamaa Village Policy Fail?" pp. 402–3.

6. Hyden, *Beyond Ujamaa in Tanzania*, pp. 146–47; J. Briggs, "Villagisation and the 1974–6 Economic Crisis in Tanzania," *Journal of Modern African Studies* 17, no. 4 (1979): 695–702.

7. Joanmarie Kalter, "The Economics of Desperation," *Africa Report* 29, no. 3 (1984): 19–23.

# Glossary

**Abāya**: Miniature of an iron bar, formerly used as money.
**Aforšēsa**: Specialist who performs the clitoridectomy operations.
**Anga**: Descent and ritual purity involving elaborate food and social taboos.
**Arike**: A distilled, alcoholic beverage.
**Atbia**: Lowest level of government jurisdiction, consisting of 130 gaša (approximately 1,100 acres).
**Atbia dagnia**: Rural small claims court.
**Awraja**: Government district.
**Balabat**: Amharic title given to traditional authorities in other ethnic groups to further the indirect rule process of the government.
**Bānko**: Deity of thunder and lightning.
**Boselo**: Lineage (literally, "near the fire").
**Čat**: Plant chewed by Muslims at prayer, the leaves of which produce a mild narcotic effect.
**Činānča:**: Subneighborhood.
**Dagnia:**: Marketplace judge.
**Dē-ro**: Taking a bride by force.
**Dī-yi**: Traditional work group.
**Dore**: Pole marking the center of ritual activities in the ceremonies for mourning the dead.
**Ediguet**: A society for socioeconomic development.
**Ensete ventricosum**: The food staple of the Sadāma. This plant is often called the false banana tree because it looks like the banana plant, but the fruit is nonedible. The outer layers of the trunk and the root are consumed as food.
**Feetōma**: Visiting and giving gifts to a wife's relatives as a sign of respect.
**Fīče**: The Sadāma new year's feast and ritual.
**Funta**: Ensete seedlings.
**Gabbar**: System of forced labor imposed after Menelik's conquest.
**Gaberuč**: A produce-marketing cooperative.
**Gaden**: The leader of a generational class.
**Gaša**: Unit of land varying in size from thirty to seventy hectares.
**Gočīsa**: Traditional form of bribery.

264

**Gumamōrra**: Bloodwealth presented to the relatives of a homicide victim.
**Gumātta**: Gifts given at the installation of a clan chief.
**Gurrī**: Clan.
**Hadīčo**: Members of the artisan clan of pottery workers.
**Halōli**: The original beliefs and values of the Sadāma, or "the true way of life."
**Hawāčo**: Members of the artisan clan of leatherworkers.
**Hecob-minne**: Lineage (literally, "house of my father"; often used in place of *boselo*).
**Hibret**: A merchandising and trade cooperative.
**Imihēšo**: Afterlife.
**Iyāni**: Spirit associated with good fortune.
**Īyānto**: Calendrical specialist who keeps track of the days and the significance of each.
**Jāla**: Young man who attends a candidate for elderhood during his period of seclusion.
**Jet-lāwa**: The assistant to the leader of a generational class.
**Kāča**: Hamlet.
**Kayīčo-witla**: Mourning ritual that takes place usually one to two months after a death.
**Kilānčo**: Practitioner of magic with a powerful spirit that enables him to have prophetic ability.
**Koro**: Amharic rank given in some parts of Sidāmoland to lineage chiefs and in other areas to those appointed by the elders' council.
**Lua**: The generational class system.
**Magāno**: The creator sky god.
**Mahabar**: Amharic term referring to associations having religious or friendship functions but used by the Sadāma to designate self-help societies.
**Mamāša**: Adult moralistic tales told during elders' council meetings to convince others and to lead to consensus.
**Mārša**: Iron bar formed into an angle, formerly used as money.
**Masāni**: Iron bar hafted to a wooden handle, formerly used as money.
**Māto**: Children's tales.
**Medāša**: Burial.
**Minne-māna**: Household.
**Morīča**: Neighborhood work leader.
**Mote**: Clan chief.
**Olau**: Grouping of households that make up a neighborhood organization, from which come the personnel for large-scale work projects and rituals.
**Orgāsse**: Specialist who performs circumcision operation.
**Radāna**: Trickster-type spirits.
**Sadāminya**: Cushitic language spoken by the Sadāma.
**Šatāna**: Spirits that possess people and that are believed to control their health and wealth.

**Sīra**: Ostracizing a person from membership in the clan into which he or she was born.

**Sōngo**: Elders' council for policy making and dispute settlement.

**Tāno**: Compact between an individual and a deity in which the person agrees to give a tangible gift in return for aid in overcoming ill health, poverty, or childlessness.

**Tārre**: Totemic object used to protect property.

**Tuntīča**: Ironworkers.

**Wallabīčo**: Term for all Sadāma cultivators, as opposed to those who belong to artisan clans.

**Wāsa**: Prepared ensete, ready to be served as food.

**Wereda**: Government subdistrict.

**Wese**: Ensete plant.

**Wōma**: Highest rank of elder, usually one who has survived two cycles of the generational class system and who meets various other criteria.

**Womāša**: Iron bar with loop, formerly used as money.

**Wo-wāte**: Ritual feast of rebellion sponsored by and for women.

**Yamarīčo**: Descendants of Bushē, one of the cofounders of the Sadāma.

Bibliography

Abate, Alula, and Tesfaye Teklu. "Land Reform and Peasant Associations in Ethiopia—Case Studies of Two Widely Differing Regions." *Northeast African Studies* 2, no. 2 (Fall 1980): 1–51.

Abir, M. "Salt, Trade, and Politics in Ethiopia in the Zāmōnā Māsafent." *Journal of Ethiopian Studies* 4, no. 2 (1966): 1–10.

Abrahams, R. G. *The Nyamwezi Today.* London: Cambridge University Press, 1981.

Adams, A. E., and J. S. Adams. *Men versus Systems.* New York: Free Press, 1971.

Amin, Samir. *Le development inégal.* Paris: Editions de Minuit, 1973.

Anderson, John. "Voluntary Associations in Hyderabad." *Anthropological Quarterly* 37 (1964): 175–90.

Arens, W. *On The Frontier of Change: Mto wa Mbu, Tanzania.* Ann Arbor: University Microfilms Press, 1979.

Ashley Montagu, M. F. *The Reproductive Development of the Female.* New York: Julian Press, 1957.

Asyeghn, Desta. "Schooling and Inequality in Prerevolutionary Ethiopia." *Ethiopianist Notes* 2, no. 2 (1978):1–12.

Baran, Paul. *The Political Economy of Growth.* New York: Monthly Review Press, 1957.

Barker, A. J. *The Civilizing Mission: A History of the Italo-Ethiopian War of 1935–1936.* New York: Dial Press, 1968.

Bath, C. Richard, and Dilmas James. "Dependency Analysis of Latin America: Some Criticisms and Suggestions." *Latin American Research Review* 11, no. 3 (1976): 3–54.

Beckman, Bjorn. "Ghana, 1951–78: The Agrarian Basis of the Post-Colonial State." In Judith Heyer, Pepe Roberts, and Gavin Williams, eds., *Rural Development in Tropical Africa.* New York: St. Martin's Press, 1981.

Bierman, Werner. "The Development of Underdevelopment: The Historical Perspective." In Ben Turok, ed., *Development in Zambia: A Reader.* London: Zed Press, 1979.

Bloch, Maurice. "The Long Term and the Short Term: The Economic and

267

Political Significance of the Morality of Kinship." In Jack Goody, ed., *The Character of Kinship*. London: Cambridge University Press, 1973.

Bohanon, Paul. *Social Anthropology*. New York: Holt, Rinehart & Winston, 1963.

Bondestan, Lars. "Notes on Foreign Investments in Ethiopia." In Carl Widstrand, ed., *Multinational Firms in Africa*. Uppsala: Scandinavian Institute of African Studies, 1975.

Braukamper, Ulrich. "The Ethnogenesis of the Sidāma." In Jean Chavaillon, ed., *Abbay: Documents pour servir à l'histoire de la civilisation ethiopienne*. Report no. 9. Paris: Centre Regional de Publications de Meudon-Bellevue, 1978.

Brett, Theodore. "Colonialism, Underdevelopment, and Class Formation in East Africa." In Chris Allen and Gavin Williams, eds., *Subsaharan Africa*. New York: Monthly Review Press, 1982.

Brietzke, Paul. "Review: Class and Revolution in Ethiopia by John Markakis and Nega Ayele." *Northeast African Studies* 1, no. 3 (Winter 1979–80): 99–105.

Briggs, J. "Villagisation and the 1974–6 Economic Crisis In Tanzania." *Journal of Modern African Studies* 17, no. 4 (1979): 695–702.

Bunker, S. G. "Forms and Functions of Government Intervention in a Uganda Cooperative Union." Paper presented at the Fourteenth Annual Meeting of the African Studies Association, 1971.

Burling, Robbins. *The Passage of Power: Studies in Political Succession*. New York: Academic Press, 1974.

Carneiro, Robert L. "Political Expansion as an Expression of the Principle of Competitive Exclusion." In Ronald Cohen and Elman R. Service, eds., *Origins of the State: The Anthropology of Political Evolution*. Philadelphia: Institute for the Study of Human Issues, 1978.

Caulk, R. A. "Firearms and Princely Power in Ethiopia in the Nineteenth Century." *Journal of African History* 13, no. 4 (1972): 609–30.

———. "The Army and Society in Ethiopia." *Ethiopianist Notes* 1, no. 3 (1978): 17–24.

Central Statistical Office. *Statistical Abstracts 1971*. Addis Ababa: Government Printer, 1971.

———. "Estimates of Rural Households and Populations in Thirteen Provinces." Addis Ababa, 1972. Mimeo.

Cerulli, Ernesta. *Peoples of South-West Ethiopia and Its Borderland*. London: International African Institute, 1956.

Chinchilla, Norma S. "Crisis and Transformation of Dependency in the World System." In Ronald H. Chilcote and Dale L. Johnson, eds., *Theories of Development: Mode of Production or Dependency*. Beverly Hills: Sage Publications, 1983.

Cliffe, Lionell. "Rural Political Economy of Africa." In Peter C. W. Gutkind and Immanuel Wallerstein, eds., *The Political Economy of Contemporary Africa*. Beverly Hills: Sage Publications, 1976.

Cohen, John. "Effects of Green Revolution Strategies on Tenants and Small-Scale Landowners in the Chilalo Region of Ethiopia." *Journal of Developing Areas* 9 (1975): 335–58.

Cohen, John M., and Dove Weintraub. *Land and Peasants in Imperial Ethiopia*. Assem: Van Gorcum, 1975.

Cohen, S. F. *Bukharin and the Bolshevik Revolution*. New York-Oxford University Press, 1980.

Coquery-Vidrovitch, Catherine. "The Political Economy of the African Peasantry and Modes of Production." In Peter C. W. Gutkind and Immanuel Wallerstein, eds., *The Political Economy of Contemporary Africa*. Beverly Hills: Sage Publications, 1976.

Cruise O'Brien, Donal B. "Cooperators and Bureaucrats: Class Formation in a Senegalese Society." *Africa*, 41, no. 4 (1971): 263–77.

Crummey, Donald. "State and Society: Nineteenth-Century Ethiopia." In Donald Crummey and C. C. Stewart, eds., *Modes of Production in Africa*. Beverly Hills: Sage Publications, 1981.

Davis, Raymond. *Fire on the Mountains*. Grand Rapids: Zondervan, 1966.

De Wolf, Jan J. *Differentiation and Integration in Western Kenya*. The Hague: Mouton, 1977.

Donham, D. L. "From Ritual Kings to Ethiopian Landlords: Malle, South-western Ethiopia, c. 1894–1974." In D. L. Donham and Wendy Jones, eds., *Working Papers on Society and History in Imperial Ethiopia: The Southern Periphery from the 1880s to 1974*. Cambridge: African Studies Center, 1980.

Dore, Ronald F. "Modern Cooperatives in Traditional Communities." In Peter Worsley, ed., *Two Blades of Grass*. London: Manchester University Press, 1971.

Downing, Theodore E. "The Internationalization of Capital in Agriculture." *Human Organization* 41, no. 3 (Fall 1982): 269–77.

Dugan, James, and Lawrence Lafore. *Days of Emperor and Clown: The Italo-Ethiopian War, 1935–1936*. Garden City: Doubleday, 1973.

Erasmus, Charles J. *In Search of the Common Good*. New York: Free Press, 1977.

Ergas, Zaki. "Why Did the Ujamaa Village Policy Fail?—Towards a Global Analysis." *Journal of Modern African Studies* 18, no. 3 (September 1980): 387–410.

Evans-Pritchard, E. E. *The Nuer*. Oxford: Clarendon Press, 1940.

Fals Borda, Orlando, Raymond Apthorpe, and Inayatullah. "The Crisis of Rural Cooperatives: Problems in Africa, Asia, and Latin America." In June Nash, Jorge Dandler, and Nicholas Hopkins, eds., *Popular Participation in Social Change*. The Hague: Mouton, 1976.

Feldman, Rayah. "Rural Social Differentiation and Political Goals in Tanzania." In Ivar Oxal, Tony Barnett, and David Booth, eds., *Beyond the Sociology of Development: Economy and Society in Latin America and Africa*. London: Routledge & Kegan Paul, 1975.

Fortes, Meyer. *Kinship and the Social Order*. Chicago: Aldine, 1969.

Fox, Robin. *Kinship and Marriage*. Middlesex: Penguin Books, 1967.

Frisch, R. E. "Population, Food Intake, and Fertility." *Science* 199 (1977): 22–30.

Gamst, Frederick. *Peasants in Complex Society*. New York: Holt, Rinehart & Winston, 1974.

Gilkes, Patrick. *The Dying Lion: Feudalism and Modernization in Ethiopia*. New York: St. Martin's Press, 1975.

Gluckman, Max. *Politics, Law, and Ritual in Tribal Society*. Chicago: Aldine, 1965.

Goody, Jack. "Introduction." In Jack Goody, ed., *Succession to High Office*. London: Cambridge University Press, 1966.

Greenfield, Richard. *Ethiopia: A New Political History*. New York: Praeger, 1965.

Groger, B. Lisa. "Of Men and Machines: Cooperation among French Family Farmers." *Ethnology* 20, no. 3 (July 1981): 163–76.

Gulilat, Taye. "Coffee in the Ethiopian Economy, II." *Journal of Ethiopian Studies* 1, no. 1 (January 1963): 47–56.

Haberland, Eike. "Special Castes in Ethiopia." In Robert L. Hess, ed., *Proceedings of the Fifth International Conference on Ethiopian Studies*. Chicago: University of Illinois at Chicago Circle, 1979.

Hamer, John. "Voluntary Associations as Structures of Change among the Sidāmo of Southwest Ethiopia." *Anthropological Quarterly* 40, no. 2 (1967): 73–91.

———. "Sidāmo Generational Class Cycles: A Political Gerontocracy." *Africa* 40, no. 1 (1970): 50–70.

———. "Myth, Ritual, and the Authority of Elders in an Ethiopian Society." *Africa* 46, no. 4 (1976): 327–39.

———. "Crisis, Moral Consensus, and the Wando Magāno Movement among the Sadāma of Southwest Ethiopia." *Ethnology* 16, no. 4 (October 1977): 399–413.

———. "Goals, Status, and the Stability of n-Achievement: A Small Sample from Southern Ethiopia." *Ethos* 6, no. 1 (1978): 46–62.

———. "The Origins of the Sadāma: A Cushitic-Speaking People of South-Western Ethiopia." In Jean Chavaillon, ed., *Abbay: Documents pour servir a l'histoire de la civilisation ethiopienne*. Report no. 9. Paris: Centre Régional de Publications de Meudon-Bellevue, 1978.

———. "Preference, Principle, and Precedent: Dispute Settlement and Changing Norms in Sidāmo Associations." *Ethnology* 19, no. 1 (January 1980): 89–109.

———. "Preconditions and Limits in the Formation of Associations: The

Self-Help and Cooperative Movement in Subsaharan Africa." *African Studies Review* 24, no. 1 (March 1981): 113–31.

———. "Rivalry and Taking Kinsmen for Granted: Limiting Factors in the Development of Voluntary Associations." *Journal of Anthropological Research* 38, no. 3 (Fall 1982): 303–14.

———. "Islam and the Sadāma." In Richard V. Weekes, ed., *Muslim Peoples: A World Ethnographic Survey*. Westport: Greenwood Press, 1984.

Hamer, John, and Irene Hamer. "Spirit Possession and Its Socio-Psychological Implications among the Sidāmo of Southwest Ethiopia." *Ethnology* 5, no. 4 (October 1966): 392–408.

Herskovits, Melville J. *Man and His Works*. New York: Random House, 1948.

Hindess, Barry, and Paul Hirst. *Pre-Capitalist Modes of Production*. London: Routledge & Kegan Paul, 1975.

Hoben, Allen. *Land Tenure among the Amhara of Ethiopia*. Chicago: University of Chicago Press,1973.

———. "Perspectives on Land Reform in Ethiopia: The Political Role of the Peasantry." *Rural Africana*, no. 28 (Fall 1975): 55–69.

Hopkins, Nicholas S. "Leadership and Consensus in Two Malian Cooperatives." In David Brokensha and Marion Pearsall, eds., *The Anthropology of Development in Sub-Saharan Africa*. Monograph 10. Lexington, Ky.: Society for Applied Anthropology, 1969.

———. "The Articulation of the Modes of Production: Tailoring in Tunisia." *American Ethnologist* 5 (1978): 468–83.

Howell, N. "Toward a Uniformitarian Theory of Human Paleo-demography." *Journal of Human Evolution* 5 (1976): 25–40.

Hudson, Grover. "Highland East Cushitic." In M. Lionel Bender, ed., *The Non-Semitic Languages of Ethiopia*. East Lansing: Michigan State University, 1976.

Hutton, Caroline, and Robin Cohen. "African Peasants and Resistance to Change: A Reconsideration of Sociological Approaches." In Ivar Oxal, Tony Barnett, and David Booth, eds., *Beyond the Sociology of Development: Economy and Society in Latin America and Africa*. London: Routledge & Kegan Paul, 1975.

Hyden, Goran. *Beyond Ujamaa in Tanzania: Underdevelopment and an Uncaptured Peasantry*. Berkeley: University of California Press, 1980.

Illy, Hans F. "How to Build in the Germs of Failure: Credit Cooperatives in French Cameroon." *Rural Africana*, no. 2 (Fall 1978): 57–67.

Johnson, Dale L. "Class Analysis and Dependency." In Ronald H. Chilcote and Dale L. Johnson, eds., *Theories of Development: Mode of Production or Dependency*. Beverly Hills: Sage Publications, 1983.

Kalter, Joanmarie. "The Economics of Desperation." *Africa Report* 29, no. 3 (1984): 19–23.

Kasfir, Nelson. "Departicipation and Political Development in Black Africa." *Political Studies in Comparative International Development* 9 (1974): 3–25.

Keesing, Roger. Kin Groups and Social Structure. New York: Holt, Rinehart & Winston, 1975.

Keller, Edmond J. "Revolution, Class, and the National Question: The Case of Ethiopia." Northeast African Studies 3, no. 1 (1981): 43–68.

Kerri, James, "Studying Voluntary Associations as Adaptive Mechanisms: A Review of Anthropological Perspectives." Current Anthropology 17, no. 1 (1976): 23–47.

King, Roger. "Cooperative Policy and Village Development in Northern Nigeria." In Judith Heyer, Pepe Roberts, and Gavin Williams, eds., Rural Development in Tropical Africa. New York: St. Martin's Press, 1981.

Knutsson, Karl Eric. Authority and Change: A Study of the Kallu Institution among the Macha Galla of Ethiopia. Göteborg: Ethnografika Museet, 1967.

Kopytoff, Igor. "Socialism and Traditional African Societies." In W. H. Friedland and Carl G. Rosberg, eds., African Socialism. Stanford: Stanford University Press, 1964.

Laird, R. D., and B. A. Laird. Soviet Communism and Agrarian Revolution. Middlesex: Penguin Books, 1970.

Lang, Gottfried O., Warren J. Roth, and Martha B. Lang. "Sukumaland Cooperatives as Mechanisms of Change." In David Brokensha and Marion Pearsall, eds., The Anthropology of Development in Sub-Saharan Africa. Monograph 10. Lexington: Society for Applied Anthropology, 1969.

Legesse, Asmarom. "Class Systems Based on Time." Journal of Ethiopian Studies 1, no. 2 (1963): 1–29.

Levine, Donald N. Wax and Gold: Tradition and Innovation in Ethiopia Culture. Chicago: University of Chicago Press, 1965.

———. Greater Ethiopia: The Evolution of a Multiethnic Society. Chicago: University of Chicago Press, 1974.

Lewin, M. Russian Peasants and Soviet Power. New York: Norton, 1975.

Liebenthal, Robert. "Certain Development Issues in Ethiopia and Their Relationship to Rural/Urban Balance: A Perspective Based on World Bank Experience." Ethiopian Notes, no. 3 (Spring 1978): 51–60.

Lirenso, Alemayehu. "Grain Marketing in Post-1974 Ethiopia: Problems and Prospects." Paper presented at the Eighth International Conference of Ethiopian Studies, Addis Ababa University, November 26–30, 1984.

Littlefield, Alice. "Exploitation and the Expansion of Capitalism: The Case of the Hammock Industry of Yucatan." American Ethnologist 5, no. 3 (1978): 495–508.

Lofchie, M.F. "Agrarian Crisis and Economic Liberalization in Tanzania." Journal of Modern African Studies 16, no. 3 (1978): 451–75.

McClellan, Charles W. "The Ethiopian Occupation of Northern Sidāmo— Recruitment and Motivation." In Robert L. Hess, ed., Proceedings of the Fifth International Conference on Ethiopian Studies. Chicago: University of Illinois at Chicago Circle, 1979.

Mair, Lucy. *Primitive Government*. Baltimore: Penguin Books, 1962.

Markakis, John. *Ethiopia: Anatomy of a Traditional Polity*. Oxford: Clarendon Press, 1974.

Markakis, John, and Nega Ayele. *Class and Revolution in Ethiopia*. Nottingham: Spokesman, 1978.

Marx, Karl, and Friedrich Engels. *Basic Writings on Politics and Philosophy*. Edited by Lewis S. Feuer. Garden City: Doubleday, 1959.

Meillassoux, Claude. "From Reproduction to Production." *Economy and Society* 1, no. 1 (February 1972): 93–105.

Middleton, John, and David Tait, eds. *Tribes without Rulers*. London: Routledge & Kegan Paul, 1958.

Migdal, J. *Peasants, Politics, and Revolution*. Princeton: University Press, 1974.

Migot-Adholla, Shem E. "Traditional Society and Cooperatives." In Carl G. Widstrand, ed., *Cooperatives and Rural Development in East Africa*. Uppsala: Almquist & Wiksell, 1970.

Milkias, Paulos. "Zemecha—An Assessment of the Political and Social Foundations of Mass Education in Ethiopia." *Northeast African Studies* 2, no. 1 (Spring 1980): 19–30.

Ministry of National Community Development. *Labour, Cooperatives, Social Welfare, and Community Development*. Addis Ababa: Commercial Printing Press, 1964.

Murdock, George. *Africa: Its Peoples and Their Culture History*. New York: McGraw-Hill, 1959.

Nag, M. *Factors Affecting Fertility in Non-Industrial Societies, A Cross-Cultural Study*. New Haven: Human Relations Area File Press, 1968.

Norbeck, Edward. "Associations and Democracy in Japan." In R. P. Dore, ed., *Aspects of Social Change in Modern Japan*. Princeton: Princeton University Press, 1967.

Nowrojee, Pheroze. "The Settlement of Disputes in Cooperative Societies." In Carl G. Widstrand, ed., *African Cooperatives and Efficiency*. Uppsala: Almquist & Wiksell, 1972.

Office of the Population and Housing Census Commission. *Ethiopia 1984: Population and Housing Census Preliminary Report*. Addis Ababa: Government Printer, 1984.

O'Laughlin, Bridget. "Marxist Approaches in Anthropology." In B. J. Segal, A. R. Beals, and S. A. Tyler, eds., *Annual Review of Anthropology*. Palo Alto: Annual Reviews, 1975.

Ottaway, Marina. "Land Reform and Peasant Associations: A Preliminary Analysis." *Rural Africana*, no. 28 (Fall 1975): 39–54.

Ottaway, Marina, and David Ottaway. *Ethiopia: Empire in Revolution*. New York: African Publishing Company, 1978.

Owusu, Maxwell. "Ethnography of Africa: The Usefulness of the Useless." *American Anthropologist* 80, no. 2 (1978): 310–34.

Pankhurst, Richard. "The Maria Theresa Dollar." *Journal of Ethiopian Studies* 1, no. 1 (January 1963): 8–26.

Popkin, Samuel L. *The Rational Peasant: The Political Economy of Rural Society in Vietnam.* Berkeley: University of California Press, 1979.

Preston, P. W. *Theories of Development.* London: Routledge & Kegan Paul, 1982.

Quick, Stephen A. "Bureaucracy and Rural Socialism in Zambia." *Journal of Modern African Studies* vol. 15 (1977): 379–400.

Radcliffe-Brown, A. R., and Daryll Forde, eds. *African Systems of Kinship and Marriage.* New York: Oxford University Press, 1950.

Raikes, Philip. "Agrarian Crisis and Economic Liberalisation in Tanzania: A Comment." *Journal of Modern African Studies* 17, no. 2 (1979): 309–16.

Raulin, Henri. "Organized Cooperation and Spontaneous Cooperation in Africa (Niger Republic)." In June Nash, Jorge Dandler, and Nicholas Hopkins, eds., *Popular Participation in Social Change.* The Hague: Mouton, 1976.

Redfield, Robert. *The Little Community and Peasant Society and Culture.* Chicago: University of Chicago Press, 1960.

Reimer, Richard. "Ethiopian Agricultural Exports: A Brief Survey." *Rural Africana,* no. 28 (Fall 1975): 119–37.

Roberts, Pepe. "Rural Development and Economy in Niger, 1900–75." In Judith Heyer, Pepe Roberts, and Gavin Williams, eds., *Rural Development in Tropical Africa.* New York: St. Martin's Press, 1981.

Rosen, Charles B. "The Dynamics of Provincial Administration in Haile Selassie's Ethiopia: 1930–1974." In Gerald M. Britan and Ronald Cohen, eds., *Hierarchy and Society: Anthropological Perspectives on Bureaucracy.* Philadelphia: Institute for the Study of Human Issues, 1980.

Rostow, W. W. *The Stages of Economic Growth.* Cambridge: Cambridge University Press, 1960.

Roth, Warren. "Three Cooperatives and a Credit Union as Examples of Culture Change." Ph.D. diss., Catholic University of America, 1966.

———. "Traditional Social Structure and the Development of a Marketing Cooperative in Tanzania." In June Nash, Jorge Dandler, and Nicholas Hopkins, eds., *Popular Participation in Social Change.* The Hague: Mouton, 1976.

Rubinson, Richard. "Introduction." In Richard Rubinson, ed., *Dynamics of World Development.* Beverly Hills: Sage Publications, 1981.

Ruel, M. "The Modern Adaptation of Associations among the Banyang of the West Cameroon." *Southwestern Journal of Anthropology* 20, no. 1 (1964): 1–14.

Sahlins, Marshall. "On the Sociology of Primitive Exchange." In Michael Banton, ed., *The Relevance of Models for Social Anthropology.* London: Tavistock Publications, 1965.

———. *Tribesmen.* Englewood Cliffs: Prentice-Hall, 1968.

―――. *Culture and Practical Reason.* Chicago: University of Chicago Press, 1976.

Samoff, Joel. "Underdevelopment and Its Grass Roots in Africa." *Canadian Journal of African Studies* 14, no. 1 (1980): 5–36.

Scaff, L., and E. Williams. "Participation and the Primacy of Politics in Development Theory." In J. Booth and M. Seligson, eds., *Political Participation in Latin America.* Vol. 1. New York: Holmes & Meier Publishers, 1978.

Schwartz, Theodore. "The Acquisition of Culture." *Ethos* 9, no. 1 (Spring 1981): 4–17.

Scott, James C. *The Moral Economy of the Peasant.* New Haven: Yale University Press, 1976.

Seibel, Hans Dieter, and Andreas Massing. *Traditional Organizations and Economic Development: Studies of Indigenous Cooperatives in Liberia.* New York: Praeger, 1974.

Service, Elman R. *Origins of the State and Civilization: The Process of Cultural Evolution.* New York: Norton, 1975.

Shack, William A. *The Gurage: A People of the Ensete Culture.* New York: Oxford University Press, 1966.

Singer, Norman. "A Traditional Legal Institution in a Modern Legal Setting: The Atbia Dagnia of Ethiopia." *U.C.L.A. Law Review* 18, no. 2 (December 1970): 308–34.

―――. "The Ethiopian Civil Code and the Recognition of Customary Law." *Huston Law Review* 9, no. 3 (January 1972): 460–94.

Smeds, Helmet. "The Ensete Planting Culture of Eastern Sidāmo, Ethiopia." *Acta Geographica* 13, no. 4 (1955): 1–39.

Tekle, Tesfai. "An Approach to Rural Development: A Case Study of the Ethiopian Package Projects." In John W. Harbeson and Paul Brietzke, eds., *Rural Development in Ethiopia.* East Lansing: Michigan State University, African Studies Center Publication, 1975.

Terray, Emmanuel. *Marxism and Primitive Societies.* New York: Monthly Review Press, 1972.

Todd, David M. "Caste in Africa?" *Africa* 47, no. 4 (1977): 398–412.

Trimingham, J. Spencer. *Islam in Ethiopia.* New York: Barnes & Noble, 1965.

United Nations. *1980 Trade Yearbook.* Rome: Food and Agriculture Organization, 1980.

Veltmeyer, Henry. "Surplus Labor and Class Formation on the Latin American Periphery." In Ronald H. Chilcote and Dale L. Johnson, eds., *Theories of Development: Mode of Production or Dependency.* Beverly Hills: Sage Publications, 1983.

Vincent, Joan. "Rural Competition and the Cooperative Monopoly: A Ugandan Case Study." In June Nash, Jorge Dandler, and Nicholas Hopkins, eds., *Popular Participation in Social Change.* The Hague: Mouton, 1976.

Von Grunebaum, G. E. *Islam: Essays in the Nature and Growth of a Cultural*

*Tradition.* American Anthropological Association. Vol. 57, no. 2, part 2, memoir no. 81 (Menasha, Wis.: Banta, 1955).

Wallerstein, Immanuel. *The Modern World System. Vol. 1, Capitalist Agriculture and the Origins of the European World Economy in the Sixteenth Century.* New York: Academic Press, 1974.

——. "The Three Stages of African Involvement in the World Economy." In Peter C. W. Gutkind and Immanuel Wallerstein, eds., *The Political Economy of Contemporary Africa.* Beverly Hills: Sage Publications, 1976.

——. *The Modern World System. Vol. 2, Mercantilism and the Consolidation of the European World Economy.* New York: Academic Press, 1980.

Welch, Claude E. "Peasants as a Focus in African Studies." In Alan K. Smith and Claude E. Welch, eds., *Peasants in Africa.* Waltham: Crossroads Press, 1978.

Williams, Gavin. "Taking the Part of Peasants: Rural Development in Nigeria and Tanzania." In Peter C. W. Gutkind and Immanuel Wallerstein, eds., *The Political Economy of Contemporary Africa.* Beverly Hills: Sage Publications, 1976.

Wilson, David. "Review Essay: Class and Revolution in Ethiopia." *Horn of Africa* 4, no. 4 (1981–82): 15–22.

Winans, Edgar V., and Angelique Hangerud. "Rural Self-Help in Kenya: The Harambee Movement." *Human Organization* 36 (1977): 334–51.

Wolde-Mariam, Mesfin. *An Introductory Geography of Ethiopia.* Addis Ababa: Berhanena Selam H.S.I. Printing Press, 1972.

Wolf, Eric R. *Peasants.* Englewood Cliffs: Prentice-Hall, 1966.

——. *Europe and the People without History.* Berkeley: University of California Press, 1982.

World Bank. *World Development Report 1982.* New York: Oxford University Press, 1980.

Worsley, Peter, *The Third World.* Chicago: University of Chicago Press, 1970.

Yeager, Rodger, and Norman N. Miller, "Food Policy in Tanzania: Issues of Production, Distribution, and Sufficiency." *Universities Field Staff International Reports,* no. 17 (1982): 1–24.

# Index

277

## About the Author

John H. Hamer received his B.A.
degree from Pennsylvania State
University, his M.A. degree from
the University of Pittsburgh, and his
Ph.D. degree from Northwestern
University. He is now a Professor of
Anthropology at The University of
Alabama at Birmingham.